Fodor's
New EDITION

Singapore

The complete guide, thoroughly up-to-date

Packed with details that will make your trip

The must-see sights, off and on the beaten path

What to see, what to skip

Vacation itineraries, walking tours, day trips

Smart lodging and dining options

Essential local do's and taboos

Transportation tips

Key contacts, savvy travel advice

When to go, what to pack

Clear, accurate, easy-to-use maps

Background essays

Excerpted from *Fodor's Southeast Asia*

Fodor's Travel Publications, Inc.
New York • Toronto • London • Sydney • Auckland
www.fodors.com

Fodor's Singapore

EDITOR: Laura M. Kidder

Editorial Contributors: Bruce Bishop, David Brown, Helayne Schiff, M.T. Schwartzman (Gold Guide editor), Ilsa Sharp

Editorial Production: Nicole Revere

Maps: David Lindroth, *cartographer*; Steven Amsterdam and Bob Blake, *map editors*

Design: Fabrizio La Rocca, *creative director*; Guido Caroti, *associate art director*; Jolie Novak, *photo editor*

Production/Manufacturing: Mike Costa

Cover Photograph: Bob Krist

Database Production: Martin Walsh

Copyright

Special Sales

Fodor's Travel Publications are available at special discounts for bulk purchases for sales promotions or premiums. Special editions, including personalized covers, excerpts of existing guides, and corporate imprints, can be created in large quantities for special needs. For more information, contact your local bookseller or write to Special Markets, Fodor's Travel Publications, 201 East 50th Street, New York, NY 10022. Inquiries from Canada should be directed to your local Canadian bookseller or sent to Random House of Canada, Ltd., Marketing Department, 2775 Matheson Boulevard East, Mississauga, Ontario L4W 4P7. Inquiries from the United Kingdom should be sent to Fodor's Travel Publications, 20 Vauxhall Bridge Road, London SW1V 2SA, England.

PRINTED IN THE UNITED STATES OF AMERICA

10 9 8 7 6 5 4 3 2 1

CONTENTS

Maps

ON THE ROAD WITH FODOR'S

WHEN I PLAN A VACATION, the first thing I do is cast around among my friends and colleagues to find someone who's just been where I'm going. That's because there's no substitute for advice from a good friend who knows your tastes, budget, and circumstances, someone who's just been there. Unfortunately, such friends are few and far between. So it's nice to know that there's *Fodor's Singapore.*

In the first place, this book won't stay home when you hit the road. It will accompany you every step of the way, steering you away from wrong turns and choices and never expecting a thing in return. Most important, it's written and assiduously updated by the kind of people you *would* hit up for travel tips. They're as choosy as your pickiest friend, except they've probably seen a lot more of Singapore. They don't send you chasing down every town and sight but have instead selected the best ones, the ones that are worthy of your time and money. To make it easy for you to put it all together in the time you have, they've created itineraries and walks that you can mix and match. Will this be the vacation of your dreams? We hope so.

About Our Writers

A resident of Toronto, **Bruce Bishop** is a freelance writer/photographer and events coordinator. He has written for Canada's *The Globe and Mail,* Delta Air Lines' *Sky* magazine, Mexicana Airlines' *Vuelo* magazine, and other publications. Bruce spent two months in Singapore researching and updating *Fodor's Singapore 10th Edition.*

Ilsa Sharp, who wrote the introduction, is a British-born Chinese studies graduate and professional writer who has lived in Singapore since 1968. She's married to a Tamil-Indian Singaporean writer and entertainer, and is the author of several books on the history, culture, and wildlife of Singapore and the Asia-Pacific region.

We'd like to thank Singapore Airlines for its gracious help; Tania Goh of the Singapore Tourism Board (STB); Gerald Lee of the STB's office in Toronto; Chia Boon Hee of BnE Travel Consultants, Singapore; and Gregory Bishop.

Connections

We're pleased that the American Society of Travel Agents continues to endorse Fodor's as its guidebook of choice. ASTA is the world's largest and most influential travel trade association, operating in more than 170 countries, with 27,000 members pledged to adhere to a strict code of ethics reflecting the Society's motto, "Integrity in Travel." ASTA shares Fodor's devotion to providing smart, honest travel information and advice to travelers, and we've long recommended that our readers—even those who have guidebooks and traveling friends—consult ASTA member agents for the experience and professionalism they bring to your vacation planning.

On Fodor's Web site (www.fodors.com), check out the Resource Center, an online companion to the Gold Guide section of this book, with useful hot links to related sites. In our forums, you can also get advice from other travelers and more tips from Fodor's experts worldwide.

How to Use This Book

Organization

Smart Travel Tips A to Z is arranged alphabetically by topic. Under each listing you'll find travel tips and addresses and phone numbers of organizations and companies that offer destination-related services.

The first chapter, Destination: Singapore, helps get you in the mood for your trip. New and Noteworthy cues you in on trends, What's Where gets you oriented, Pleasures and Pastimes discusses things that make Singapore unique, Great Itineraries lays out a selection of trips, Fodor's Choice cites our top picks, and Festivals and Seasonal Events alerts you to happenings.

The Exploring chapter is divided by neighborhood, and each has a tour and sights, which are listed alphabetically. The remaining chapters are arranged in alphabetical order by subject. At the end of the book is Portraits, with illuminating essays on Singapore, including an excerpt from Stan Sesser's book *The Lands of Charm and Cruelty.*

Icons and Symbols

★	Our special recommendations
✕	Restaurant
🏨	Lodging establishment
🐤	Good for kids (rubber duck)
☞	Sends you to another section of the guide for more information
✉	Address
☎	Telephone number
◷	Opening and closing times
🎫	Admission prices (for adults; substantially reduced fees are usually available for children, students, and senior citizens)

Numbers in white and black circles (e.g., ③ or ❸) on maps, in margins, and in tours correspond to one another.

Dining and Lodging

The restaurants and lodgings we list are the cream of the crop. Price categories are as follows:

For restaurants:

CATEGORY	COST*
$$$$	over S$60
$$$	S$35–S$60
$$	S$15–S$35
$	under S$15

All prices are per person for a three-course meal excluding tax, service charge, and drinks.

For hotels:

CATEGORY	COST*
$$$$	over S$375
$$$	S$275–S$375
$$	S$175–S$275
$	under S$175

All prices are for a standard double room, excluding 4% tax and 10% service charge.

Hotel Facilities

We always list available facilities, but we don't specify whether you'll be charged extra for them: when pricing hotels, ask what's included. Assume that rooms have private baths unless noted otherwise. When you book, be sure to mention if you have a disability or are traveling with children, if you prefer a private bath or a certain type of bed, or if you have specific dietary needs or other concerns.

Assume that hotels operate on the **European Plan** (EP, with no meals) unless we specify that they use the **Continental Plan** (CP, with a Continental breakfast daily), **Breakfast Plan** (BP, with a full breakfast daily), **Modified American Plan** (MAP, with breakfast and dinner daily), or the **Full American Plan** (FAP, with all meals).

Restaurant Reservations and Dress Codes

Reservations are always a good idea; we mention them only when they're essential or aren't accepted. Book as far ahead as you can, and reconfirm. Unless otherwise noted, the restaurants listed are open daily for lunch and dinner. We mention dress only when men must wear a jacket and/or tie.

Credit Cards

The following abbreviations are used: **AE,** American Express; **DC,** Diners Club; **MC,** MasterCard; and **V,** Visa.

Don't Forget to Write

You can use this book in the confidence that all prices and opening times are based on information supplied to us at press time; Fodor's cannot accept responsibility for any errors. Time inevitably brings changes, so always confirm information when it matters.

Were the restaurants we recommended as described? Did our hotel picks exceed your expectations? Did you find a museum we recommended a waste of time? Keeping a travel guide fresh and up-to-date is a big job, and we welcome your feedback, positive *and* negative. If you have complaints, we'll look into them and revise our entries when the facts warrant it. If you've discovered a special place that we haven't included, we'll pass the information along to our correspondents and have them check it out. So send us your thoughts via E-mail at editors@fodors.com (specifying the name of the book on the subject line) or on paper in care of the Singapore editor at Fodor's, 201 East 50th Street, New York, New York 10022. In the meantime, have a wonderful trip!

Karen Cure

Karen Cure
Editorial Director

CHINA

Guangzhou

Macao HONG
KONG

Mandalay

Hanoi

Luang
Prabang

Haiphong

UNION OF
MYANMAR
(BURMA)

LAOS

HAINAN

Vientiane

Pegu

Chiang
Mai

Yangon
(Rangoon)

Hue
Danang

THAILAND

Bangkok

VIETNAM

Angkor Wat

Andaman
Sea

CAMBODIA

Phnom Penh

Ho Chi Minh City
(Saigon)

Isthmus of
Kra

Gulf of
Thailand

South China
Sea

Songkhla

Georgetown

Bandar Seri
Begawan

PENINSULAR
MALAYSIA

MALAYSIA

BRUNEI

INDIAN OCEAN

Medan

Kuala Lumpur

SARAWAK

Strait of Melaka (Malacca)

Johor Bahru

Kuching

SINGAPORE

BORNEO

SUMATRA

KALIMANTAN

Karimata

Jambi

INDONESIA

KEPULAÜAN

Palembang

Strait

Banjarmasin

GREATER SUNDA ISLANDS

Jakarta

Java Sea

0   500 miles

Bandung

Surabaya

0   750 km

Yogyakarta JAVA

Malang

BALI

N

Singapore Island

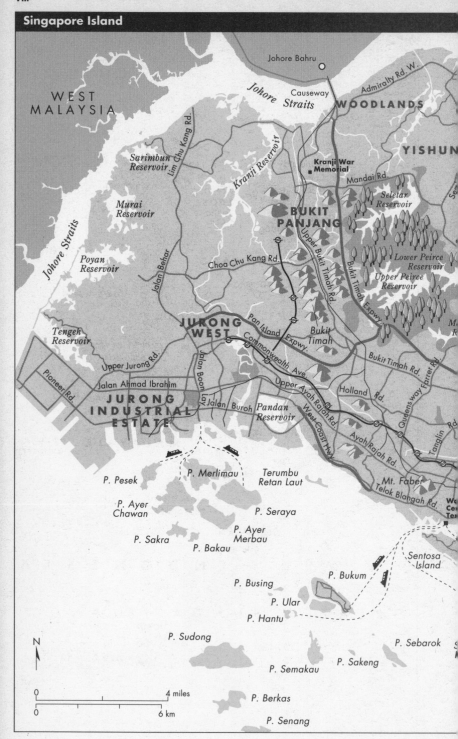

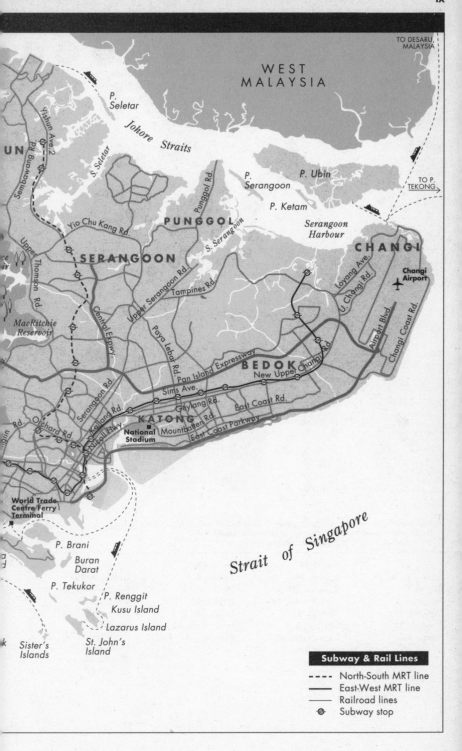

Subway & Rail Lines

- - - - North-South MRT line
───── East-West MRT line
───── Railroad lines
⊖ Subway stop

x

World Time Zones

Numbers below vertical bands relate each zone to Greenwich Mean Time (0 hrs.).
Local times frequently differ from these general indications,
as indicated by light-face numbers on map.

Algiers, **29**
Anchorage, **3**
Athens, **41**
Auckland, **1**
Baghdad, **46**
Bangkok, **50**
Beijing, **54**

Berlin, **34**
Bogotá, **19**
Budapest, **37**
Buenos Aires, **24**
Caracas, **22**
Chicago, **9**
Copenhagen, **33**
Dallas, **10**

Delhi, **48**
Denver, **8**
Djakarta, **53**
Dublin, **26**
Edmonton, **7**
Hong Kong, **56**
Honolulu, **2**

Istanbul, **40**
Jerusalem, **42**
Johannesburg, **44**
Lima, **20**
Lisbon, **28**
London (Greenwich), **27**
Los Angeles, **6**
Madrid, **38**
Manila, **57**

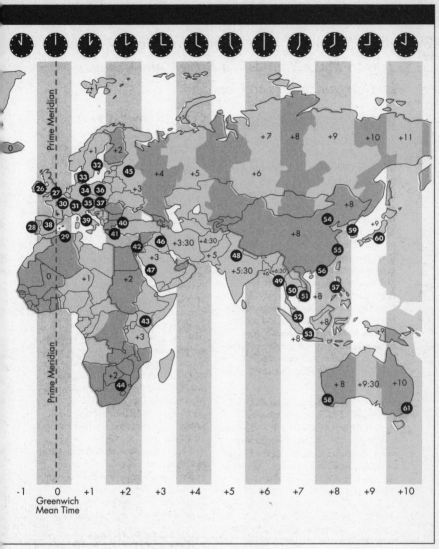

SMART TRAVEL TIPS A TO Z

Basic Information on Traveling in Singapore, Savvy Tips to Make Your Trip a Breeze, and Companies and Organizations to Contact

AIR TRAVEL

MAJOR AIRLINE OR LOW-COST CARRIER?

Major airlines offer the greatest number of departures; smaller airlines—including regional, low-cost, and no-frill airlines—usually have a more limited number of flights daily. Major airlines have frequent-flyer partners that allow you to credit mileage earned on one airline to your account with another. Low-cost airlines offer price advantages and fewer restrictions, such as advance-purchase requirements. Safety-wise, low-cost carriers have a good history, but **check the safety record before booking** any low-cost carrier; call the Federal Aviation Administration's (FAA's) Consumer Hotline (☞ Airline Complaints, *below*).

➤ AIRLINES: **Air New Zealand** (☎ 800/663–5494 in North America), **British Airways** (☎ 800/247–9297 in North America), **Cathay Pacific Airways** (☎ 800/233–2742 in the U.S. or 800/268–6868 in Canada). **China Airlines** (☎ 800/227–5118 in North America). **Japan Airlines** (☎ 800/525–3663 in North America). **Korean Air** (☎ 800/438–5000 in North America). **Malaysia Airlines** (☎ 800/552–9264 in the U.S.). **Northwest** (☎ 800/447–4747 in North America). **Qantas** (☎ 800/227–4500 in North America). **Singapore Airlines** (☎ 800/742–3333 in the U.S. and 800/387–0038 or 800/663–3046 in Canada). **Thai International Airways** (☎ 800/668–8103 in North America). **United Airlines** (☎ 800/241–6522 in North America).

➤ FROM THE U.K.: **British Airways** (☎ 0181/897–4000 or 0345/222111). **Qantas** (☎ 0800/747–767 or 0345/747767). **Singapore Airlines** (☎ 0171/439–8111). **Thai International Airways** (☎ 0171/499–9113).

GET THE LOWEST FARE

The least-expensive airfares to Singapore are priced for round-trip travel. Major airlines usually require that you **book far in advance and stay at least seven days** and no more than 30 to get the lowest fares. Ask about "ultrasaver" fares, which are the cheapest; they must be booked 90 days in advance and are nonrefundable. A little more expensive are "supersaver" fares, which require only a 30-day advance purchase. Remember that penalties for refunds or scheduling changes are stiffer for international tickets, usually about $150. International flights are also sensitive to the season: **plan to fly in the off season** for the cheapest fares. If your destination or home city has more than one gateway, **compare prices to and from different airports.** Also price flights scheduled for off-peak hours, which may be significantly less expensive. To save money on flights from the United Kingdom and back, **look into an APEX or Super-PEX ticket.** APEX tickets must be booked in advance and have certain restrictions. Super-PEX tickets can be purchased at the airport on the day of departure—subject to availability.

DON'T STOP UNLESS YOU MUST

Singapore is the transport hub of Asia. Fifty-two airlines link the republic with 111 cities in 54 countries. The distance between Singapore and North America is too great for planes to fly without refueling and changing crews. There are, however, "direct" flights with no change of airplane, but one or two stops in major cities. Try to **avoid connecting flights,** which require a change of plane. Two airlines may jointly operate a connecting flight, so ask if your airline operates every segment—you may find that your preferred carrier flies you only part of the way.

USE AN AGENT

Travel agents, especially those who specialize in finding the lowest fares (☞ Discounts & Deals, *below*), can be especially helpful when booking a plane ticket. When you're quoted a price, **ask your agent if the price is likely to get any lower.** Good agents know the seasonal fluctuations of airfares and can usually anticipate a sale or fare war. However, waiting can be risky: The fare could go *up* as seats become scarce, and you may wait so long that your preferred flight sells out. A wait-and-see strategy only works if your plans are flexible.

CHECK WITH CONSOLIDATORS

Consolidators buy tickets for scheduled flights at reduced rates from the airlines then sell them at prices that beat the best fare available directly from the airlines, usually without advance restrictions. Sometimes you can even get your money back if you need to return the ticket. Carefully read the fine print detailing penalties for changes and cancellations, and **confirm your consolidator reservation with the airline.**

➤ Consolidators: **United States Air Consolidators Association** (✉ 925 L St., Suite 220, Sacramento, CA 95814, ☎ 916/441–4166, ℻ 916/441–3520).

Airlines routinely overbook planes, knowing that not everyone with a ticket will show up, but sometimes everyone does. When that happens, airlines ask for volunteers to give up their seats. In return these volunteers usually get a certificate for a free flight and are rebooked on the next flight out. If there aren't enough volunteers the airline must choose who will be denied boarding. The first to get bumped are passengers who checked in late and those flying on discounted tickets, so **get to the gate and check in as early as possible,** especially during peak periods. Always **bring a photo ID to the airport.** You may be asked to show it before you're allowed to check in.

ENJOY THE FLIGHT

For more legroom, **request an emergency-aisle seat**; don't however, sit in the row in front of the emergency aisle or in front of a bulkhead, where seats may not recline. If you don't like airline food, **ask for special meals when booking.** These can be vegetarian, low-cholesterol, or kosher, for example.

To avoid jet lag try to maintain a normal routine while traveling. At night **get some sleep.** By day **eat light meals, drink water (not alcohol), and move about the cabin** to stretch your legs. Some carriers have prohibited smoking throughout their systems; others allow smoking only on certain routes or even certain departures from that route, so **contact your carrier regarding its smoking policy.**

COMPLAIN IF NECESSARY

If your baggage goes astray or your flight goes awry, complain right away. Most carriers require that you file a claim immediately.

➤ Airline Complaints: **U.S. Department of Transportation Aviation Consumer Protection Division** (✉ C-75, Room 4107, Washington, DC 20590, ☎ 202/366–2220). **FAA Consumer Hotline** (☎ 800/322–7873).

AIRPORTS & TRANSFERS

The major airport is Changi International Airport, which is on the eastern end of the island, about 30 minutes by car from the city center. It consistently ranks as one of the best airports in the world. Superb shopping, efficient arrival and departure check-in, a host of entertainment activities and food and beverage outlets make Changi a visit unto itself.

Flying west, Singapore is 22 hours from Chicago, 18 hours from Los Angeles, 17 hours from Vancouver, 10½ hours from Auckland and Christchurch, and 8 hours from Sydney. The flying time east from New York is 19 hours; from London it's 13 hours.

➤ Airport Information: **Changi International Airport** (☎ 541–9828).

TRANSFERS

The trip by taxi usually takes 20 to 30 minutes. Fares range from S$13 to S$20, plus a S$3 airport surcharge

THE GOLD GUIDE / SMART TRAVEL TIPS

(not applicable for trips *to* the airport, but **be wary of taxi drivers who try to impose this charge anyway**). Other surcharges apply when baggage is stored in the trunk or when more than two adults travel in the same cab.

AIRBUS is a premier airport coach service that stops at hotels along Orchard Road, Marina Square, and Victoria Street. Buses leave every 20 minutes, and the fare is S$5. Tickets are available from selected hotels and AIRBUS counters in the arrival hall of Changi Airport Terminals 1 and 2. You can also buy the ticket aboard the bus.

Should you wish to rent a car, major agencies are represented at the airport's car-rental counter (☞ Car Rental, *below*).

BICYCLE RICKSHAWS

Once the major method of getting around the city, rickshaws are now driven mostly by elderly Chinese, and there are only a few dozen left. You'll most likely find them on Orchard Road, before the National Museum, and at Bugis Junction. **Bargain for the fare**; you should not pay more than S$15 for a 45-minute ride. The best time to take a rickshaw ride is early evening, after rush hour.

BOAT TRAVEL

Harbor cruises and ferries to Singapore's outer islands, Malaysia, and the Indonesian Riau islands depart from the Singapore Cruise Centre, a 10-minute drive from the city center and the Tanah Merah Ferry Terminal on Singapore's east coast.

Daily ferries ply the World Trade Centre and Sentosa Island every 15 minutes starting at 9:30 AM; the crossing takes four minutes, and the one-way fare is S$1.30. The last ferry back from Sentosa departs at 9 PM Monday through Thursday; Friday through Sunday and holidays, there are two extra return ferries—one at 11:15 PM, the other at midnight. Monday through Saturday, two ferries—one at 10 AM and another at 1:30 PM—leave for Kusu from the Singapore Cruise Centre at the World Trade Centre; on Sunday and holidays there are six ferries, with the

first departing at 6 AM and the last at 8 PM. The trip takes about 30 minutes and costs S$6.20 each way. The same ferries that go to Kusu run to St. John's, a trip that takes a little over an hour and costs S$6.20.

Bumboats are motorized launches that serve as inexpensive taxis. Sailors use them to shuttle between Singapore and their ships, but you can hire a bumboat for a trip to Pulau Ubin. Take SBS Bus 2 from the Tanah Merah MRT station to Changi Point. Then take a bumboat (S$1.50) from the Changi Jetty nearby. To reach Sisters Island, hire a water taxi (S$50 an hour) at the Jardine Steps or Clifford Pier. (Note that water taxis are larger than bumboats and can comfortably accommodate six people.)

Ferries to any of the resorts on Bintan leave regularly from Singapore's Tanah Merah Ferry Terminal. The round-trip fare for the 45-minute trip to the island is S$45. Do not go without a hotel reservation and arrangements for land transfer, and remember to bring your passport. Regular ferries to Bintan's main town, Tanjung Pinang, also depart from the Tanah Merah terminal; the trip takes 1½ hours and costs about S$58 return. Companies that offer service include Auto Batam Ferries and Bintan Resort Ferries.

To Tanjong Belungkor and Mersing on the east coast of Peninsular Malaysia, Ferrylink ferries leave from Changi Point. Auto Batam Ferries & Tours has ferries to Tioman Island in Malaysia that leave from Singapore's Tanah Merah Ferry Terminal daily at 8:30 AM. Ferries to the nearby Indonesian islands of Batam and Bintan are available daily from the World Trade Centre and the Tanah Merah Ferry Terminal. As the ferry services have different schedules and ticket prices, contact the operators for updated information on prices and schedules.

➤ INFORMATION AND RESERVATIONS: **Auto Batam Ferries & Tours** (☎ 542–7105 at Tanah Merah terminal or 271–4866 at World Trade Centre terminal). **Bintan Resort Ferries** (☎ 345–1210 at Tanah Merah). **Channel Holidays** (☎ 270–2228 at World Trade Centre). **Ferrylink** (☎ 545–

3600 or 733–6744). **Singapore Cruise Centre** (☎ 270–3918). **Tanah Merah Ferry Terminal** (☎ 345–1210).

BOOKS ON SINGAPORE

A great book to take home with you is *Singapore,* with wonderful photographs by Ian Lloyd and text by Betty Rabb Schafer (Times Editions, 1988). It's available in most Singapore bookstores. Other books on Singapore include the following: *A History of Singapore, 1819–1975,* by Constance M. Turnbull (Oxford University Press, 1977); *The Worst Disaster: The Fall of Singapore,* by Raymond A. Callahan (University of Delaware Press, 1977); *Raffles of the Eastern Isles,* by Charles Wurtzburg (Oxford University Press, 1984); and *Saint Jack,* a novel set in Singapore, by Paul Theroux (Houghton Mifflin, 1984). If you are staying any length of time in Singapore, or must conduct business there, JoAnn Meriwether Craig's *Culture Shock! Singapore* is a must-have (Graphic Arts Center Publishing Co., 1993). *See also* English-Language Bookstores, *below.*

BUS TRAVEL

Air-conditioned buses are a convenient way to travel between Singapore and three main destinations in Malaysia. The nearest city to Singapore is Johor Bahru (everyone calls it "JB"). The Singapore–Johor Bahru Express runs every seven minutes from 6:30 AM to midnight; the cost is only S$2.10 one way. The Kuala Lumpur–Singapore Express leaves daily at 9 AM, 1 PM, and 10 PM from Singapore, at S$25 one way, and takes about six hours. The Malacca–Singapore Express takes about 4½ hours, costs S$11 one way, and leaves at 8 AM, 9 AM, 10 AM, 11 AM, 2 PM, 3 PM, and 5 PM.

Within Singapore buses are much cheaper than taxis and—with a little practice—easy to use. During rush hours, they can be quicker than cabs, since there are special bus lanes along the main roads. Some buses are air-conditioned, and service is frequent—usually every 5 to 10 minutes on most routes. Even without the excellent *TransitLink Guide,* available for S$1.40 at any bookstore, finding your way around is relatively easy. The minimum fare is S$.60, the maximum S$1.20 for non-air-conditioned buses, S$.70–S$1.50 for air-conditioned ones. **Deposit exact change** in the box as you enter the bus (conductors cannot give change), and **remember to collect your ticket.** Bus numbers are clearly marked, and most stops have a list of destinations with the numbers of the buses that serve them. Most buses run from 6 AM until around midnight; a few run all night.

The Singapore Trolley bus service plys between the Orchard Road shopping belt, the colonial district, the Singapore River, the Raffles Hotel, Boat Quay, Clarke Quay, Marina Square, and Suntec City. It's expensive (S$9), but it makes 22 stops, and your ticket is good for a full day of unlimited travel. You can buy a ticket when you board (you'll need exact change) or from your hotel concierge.

To reach Sentosa Island by bus, first take one to the World Trade Centre—number 10, 97, 100, or 125 from Shenton Way, or number 65 or 143 from Orchard Road—and transfer from there onto a shuttle bus across the causeway. The S$6 round-trip fare includes admission to the island. The shuttle operates 7 AM–11 PM (midnight on weekends).

➤ INFORMATION: **Singapore Bus Service Passenger Relations Center** (☎ 287–2727). **Singapore Explorer** (☎ 338–6833). For buses to Malaysia, contact **Singapore-Johor Bahru Express** (☎ 292–8149), **Kuala Lumpur-Singapore Express** (☎ 292–8254), or **Malacca-Singapore Express** (☎ 293–5915).

DISCOUNT PASSES

You can **purchase a Singapore Explorer Bus Ticket** at most major hotels; it lets you travel anywhere on the island on any bus operated by Singapore Bus Service (SBS, the red-and-white buses) or Trans Island Bus Service (TIBS, the orange-and-yellow buses). You may embark and disembark as frequently as you like, flashing your pass as you board. A one-day pass costs S$5 and a three-day pass costs S$12. With this ticket you also receive an Explorer Bus Map with color-coded routes showing bus stops and all major points of interest. Most major hotels, travel agents, money changers, convenience stores and TransitLink Sales Offices at subway (MRT) stations (Raffles Place, City Hall, Bugis, Dhoby Ghaut, Somerset, Orchard and Newton) sell Explorer tickets.

Use the TransitLink farecard, a prepaid mass-transit ticket. You can purchase one for S$12 to S$52 (including a S$2 deposit), from TransitLink sales offices at MRT stations and at bus interchanges. The card lets you travel on the trains and on many buses; the fare for each trip is deducted from the balance on the card. Any unused fare and the deposit can be refunded at TransitLink offices.

BUSINESS HOURS

Businesses are generally open weekdays 9 or 9:30 to 5 or 5:30; a few are also open on Saturday morning. Banking hours are weekdays 9:30–3, Saturday 9:30–1, though branches of the Development Bank of Singapore stay open until 3 PM on Saturday, and the bank at Changi International Airport is open whenever there are flights. Many museums close on Monday; otherwise, they're generally open 9–5. Pharmacies in the major shopping centers stay open until 10 PM. Prescriptions must be written by locally registered doctors (hospitals can fill prescriptions 24 hours a day). There are 87 post offices on the island, most of them open weekdays 8:30–5 and Saturday 8:30–1. The branches at the airport and Takashimaya are open daily 8–8. Department stores and many shops in big centers are generally open seven days a week from about 10 AM to 9 PM (later some evenings). Smaller shops tend to close on Sunday.

CABLE CARS

You can catch a cable car to Sentosa Island from one of two terminals on the Singapore side: the Cable Car Towers, next to the World Trade Centre, and the Mt. Faber Cable Car Station. The trip from Cable Car Towers starts at the edge of the sea and is shorter than that from Mt. Faber. However, the trip from Mt. Faber offers better views. There's no bus to the Mt. Faber station, and it's a long walk up the hill, so a taxi is the best way to get there. The Cable Car Towers station is accessible by bus: from Orchard Road, take Bus 10 or 143; from Collyer Quay, Bus 10, 20, 30, 97, 125, or 146. Cable cars run regularly Monday–Saturday 8:30 AM–9 PM and Sundays and holidays 9–9; fares are S$6.90 round-trip, S$5.90 one-way.

➤ INFORMATION: **Cable Car Towers** (☎ 270–8855). **Mt. Faber Cable Car Station** (☎ 275–0248).

CAMERAS, CAMCORDERS, & COMPUTERS

Always **keep your film, tape, or computer disks out of the sun.** Carry an extra supply of batteries, and **be prepared to turn on your camera, camcorder, or laptop** to prove to security personnel that the device is real. Always **ask for hand inspection of film,** which becomes clouded after successive exposure to airport x-ray machines, and **keep videotapes and computer disks away from metal detectors.**

➤ PHOTO HELP: **Kodak Information Center** (☎ 800/242–2424). *Kodak Guide to Shooting Great Travel Pictures,* available in bookstores or from Fodor's Travel Publications (☎ 800/533–6478; $16.50 plus $4 shipping).

CUSTOMS

Before departing, **register your foreign-made camera or laptop with U.S. Customs** (☞ Customs & Duties, *below*). If your equipment is U.S.-made, call the consulate of the country you'll be visiting to find out whether the device should be registered with local customs upon arrival.

CAR RENTAL

Rates in Singapore begin at US$91 a day and US$548 a week for an economy car with unlimited mileage. This does not include tax on car rentals, which is 3%.

➤ MAJOR AGENCIES: **Avis** (☎ 800/331–1084 or 800/879–2847 in Canada). **Budget** (☎ 800/472–3325 in North America). **Hertz** (☎ 800/654–3131, 800/263–0600 in Canada, 0990/996699 in the U.K.). **National** (☎ 800/227–3876).

➤ LOCAL AGENCIES: Should you want to look up firms in the Singapore Yellow Pages, check under "Motorcar Renting and Leasing." The following are some local branches of international agencies: **Avis** and **National** (✉ Changi Airport, ☏ 543–2331 or 542–8855; ✉ Boulevard Hotel, 200 Orchard Blvd., ☏ 737–1668), **Budget** (✉ Pan Pacific Hotel, ground floor, ☏ 334–0019), **Hertz** (✉ Changi Airport, Terminal 2, ☏ 542–5300; ✉ Tudor Court Shopping Gallery, 125 Tanglin Rd., ☏ 800/734–4646), and **Sintat** (✉ Changi Airport, Terminal 1, ☏ 542–7288; ✉ 60 Bendemeer Rd., ☏ 295–2211 or 295–6288).

CUT COSTS

To get the best deal, **book through a travel agent who's willing to shop around.** Also **ask your travel agent about a company's customer-service record.** How has it responded to late plane arrivals and vehicle mishaps? Are there often lines at the rental counter, and, if you're traveling during a holiday period, does a confirmed reservation guarantee you a car?

NEED INSURANCE?

When driving a rented car you are generally responsible for any damage to or loss of the vehicle. You also are liable for any property damage or personal injury that you may cause while driving. Before you rent, **see what coverage you already have** under the terms of your personal auto-insurance policy and credit cards.

BEWARE SURCHARGES

Before you pick up a car in one city and leave it in another, **ask about drop-off charges or one-way service fees,** which can be substantial. Note, too, that some rental agencies charge extra if you return the car before the time specified on your contract. To avoid a hefty refueling fee, **fill the tank just before you turn in the car,** but be aware that gas stations near the rental outlet may overcharge.

MEET THE REQUIREMENTS

In Singapore your own driver's license is acceptable. An International Driver's Permit is a good idea; it's available from the American or Cana-dian automobile association, or, in the United Kingdom, from the Automobile Association or Royal Automobile Club.

CHILDREN & TRAVEL

CHILDREN IN SINGAPORE

Be sure to plan ahead and **involve your youngsters** as you outline your trip. When packing, include things to keep them busy en route. On sightseeing days try to schedule activities of special interest to your children. If you are renting a car don't forget to **arrange for a car seat** when you reserve. Most hotels in Singapore allow children under a certain age to stay in their parents' room at no extra charge, but others charge them as extra adults; be sure to **ask about the cutoff age for children's discounts.**

FLYING

As a general rule, infants under two not occupying a seat fly at greatly reduced fares and occasionally for free. If your children are two or older **ask about children's airfares.** In general the adult baggage allowance applies to children paying half or more of the adult fare. When booking, **ask about carry-on allowances for those traveling with infants.** In general, for babies charged 10% of the adult fare you are allowed one carry-on bag and a collapsible stroller, which may have to be checked; you may be limited to less if the flight is full.

According to the FAA it's a good idea to use safety seats aloft for children weighing less than 40 pounds. Airlines, however, can set their own policies: U.S. carriers allow FAA-approved models but usually require that you buy a ticket, even if your child would otherwise ride free, since the seats must be strapped into regular seats. Airline rules vary regarding their use, so it's important to **check your airline's policy about using safety seats during takeoff and landing.** Safety seats cannot obstruct any of the other passengers in the row, so get an appropriate seat assignment as early as possible.

When making your reservation, **request children's meals or a free-standing bassinet** if you need them;

the latter are available only to those seated at the bulkhead, where there's enough legroom. Remember, however, that bulkhead seats may not have their own overhead bins, and there's no storage space in front of you—a major inconvenience.

GROUP TRAVEL

If you're planning to take your kids on a tour, look for companies that specialize in family travel.

➤ TOUR COMPANY: **Rascals in Paradise** (✉ 650 5th St., Suite 505, San Francisco, CA 94107, ☎ 415/978–9800 or 800/872–7225, FAX 415/442–0289).

CONSUMER PROTECTION

Whenever possible, **pay with a major credit card** so you can cancel payment if there's a problem, provided that you can provide documentation. This is a good practice whether you're buying travel arrangements before your trip or shopping at your destination.

If you're doing business with a particular company for the first time, **contact your local Better Business Bureau and the attorney general's offices** in your state and the company's home state, as well. Have any complaints been filed?

Finally, if you're buying a package or tour, always **consider travel insurance** that includes default coverage (☞ Insurance, *below*).

➤ LOCAL BBBs: **Council of Better Business Bureaus** (✉ 4200 Wilson Blvd., Suite 800, Arlington, VA 22203, ☎ 703/276–0100, FAX 703/525–8277).

CRUISES

Singapore is trying to attract more cruise ships to the island. Right now, you can take one- to seven-day cruises to nowhere, or to destinations in Malaysia, Thailand, or Indonesia. Trips start at around S$399 on the two main ships, the *Star Aquarius* and the *Superstar Gemini*. The *Star Aquarius* has karaoke, swimming, discos, and restaurants on board. The smaller *Superstar Gemini* has similar facilities, but bigger rooms. It takes longer trips up Malaysia's west coast and on to Sumatra and Thailand. Sun Cruises, a new Singapore-owned

cruise company, began offering similar trips in 1998, and plans to expand its fleet. To get the best deal on a cruise, **consult a cruise-only travel agency.**

➤ INFORMATION: **Star Cruises** (✉ No. 21-01, Ngee Ann City, Tower B, 391B Orchard Rd., , ☎ 733–6388). **Sun Cruises** (✉ No. 05-02 Lucky Plaza, 304 Orchard Rd., ☎ 830–8800).

CUSTOMS & DUTIES

When shopping, **keep receipts** for all of your purchases. Upon reentering the country, **be ready to show customs officials what you've bought.** If you feel a duty is incorrect, appeal the assessment. If you object to the way your clearance was handled, get the inspector's badge number. In either case, first ask to see a supervisor, then write to the port director at the address listed on your receipt. Send a copy of the receipt and other appropriate documentation. If you still don't get satisfaction you can take your case to customs headquarters in Washington.

ENTERING SINGAPORE

Duty-free customs allowances in Singapore are in line with those of other countries in the region: visitors over 18 are allowed to bring in up to 1 liter of spirits, wine, or beer; all personal effects; and less than S$50 in foodstuffs such as chocolates, biscuits, and cakes. Singapore doesn't permit importing any duty-free cigarettes; pornography (including such publications as *Playboy*); toy coins and currency notes; cigarette lighters of pistol/revolver shapes; or reproductions of copyrighted publications, videotapes, records, or cassettes. The sale of chewing gum is banned, but you can usually bring in a few packs for your own use. Special import permits are required for animals, live plants, meats, arms, and controlled drugs. Penalties for drug abuse are very severe in Singapore and rigidly enforced. Customs is also extremely strict regarding the import of any form of arms, including such items as ceremonial daggers purchased as souvenirs in other countries. These are held in bond and returned to you on your departure.

There are no restrictions or limitations on the amount of cash, foreign currencies, checks, and drafts.

ENTERING THE U.S.

You may bring home $400 worth of foreign goods duty-free if you've been out of the country for at least 48 hours and haven't already used the $400 allowance or any part of it in the past 30 days.

Travelers 21 and older may bring back 1 liter of alcohol duty-free. In addition, regardless of your age, you are allowed 200 cigarettes and 100 non-Cuban cigars. (At press time, a federal rule restricting tobacco access to persons 18 years and older did not apply to importation.) Antiques, which the U.S. Customs Service defines as objects more than 100 years old, enter duty-free, as do original works of art done entirely by hand, including paintings, drawings, and sculptures.

You may also send packages home duty-free: up to $200 worth of goods for personal use, with a limit of one parcel per addressee per day (and no alcohol or tobacco products or perfume worth more than $5); label the package PERSONAL USE, and attach a list of its contents and their retail value. Do not label the package UNSOLICITED GIFT, or your duty-free exemption will drop to $100. Mailed items do not affect your duty-free allowance on your return.

➤ INFORMATION: **U.S. Customs Service** (✉ Inquiries, Box 7407, Washington, DC 20044, ☎ 202/927–6724; complaints, ✉ Office of Regulations and Rulings, 1301 Constitution Ave. NW, Washington, DC 20229; registration of equipment, ✉ Resource Management, 1301 Constitution Ave. NW, Washington, DC 20229, ☎ 202/927–0540).

ENTERING CANADA

If you've been out of Canada for at least seven days you may bring in C$500 worth of goods duty-free. If you've been away for fewer than seven days but more than 48 hours, the duty-free allowance drops to C$200; if your trip lasts 24–48 hours, the allowance is C$50. You

may not pool allowances with family members. Goods claimed under the C$500 exemption may follow you by mail; those claimed under the lesser exemptions must accompany you.

Alcohol and tobacco products may be included in the seven-day and 48-hour exemptions but not in the 24-hour exemption. If you meet the age requirements of the province or territory through which you reenter Canada you may bring in, duty-free, 1.14 liters (40 imperial ounces) of wine or liquor *or* 24 12-ounce cans or bottles of beer or ale. If you are 16 or older you may bring in, duty-free, 200 cigarettes and 50 cigars; these items must accompany you.

You may send an unlimited number of gifts worth up to C$60 each duty-free to Canada. Label the package UNSOLICITED GIFT—VALUE UNDER $60. Alcohol and tobacco are excluded.

➤ INFORMATION: **InfoCentre, Dept. of Foreign Affairs and International Trade** (✉ 125 Sussex Dr., Ottawa, Ontario K1A 0G2, ☎ 613/944–4000 or 800/267–8376). To determine what you types of products made from plants and animals you can and can't legally bring back into Canada, call **Environment Canada** (☎ 819/997–1840).

ENTERING THE U.K.

From countries outside the EU, including Singapore, you may import, duty-free, 200 cigarettes or 50 cigars; 1 liter of spirits or 2 liters of fortified or sparkling wine or liqueurs; 2 liters of still table wine; 60 milliliters of perfume; 250 milliliters of toilet water; plus £136 worth of other goods, including gifts and souvenirs.

➤ INFORMATION: **HM Customs and Excise** (✉ Dorset House, Stamford St., London SE1 9NG, ☎ 0171/202–4227).

DISABILITIES & ACCESSIBILITY

ACCESS IN SINGAPORE

Singapore is the easiest place in Southeast Asia for people with disabilities to visit. Most new major hotels, office buildings, and tourist attractions have wheelchair access and grab bars in the public toilets. Traffic lights (mostly

THE GOLD GUIDE / SMART TRAVEL TIPS

within the city) make a chirping sound when the signal turns to WALK. For more information, get a copy of "Access Singapore" from the Singapore Council of Social Services.

➤ LOCAL RESOURCES: Contact the **Singapore Council of Social Services** (✉ 11 Penang La., ☎ 336–1544 or 331–5417).

TIPS AND HINTS

When discussing accessibility with an operator or reservationist, **ask hard questions.** Are there any stairs, inside *or* out? Are there grab bars next to the toilet *and* in the shower/tub? How wide is the doorway to the room? To the bathroom? For the most extensive facilities meeting the latest legal specifications, **opt for newer accommodations,** which are more likely to have been designed with access in mind. Older buildings or ships may offer more limited facilities. Be sure to **discuss your needs before booking.**

➤ COMPLAINTS: **Disability Rights Section** (✉ U.S. Department of Justice, Box 66738, Washington, DC 20035-6738, ☎202/514–0301 or 800/514–0301; 202/514–0383 TTY, 800/514–0383 TTY, FAX 202/307–1198) for general complaints. **Aviation Consumer Protection Division** (☞ Air Travel, *above*) for airline-related problems. **Civil Rights Office** (✉ U.S. Department of Transportation, Departmental Office of Civil Rights, S-30, 400 7th St. SW, Room 10215, Washington, DC, 20590, ☎ 202/366–4648) for problems with surface transportation.

TRAVEL AGENCIES & TOUR OPERATORS

The Americans with Disabilities Act requires that travel firms serve the needs of all travelers. That said, you should note that some agencies and operators specialize in making travel arrangements for individuals and groups with disabilities.

➤ TRAVELERS WITH MOBILITY PROBLEMS: **Access Adventures** (✉ 206 Chestnut Ridge Rd., Rochester, NY 14624, ☎ 716/889–9096), run by a former physical-rehabilitation counselor. **Accessible Journeys** (✉ 35 W. Sellers Ave., Ridley Park, PA 19078, ☎ 610/521–0339 or 800/846–4537,

FAX 610/521–6959), for escorted tours exclusively for travelers with mobility impairments. **Flying Wheels Travel** (✉ 143 W. Bridge St., Box 382, Owatonna, MN 55060, ☎ 507/451–5005 or 800/535–6790, FAX 507/451–1685), a travel agency specializing in European cruises and tours. **Hinsdale Travel Service** (✉ 201 E. Ogden Ave., Suite 100, Hinsdale, IL 60521, ☎ 630/325–1335, FAX 630/325–1342), a travel agency that benefits from the advice of wheelchair traveler Janice Perkins. **Wheelchair Journeys** (✉ 16979 Redmond Way, Redmond, WA 98052, ☎ 425/885–2210 or 800/313–4751, FAX 425/881–5538), for general travel arrangements.

➤ TRAVELERS WITH DEVELOPMENTAL DISABILITIES: Every two years, **New Directions** (✉ 5276 Hollister Ave., Suite 207, Santa Barbara, CA 93111, ☎ 805/967–2841, FAX 805/964–7344) covers Singapore. **Sprout** (✉ 893 Amsterdam Ave., New York, NY 10025, ☎ 212/222–9575 or 888/222–9575, FAX 212/222–9768).

DISCOUNTS & DEALS

Be a smart shopper and **compare all your options before making a choice.** A plane ticket bought with a promotional coupon may not be cheaper than the least expensive fare from a discount ticket agency. For high-price travel purchases, such as packages or tours, keep in mind that what you get is just as important as what you save. Just because something is cheap doesn't mean it's a bargain.

LOOK IN YOUR WALLET

When you use your credit card to make travel purchases you may get free travel-accident insurance, collision-damage insurance, and medical or legal assistance, depending on the card and the bank that issued it. American Express, MasterCard, and Visa provide one or more of these services, so **get a copy of your credit card's travel-benefits policy.** If you are a member of the American Automobile Association (AAA) or an oil-company-sponsored road-assistance plan, always **ask hotel or car-rental reservationists about auto-club discounts.** Some clubs offer additional discounts on tours, cruises, or admission to attractions. And don't forget that auto-club membership entitles you to free maps and trip-planning services.

DIAL FOR DOLLARS

To save money, **look into "1-800" discount reservations services,** which use their buying power to get a better price on hotels, airline tickets, even car rentals. When booking a room, always **call the hotel's local toll-free number** (if one is available) rather than the central reservations number—you'll often get a better price. Always ask about special packages or corporate rates.

When shopping for the best deal on hotels and car rentals **look for guaranteed exchange rates,** which protect you against a falling dollar. With your rate locked in you won't pay more even if the price goes up in the local currency.

➤ AIRLINE TICKETS: ☎ **800/FLY-4-LESS.**

➤ HOTEL ROOMS: **Steigenberger Reservation Service** (☎ 800/223-5652). **Travel Interlink** (☎ 800/888-5898). **VacationLand** (☎ 800/245-0050).

SAVE ON COMBOS

Packages and guided tours can both save you money, but don't confuse the two. When you buy a package your travel remains independent, just as though you had planned and booked the trip yourself. Fly/drive packages, which combine airfare and car rental, are often a good deal.

JOIN A CLUB?

Many companies sell discounts in the form of travel clubs and coupon books, but these cost money. You must use participating advertisers to get a deal, and only after you recoup the initial membership cost or book price do you begin to save. If you plan to use the club or coupons frequently you may save considerably. Before signing up, find out what discounts you get for free.

➤ DISCOUNT CLUBS: **Entertainment Travel Editions** (✉ 2125 Butterfield Rd., Troy, MI 48084, ☎ 800/445-4137; $23-$48, depending on destination). **Great American Trav**eler (✉ Box 27965, Salt Lake City, UT 84127, ☎ 800/548-2812; $49.95 per year). **Moment's Notice Discount Travel Club** (✉ 7301 New Utrecht Ave., Brooklyn, NY 11204, ☎ 718/234-6295; $25 per year, single or family). **Privilege Card International** (✉ 237 E. Front St., Youngstown, OH 44503, ☎ 330/746-5211 or 800/236-9732; $74.95 per year). **Sears's Mature Outlook** (✉ Box 9390, Des Moines, IA 50306, ☎ 800/336-6330; $14.95 per year). **Travelers Advantage** (✉ CUC Travel Service, 3033 S. Parker Rd., Suite 1000, Aurora, CO 80014, ☎ 800/548-1116 or 800/648-4037; $49 per year, single or family). **Worldwide Discount Travel Club** (✉ 1674 Meridian Ave., Miami Beach, FL 33139, ☎ 305/534-2082; $50 per year family, $40 single).

DRIVING

It's really unnecessary to rent a car or hire a chauffeur to get around in Singapore. Distances are short, besides which, parking is very expensive, especially in the central business district (CBD). Taxis and public transportation are far more convenient and less expensive. And almost everything worth seeing is accessible by bus.

Singapore's speed limits are 80 kph (50 mph) on expressways unless otherwise posted, and 50 kph (31 mph) on other roads. One rule to keep in mind: **Yield right of way at rotaries. Drive on the left-hand side of the road** in both Malaysia and Singapore. Unleaded gas starts at S$1.25 per liter in Singapore, significantly less in Malaysia. A government ruling requires any car passing the Causeway out of Singapore to **drive with at least three-quarters of a tank of gas or be fined**; the republic's huge losses in revenue as a result of Singaporeans' driving to Malaysia to gas up cheaply led to the understandably unpopular ruling.

Speed cameras are installed throughout the island and as such you are advised to drive within the speed limit. Bus lanes or extreme left lanes marked by unbroken yellow lines are not to be used by cars and motorcycles during morning and evening rush hours during the week, and morning and noon hours on Saturday. Your car must have an Area Licensing Scheme (ALS) sticker for entering the CBD. A Road Pricing Scheme (RPS) sticker must be displayed when traveling along the expressways during morning peak hours. Both licenses are available at gas stations, ALS/RPS booths, post offices, and 7-Eleven stores.

➤ AUTO CLUBS: In the U.S., **American Automobile Association** (☎ 800/564–6222). In the U.K., **Automobile Association** (AA, ☎ 0990/500–600), **Royal Automobile Club** (RAC, ☎ 0990/722–722 membership; 0345/121–345 insurance). In Singapore, **Automobile Association of Singapore** (AAS; ☎ 748–9911).

ELECTRICITY

To use your U.S.-purchased electric-powered equipment, **bring a converter and adapter.** The electrical current in Singapore 220 volts, 50 cycles alternating current (AC); wall outlets take plugs with two round oversize prongs or plugs with three prongs. If your appliances are dual-voltage, you'll need only an adapter. Many hotels will provide this for you. Don't use 110-volt outlets, marked FOR SHAVERS ONLY, for high-wattage appliances such as blow dryers. Most laptops operate equally well on 110 and 220 volts and so require only an adapter.

EMBASSIES & EMERGENCIES

EMBASSIES

Most countries maintain embassies, consulates, or high commissions in Singapore. Phone ahead to confirm their hours. If you decide to travel to other countries in the area but did not obtain the appropriate visas before leaving home, be aware that the visa-application process at one of these Singapore consular offices may take several days. Note that most offices are open from 9 to noon and then from 2 to 4 or 4:30.

➤ INFORMATION: **Australia** (⊠ 25 Napier Rd., ☎ 737–9311). **United Kingdom** (⊠ 100 Tanglin Rd., ☎ 473–9333). **Canada** (⊠ 80 Anson Rd., ☎ 325–3200). **New Zealand** (⊠ No. 15-06/10 Tower A, 391A Orchard Rd., ☎ 235–9966). **United States of America** (⊠ 27 Napier Rd.,

☎ 476–9100), open weekdays 8:30–noon and 2–3:30.

EMERGENCIES

Police: ☎ 999; Sentosa Island Ranger Station: ☎ 279–1155. **Ambulance and fire:** ☎ 995. **Hospitals and doctors:** Alexandra Hospital (⊠ Alexandra Rd., ☎ 473–5222), Singapore General Hospital (⊠ Outram Rd., ☎ 222–3322), and Raffles Medical Group (⊠ 182 Clemenceau Ave., ☎ 331–5888 24-hour clinic/emergency center or 334–3333 SurgiCentre).

ENGLISH-LANGUAGE BOOKSTORES

Since English is the lingua franca, all regular bookstores carry English-language books, and there are bookstores in most of the larger shopping centers. Most major hotels also have a bookstore/newsstand, though selections are often limited. The Shangri-La and the Four Seasons have good collections of magazines and newspapers from around the world, as does Borders bookstore at Orchard and Scotts Roads in the Wheelock Center. The three-story MPH Bookstore at the corner of Stamford Road and Armenian Street is one of the best English-language bookshops in Asia. Other MPH outlets are scattered over the island.

Should you have trouble finding a book, try the **Times Bookstore** head office (☎ 284–8844), which will tell you whether any of its branches carries the title. Its main shops are at the Centrepoint, Lucky Plaza, Specialists Centre, Raffles City, and Marina Square shopping complexes.

Be aware that Singapore has a policy of censorship. Certain books and magazines are banned from being sold or even owned. Only one serious English-language newspaper, the *Straits Times,* is published in Singapore. It concentrates on local news but has international coverage as well. Editorially, it speaks for the ruling People's Action Party, and its reporting is highly biased.

The same company, Singapore Press Holdings, owns all the major newspapers and magazines on the island, most of which give similar fawning coverage to the government, but in different languages. The same publisher prints the *Business Times*. A popular newcomer, *The New Paper*, is a daily tabloid with a focus on local news and sports. For more international news coverage, seek out the *International Herald Tribune* or the *Asian Wall Street Journal*. Usually, both are available at the newsstands of leading hotels, though it is wise to reserve your copy ahead of time. Occasionally, in a fit of pique over an article, the government will ban a foreign publication, but the favored mode of censorship these days is lawsuits.

GAY & LESBIAN TRAVEL

The rights of gays and lesbians are not protected in Singapore, so employment and housing discrimination is not uncommon. There is no gay neighborhood per se, although a couple of gay and lesbian bars do exist, unadvertised as such. You may see a nightclub or disco listing in one of the entertainment weeklies mentioning "Boys' Night," which usually means gays are welcome and will be in the majority. "Women's Night" may refer to lesbians welcome, although "Ladies' Night" would mean heterosexual women get in free or receive discounted drinks. It may be confusing, but a sympathetic STB employee should be able to steer you in the right direction. Be discreet, as the "don't ask, don't tell" attitude seems to prevail.

➤ TOUR OPERATORS: **R.S.V.P. Travel Productions** (⊠ 2800 University Ave. SE, Minneapolis, MN 55414, ☎ 612/379–4697 or 800/328–7787, FAX 612/379–0484), for cruises and resort vacations for gays. **Hanns Ebensten Travel** (⊠ 513 Fleming St., Key West, FL 33040, ☎ 305/294–8174), one of the oldest operators in the gay market.

➤ GAY- AND LESBIAN-FRIENDLY TRAVEL AGENCIES: **Advance Damron** (⊠ 1 Greenway Plaza, Suite 800, Houston, TX 77046, ☎ 713/850–1140 or 800/695–0880, FAX 713/888–1010). **Club Travel** (⊠ 8739 Santa Monica Blvd., West Hollywood, CA 90069, ☎ 310/358–2200 or 800/429–8747, FAX 310/358–2222). **Islanders/Kennedy Travel** (⊠ 183 W. 10th St., New York, NY

10014, ☎ 212/242–3222 or 800/988–1181, FAX 212/929–8530). **Now Voyager** (⊠ 4406 18th St., San Francisco, CA 94114, ☎ 415/626–1169 or 800/255–6951, FAX 415/626–8626). **Yellowbrick Road** (⊠ 1500 W. Balmoral Ave., Chicago, IL 60640, ☎ 773/561–1800 or 800/642–2488, FAX 773/561–4497). **Skylink Women's Travel** (⊠ 3577 Moorland Ave., Santa Rosa, CA 95407, ☎ 707/585–8355 or 800/225–5759, FAX 707/584–5637), serving lesbian travelers.

HEALTH

STAYING WELL

There are no serious health risks associated with travel to Singapore. Proof of vaccination against yellow fever is required if you're entering from an infected area (e.g., often, Africa or South America). Occasionally though, there are reports of outbreaks of malaria or dengue fever, both spread by mosquitoes. If you are out exploring Singapore's wilder parks, **use insect repellent.** Tap water is safe to drink, and every eating establishment—from the most elegant hotel dining room to the smallest sidewalk stall—is regularly inspected by the very strict health authorities.

MEDICAL PLANS

No one plans to get sick while traveling, but it happens, so **consider signing up with a medical-assistance company.** Members get doctor referrals, emergency evacuation or repatriation, 24-hour telephone hot lines for medical consultation, cash for emergencies, and other personal and legal assistance. Coverage varies by plan, so **review the benefits carefully.**

➤ MEDICAL-ASSISTANCE COMPANIES: **International SOS Assistance** (⊠ Box 11568, Philadelphia, PA 19116, ☎ 215/244–1500 or 800/523–8930; ⊠ 1255 University St., Suite 420, Montréal, Québec H3B 3B6, ☎ 514/874–7674 or 800/363–0263; ⊠ 7 Old Lodge Pl., St. Margarets, Twickenham TW1 1RQ, England, ☎ 0181/744–0033). **MEDEX Assistance Corporation** (⊠ Box 5375, Timonium, MD 21094-5375, ☎ 410/453–6300 or 800/537–2029). **Traveler's Emergency Network** (⊠ 3100 Tower Blvd., Suite 1000B, Durham, NC

27707, ☎ 919/490–6055 or 800/275–4836, FAX 919/493–8262). **TravMed** (✉ Box 5375, Timonium, MD 21094, ☎ 410/453–6380 or 800/732–5309). **Worldwide Assistance Services** (✉ 1133 15th St. NW, Suite 400, Washington, DC 20005, ☎ 202/331–1609 or 800/821–2828, FAX 202/828–5896).

HOLIDAYS

Singapore has 10 public holidays. Some dates vary from year to year, so check with the STB for schedules: New Year's Day (Jan. 1), Hari Raya Puasa (Jan. 19, 1999; Jan. 8, 2000), Chinese New Year (Feb. 16–17, 1999; Feb. 5–6, 2000), Good Friday (Apr. 2, 1999; Apr. 21, 2000), Hari Raya Haji (Mar. 28, 1999; Mar. 16, 2000), Labor Day (May 1), Vesak Day (May), National Day (Aug. 9), Deepvali (Oct.–Nov.), and Christmas Day (Dec. 25).

INSURANCE

Travel insurance is the best way to **protect yourself against financial loss.** The most useful policies are trip-cancellation-and-interruption, default, medical, and comprehensive insurance.

Without insurance you will lose all or most of your money if you cancel your trip, regardless of the reason. It's essential that you **buy trip-cancellation-and-interruption insurance,** particularly if your airline ticket, cruise, or package tour is nonrefundable and cannot be changed. When considering how much coverage you need, look for a policy that will cover the cost of your trip plus the nondiscounted price of a one-way airline ticket, should you need to return home early. Also **consider default or bankruptcy insurance,** which protects you against a supplier's failure to deliver.

Medicare generally does not cover health-care costs outside the United States, nor do many privately issued policies. If your own policy does not cover you outside the United States, **consider buying supplemental medical coverage.** Remember that travel health insurance is different from a medical-assistance plan (☞ Health, *above*).

Citizens of the United Kingdom can buy an annual travel-insurance policy valid for most vacations during the year in which it's purchased. If you are pregnant or have a preexisting medical condition, make sure you're covered.

If you have purchased an expensive vacation, particularly one that involves travel abroad, comprehensive insurance is a must. **Look for comprehensive policies that include trip-delay insurance,** which will protect you in the event that weather problems cause you to miss your flight, tour, or cruise. A few insurers sell waivers for preexisting medical conditions. Companies that offer both features include Access America, Carefree Travel, Travel Insured International, and Travel Guard (☞ *below*).

Always **buy travel insurance directly from the insurance company;** if you buy it from a travel agency or tour operator that goes out of business you probably will not be covered for the agency or operator's default, a major risk. Before you make any purchase, **review your existing health and home-owner's policies** to find out whether they cover expenses incurred while traveling.

➤ TRAVEL INSURERS: In the U.S., **Access America** (✉ 6600 W. Broad St., Richmond, VA 23230, ☎ 804/285–3300 or 800/284–8300), **Carefree Travel Insurance** (✉ Box 9366, 100 Garden City Plaza, Garden City, NY 11530, ☎ 516/294–0220 or 800/323–3149), **Near Travel Services** (✉ Box 1339, Calumet City, IL 60409, ☎ 708/868–6700 or 800/654–6700), **Travel Guard International** (✉ 1145 Clark St., Stevens Point, WI 54481, ☎ 715/345–0505 or 800/826–1300), **Travel Insured International** (✉ Box 280568, East Hartford, CT 06128-0568, ☎ 860/528–7663 or 800/243–3174), **Travelex Insurance Services** (✉ 11717 Burt St., Suite 202, Omaha, NE 68154-1500, ☎ 402/445–8637 or 800/228–9792, FAX 800/867–9531), **Wallach & Company** (✉ 107 W. Federal St., Box 480, Middleburg, VA 20118, ☎ 540/687–3166 or 800/237–6615). In Canada, **Mutual of Omaha** (✉ Travel Division, 500 University Ave., Toronto, Ontario M5G 1V8, ☎ 416/598–4083, 800/268–8825 in Canada). In the U.K., **Association of British Insurers** (✉ 51

Gresham St., London EC2V 7HQ,
☎ 0171/600–3333).

LANGUAGE, CULTURE, & ETIQUETTE

Singapore is a multiracial society with four official languages: Malay, Mandarin, Tamil, and English. The national language is Malay, but the lingua franca is English. It's used in administration, it's a required course for every schoolchild, and it's used in entrance exams for universities. Hence, virtually all Singaporeans speak English with varying degrees of fluency. Mandarin is increasingly replacing the other Chinese dialects. However, many older Chinese do not speak Mandarin and communicate in "Singlish," a Singaporean version of English that has its own grammar.

You'd do well to bring along a stash of business cards—it seems like everyone exchanges them, even people who are on vacation. It's proper to offer your business card using both hands with the card facing the recipient. Likewise, when a card is offered to you, accept it in both hands and make a point to read the card. This shows your respect for the person's title and position.

Don't use your left hand for shaking or giving something to a Malay or an Indonesian, as both countries are predominantly Muslim. It's also improper for a male to kiss a female acquaintance on the cheek; and a man shouldn't offer his hand to most women until she has offered hers first. Do not be surprised or shocked to see members of the same sex hold hands, link arms, or act affectionate with one another. This is purely social behavior, not sexual.

If you're invited for dinner by Chinese friends or business acquaintances, it's proper etiquette to leave some food on the plate or in the bowl, to indicate your host has been so generous with ordering or preparing the food, you cannot eat any more. It is common for non-Asians to ask for a knife and fork instead of chopsticks. Tea is generally served at the beginning and probably throughout the meal, and it's good form to drink or at least sip the tea.

LODGING

Types of lodging run the gamut from ultraluxurious hotels to youth hostels. There are more than 30,000 rooms on the island, so it shouldn't be hard to find a place that suits your tastes and budget. Many hotels offer promotional rates, weekend rates, corporate rates, and seasonal specials; always **ask about discounts before making a reservation.** If you're looking for affordable lodgings, the STB publishes a brochure titled "Budget Hotels"; although it doesn't have objective reviews, it does list each hotel's amenities. If you arrive in Singapore without a hotel reservation, the STB and the Singapore Hotel Association both have desks at the airport, and can help you find accommodations on the spot.

APARTMENT AND VILLA RENTALS

If you want a home base that's roomy enough for a family and comes with cooking facilities, **consider a furnished rental.** These can save you money, however some rentals are luxury properties, economical only when your party is large. Home-exchange directories list rentals (often second homes owned by prospective house swappers), and some services search for a house or apartment for you (even a castle if that's your fancy) and handle the paperwork. Some send an illustrated catalog; others send photographs only of specific properties, sometimes at a charge. Up-front registration fees may apply.

► RENTAL AGENTS: **At Home Abroad** (✉ 405 E. 56th St., Suite 6H, New York, NY 10022, ☎ 212/421–9165, FAX 212/752–1591). **Drawbridge to Europe** (✉ 5456 Adams Rd., Talent, OR 97540, ☎ 541/512–8927 or 888/268–1148, FAX 541/512–0978). **Europa-Let/Tropical Inn-Let** (✉ 92 N. Main St., Ashland, OR 97520, ☎ 541/482–5806 or 800/462–4486, FAX 541/482–0660). **Interhome** (✉ 124 Little Falls Rd., Fairfield, NJ 07004, ☎ 201/882–6864, FAX 201/808–1742). **Property Rentals International** (✉ 1008 Mansfield Crossing Rd., Richmond, VA 23236, ☎ 804/378–6054 or 800/220–3332, FAX 804/379–2073). **Rent-a-Home International** (✉ 7200 34th

Ave. NW, Seattle, WA 98117, ☎ 206/
789–9377 or 800/488–7368, FAX 206/
789–9379). **Vacation Home Rentals
Worldwide** (✉ 235 Kensington Ave.,
Norwood, NJ 07648, ☎ 201/767–
9393 or 800/633–3284, FAX 201/767–
5510). **Villas and Apartments Abroad**
(✉ 420 Madison Ave., Suite 1003,
New York, NY 10017, ☎ 212/759–
1025 or 800/433–3020, FAX 212/755–
8316).

HOME EXCHANGES

If you would like to exchange your
home for someone else's, **join a home-
exchange organization,** which will
send you its updated listings of available exchanges for a year and will
include your own listing in at least
one of them. Making the arrangements is up to you.

➤ EXCHANGE CLUBS: **HomeLink International** (✉ Box 650, Key West, FL
33041, ☎ 305/294–7766 or 800/638–
3841, FAX 305/294–1148) charges $83
per year.

MAIL

Most hotels sell stamps and mail
guests' letters. You can buy postage,
stationery, and certain types of driving
permits at some post offices. Postage
on local letters up to 20 grams (0.8
ounces) is S$0.22. Airmail takes about
seven business days to reach North
America and Great Britain. An airmail
postcard costs S$0.50; larger cards are
S$1. A letter up to 20 grams is S$.35
to Malaysia or Brunei, S$.40 to other
foreign countries. Printed aerogram
letters (available at most post offices)
are S$.45. Note that delivery of small
packets, printed paper, and parcels
(both international and domestic mail)
isn't regulated; service for such items
is provided by several courier companies as well as Singapore Post.

➤ INFORMATION: **General Post Office**
(GPO; ☎ 448–7733).

RECEIVING MAIL

If you know which hotel you'll be
staying at, have mail sent there marked
"Hold for Arrival." American Express
cardholders or traveler's-check users
can have mail sent c/o **American
Express International** (✉ 300 Beach
Rd., No. 18-01/07, The Concourse,
Singapore 199555, ☎ 299–8133).

Envelopes should be marked "Client
Mail."

WRITING TO SINGAPORE

In 1997, Singapore began using a six-
digit postal code; it's important to
include this on any correspondence.
Addresses can be written either with
the number and street following the
name of the person or company, with
the second or third line being used for
the name of the building: "XYZ Sales
Office, No. 16-00 Cable Car Towers, 3
Maritime Square, Singapore 099254"
or "ABC Cable Car (Pte) Ltd., 333
Orchard Rd., No. 03-10 Mandarin
Hotel Shopping Arcade, Singapore
238867." Note that in the last address,
"03-10" refers to the third floor, office
number 10; the abbreviation "Pte"
(which is used in many business
names) indicates that a company is
owned privately rather than by the
government.

MONEY

The local currency is the Singapore
dollar (S$), which is divided into 100
cents. Notes in circulation are S$1,
S$2, S$5, S$10, S$20, S$50, S$100,
S$500, S$1,000, and S$10,000.
Coins: S$.01, S$.05, S$.20, S$.50,
and S$1. At press time, the exchange
rate was S$1.02 to the Canadian
dollar, S$1.40 to the U.S. dollar, and
S$2.16 to the pound sterling.

ATMS

Before leaving home, **make sure that
your credit cards have been pro-
grammed for ATM use in Singapore.**
Note that Discover is accepted mostly
in the United States. Local bank cards
often do not work overseas or may
access only your checking account;
**ask your bank about a MasterCard/
Cirrus or Visa debit card,** which works
like a bank card but can be used at
any ATM displaying a MasterCard/
Cirrus or Visa logo. These cards, too,
may tap only your checking account;
check with your bank about their
policy.

➤ ATM LOCATIONS: **Cirrus** (☎ 800/
424–7787). A list of **Plus** locations is
available at your local bank.

COSTS

Singapore ranks up there with other
world capitals as far as expenses go.

Although a gastronomical delight is still a little less than you would pay in Paris, hotel rooms are in the New York and London range. You can **keep costs down by eating at the inexpensive but hygienic hawker food centers,** especially those in the major shopping malls, and using the efficient, clean public transportation system, which provides easy access around the city of Singapore and the island very inexpensively.

CURRENCY EXCHANGE

For the most favorable rates, **change money at banks.** Although fees charged for ATM transactions may be higher abroad than at home, Cirrus and Plus exchange rates are excellent, because they are based on wholesale rates offered only by major banks. You won't do as well at exchange booths in airports or rail and bus stations, in hotels, in restaurants, or in stores, although you may find their hours more convenient. To avoid lines at airport exchange booths, **get a small amount of local currency before you leave home.**

➤ EXCHANGE SERVICES: International Currency Express (☎ 888/842–0880 or 888/278–6628). **Thomas Cook Currency Services** (☎ 800/287–7362 for phone orders and locations).

TRAVELER'S CHECKS

Whether or not to buy traveler's checks depends on where you are headed. **Take cash if your trip includes rural areas** and small towns, traveler's checks to cities. If your checks are lost or stolen, they can usually be replaced within 24 hours. To ensure a speedy refund, buy your checks yourself (don't ask someone else to make the purchase). When making a claim for stolen or lost checks, the person who bought the checks should make the call.

PACKING FOR SINGAPORE

Take casual, loose-fitting clothes made of natural fabrics to see you through days of heat and high humidity (you'll have to wash them often). Walking shorts, T-shirts, slacks, and sundresses are acceptable everywhere. Immodest clothing is frowned upon. You'll need a sweater or jacket to cope with air-conditioning in hotels

and restaurants that sometimes borders on the glacial. Evening wear is casual; few restaurants require jacket and tie. The standard businessman's outfit in Singapore is trousers, a dress shirt, and a tie. Businesswomen wear lightweight suits. Same-day laundry service is available at most hotels, but it can be expensive.

It's advisable to **wear a hat, sunglasses, sunblock, and—of course—comfortable shoes while sightseeing.** You'll need an umbrella all year long; you can pick up inexpensive ones locally. Leave the plastic or nylon raincoats at home—the high humidity makes them extremely uncomfortable.

Bring an extra pair of eyeglasses or contact lenses in your carry-on luggage, and if you have a health problem, **pack enough medication** to last the entire trip or have your doctor write you a prescription using the drug's generic name, because brand names vary from country to country. It's important that you **don't put prescription drugs or valuables in luggage to be checked**: it might go astray. To avoid problems with customs officials, carry medications in the original packaging. Also, don't forget the addresses of offices that handle refunds of lost traveler's checks.

LUGGAGE

In general, you are entitled to check two bags on flights within the United States and on international flights leaving the United States. A third piece may be brought on board, but it must fit easily under the seat in front of you or in the overhead compartment.

If you are flying between two foreign destinations, note that baggage allowances may be determined not by piece but by weight—generally 88 pounds (40 kilograms) in first class, 66 pounds (30 kilograms) in business class, and 44 pounds (20 kilograms) in economy. If your flight between two cities abroad *connects* with your transatlantic or transpacific flight, the piece method still applies.

Airline liability for baggage is limited to $1,250 per person on flights within the United States. On international flights it amounts to $9.07 per pound or $20 per kilogram for checked baggage (roughly $640 per 70-pound bag) and $400 per passenger for unchecked baggage. Insurance for losses exceeding these amounts can be bought from the airline at check-in for about $10 per $1,000 of coverage; note that this coverage excludes a rather extensive list of items, which is shown on your airline ticket.

Before departure, **itemize your bags' contents** and their worth, and label the bags with your name, address, and phone number. (If you use your home address, cover it so that potential thieves can't see it readily.) Inside each bag, **pack a copy of your itinerary.** At check-in, **make sure that each bag is correctly tagged** with the destination airport's three-letter code. If your bags arrive damaged or fail to arrive at all, file a written report with the airline before leaving the airport.

PASSPORTS & VISAS

All U.S., Canadian, U.K., Australian, and New Zealand citizens need only a valid passport for stays up to 14 days in Singapore. You may automatically be given a 30-day social visit pass upon your arrival if you come from any of these countries; if you arrive in Singapore from Malaysia, Indonesia, or Thailand, your passport may only be stamped for 14 days. If you require a longer stay, you may apply to Singapore Immigration after your arrival. Women who are in an advanced state of pregnancy (six months or more) should make prior application to the nearest Singapore overseas mission or the Singapore Immigration Department.

To visit Bintan Island, Indonesia, citizens of Great Britain, Canada, the United States, Australia, and New Zealand need only a passport for stays of up to one month.

Once your travel plans are confirmed, **check the expiration date of your passport.** It's also a good idea to **make photocopies of the data page;** leave one copy with someone at home and keep another with you, separated from your passport. If you lose your passport, promptly call the nearest embassy or consulate and the local police; having a copy of the data page can speed replacement.

➤ INFORMATION: **Singapore Immigration** (✉ 10 Kellang Rd., ☎ 800/391–6400). **U.S. Office of Passport Services** (☎ 202/647–0518). **Canadian Passport Office** (☎ 819/994–3500 or 800/567–6868). **London Passport Office** (☎ 0990/21010) for fees and documentation requirements and to request an emergency passport.

SAFETY

Although Singapore is probably the safest city in Asia to walk around at night unaccompanied, it is advisable to be cautious after midnight, particularly because the bus and subway service stops at that time. Taxis can be flagged, but you will see more of them in the city center than in the suburbs. During the day, although everyone seems to jaywalk, you do so at your own risk. Singapore drivers will not slow down or stop to let you cross the street. When swimming the waters of Singapore's offshore islands, be not only aware of the water quality but also the strong undercurrents in some places.

SENIOR-CITIZEN TRAVEL

Singapore is an ideal place for mature travelers to get a taste of Asia. Nearly everyone speaks English; getting around by public transit is safe, clean, and inexpensive; world-class medical facilities abound; the water is safe to drink, even from the tap (this reflects the high standard of hygiene found almost everywhere); and cultural, historical, and shopping sites are numerous. The weather, albeit warm and humid most of the time, is pleasant, and virtually all indoor public places are air-conditioned. You may even want to pack a light sweater for some of the cooler spots! Add to this the level of respect with which Asians treat senior citizens, and you're sure to feel even more like an honored guest.

To qualify for age-related discounts, **mention your senior-citizen status up front** when booking hotel reservations (not when checking out) and before you're seated in restaurants (not when paying the bill). Note that discounts may be limited to certain menus, days, or hours. When renting a car, **ask about promotional car-rental** discounts, which can be cheaper than senior-citizen rates.

➤ EDUCATIONAL TRAVEL PROGRAMS: Elderhostel (✉ 75 Federal St., 3rd floor, Boston, MA 02110, ☎ 617/426–8056). Interhostel (✉ University of New Hampshire, 6 Garrison Ave., Durham, NH 03824, ☎ 603/862–1147 or 800/733–9753, FAX 603/862–1113). Folkways Institute (✉ 14600 Southeast Aldridge Rd., Portland, OR 97236-6518, ☎ 503/658–6600, FAX 503/658–8672).

SIGHTSEEING

A wide range of sightseeing tours covers the highlights of Singapore and can be a good introduction to the island. Tours can take two hours or the whole day, and prices range from S$28 to S$80. Most are operated in comfortable, air-conditioned coaches with guides and include pickup and return. Tour agencies can also arrange private-car tours with guides; these are considerably more expensive. There's no need to book tours in advance of your visit; they can be easily arranged through the tour desks in hotels. Also, if you're only in Singapore on a six-hour stopover, the tourist board offers free city tours from Changi Airport. See the tourist board desk at the airport.

Singapore Sightseeing Tours East can arrange half- and full-day trips that include a visit to Changi Prison. Although it's easy to get around Sentosa Island on your own, Sentosa Discovery Tours offers three-hour guided trips that cover the major attractions. The tours commence every 3½ hours, beginning at 9:30 AM; tickets cost S$39. If your itinerary includes a trip to Bintan Island in Indonesia, book a day with Riau Island Adventures. You can make reservations before leaving Singapore or through the concierge at your resort on Bintan. The company's "Pinang–Penyengat Adventure Cruise" takes you to Busung, Tanjung Pinang, and Pulau Penyengat. The S$100 per person cost for this tour includes lunch and all transportation.

➤ TOUR COMPANIES: Gray Line Tours (☎ 331–8244). Holiday Tours (☎ 738–2622). Malaysia and Singapore Travel Centre (☎ 737–8877). Riau Island Adventures (☎ 270–9937 or 270–3397). RMG Tours (☎ 220–1661). Sentosa Discovery Tours (☎ 277–9654 or 275–0248). Singapore Sightseeing Tour East (☎ 332–3755). Singapore Trolley (☎ 339–6833).

STUDENTS

The tourist board publishes a brochure called "Budget Hotels" about once a year. The booklet divides hotels into four price categories: from S$120 to S$81; from S$80 to S$61; from S$60 to S$41; and hotels S$40 and below.

You may notice "student" rates for ferries, for example—this only refers to people ages 12 to 18. Carry your international student ID with you at all times, though, as entertainment venues may offer discounts. Pick up a copy of *I.S.*, the free weekly tabloid, written for people from 18 to 40.

To save money, **look into deals available through student-oriented travel agencies.** To qualify you'll need a bona fide student ID card. Members of international student groups are also eligible.

➤ STUDENT IDs AND SERVICES: Council on International Educational Exchange (✉ CIEE, 205 E. 42nd St., 14th floor, New York, NY 10017, ☎ 212/822–2600 or 888/268–6245, FAX 212/822–2699), for mail orders only, in the United States. Travel Cuts (✉ 187 College St., Toronto, Ontario M5T 1P7, ☎ 416/979–2406 or 800/667–2887) in Canada.

➤ HOSTELING: Hostelling International—American Youth Hostels (✉ 733 15th St. NW, Suite 840, Washington, DC 20005, ☎ 202/783–6161, FAX 202/783–6171). Hostelling International—Canada (✉ 400-205 Catherine St., Ottawa, Ontario K2P 1C3, ☎ 613/237–7884, FAX 613/237–7868). Youth Hostel Association of England and Wales (✉ Trevelyan House, 8 St. Stephen's Hill, St. Albans, Hertfordshire AL1 2DY, ☎ 01727/855215 or 01727/845047, FAX 01727/844126). Membership in the U.S., $25; in Canada, C$26.75; in the U.K., £9.30.

SUBWAY TRAVEL

The superb subway system, known as the MRT, consists of two lines that run north–south and east–west and cross at the City Hall and Raffles Place interchanges. The MRT includes a total of 42 stations along 67 km (42 mi). All cars and underground stations are air-conditioned, and the trains operate between 6 AM and midnight daily, at frequencies of three to eight minutes. Like everywhere else in Singapore, there are rules. Durians, the infamous "smelly" fruit of Singapore, aren't allowed on the trains or buses. There are signs posted at all stations listing the fines that can be levied if you are caught smoking, eating, drinking or littering anywhere on the transit system.

Tickets may be purchased in the stations from vending machines (which give change) or at a booth. Large maps showing the station locations and the fares between them hang above each vending machine. There's a S$2 fine for underpaying, so **make sure you buy the right ticket for your destination.** The magnetic tickets are inserted in turnstiles to let you on and off the platform. Fares start at S$.70 for about two stations; the maximum fare is S$1.60. The fare between Orchard Road Station and Raffles Place Station (in the business district) is S$.70. **Look into the TransitLink farecard** (☞ Bus Travel, *above*), a prepaid mass-transit ticket that lets you travel on trains and on many buses.

➤ INFORMATION AND SCHEDULES: TransitLink (☎ 800/779–9345). Singapore MRT Ltd. (☎ 800/336–8900).

TAXES

There's a S$15 airport departure tax (for travelers to Malaysia, the tax is S$5). If not already included with the price of your ticket, it's payable at the airport. To save time and avoid standing in line, buy a tax voucher at your hotel or any airline office.

There's a 3% sales tax, called the GST. You can get refunds for purchases over S$300 at the airport as you leave the country. You can expedite refunds by shopping in stores that have a TAX FREE FOR TOURISTS sticker in their windows. (Ask for a Tax Free Shopping Cheque to be completed, and show the goods and the checks at the airport departure

terminal for customs inspection. You can cash the checks at the Cash Refund Counters in Changi Airport; opt for a bank check via mail; or ask for a refund to a specific credit card, although a surcharge may be levied for this.) This government tax is added to restaurant and hotel bills as is a 10% service charge (except by hawker stalls and small restaurants). You're also subject to a S$15 airport departure tax (for travelers to Malaysia, the tax is S$5), which—if it's not already included in the price of your ticket—is payable at the airport (to save time and avoid standing in line, buy a tax voucher at your hotel or any airline office).

TAXIS

There are more than 15,000 strictly regulated, metered taxis in Singapore. The starting fare is S$2.40 for the first kilometer (0.9 mi) and S$.10 for each subsequent 240 meters (900 ft). After 10 km (6 mi) the rate increases to S$.10 for every 225 meters (820 ft). Every 30 seconds of waiting time carries a S$.10 charge. Drivers carry tariff cards, which you may see if you want clarification of your tab. You can **catch cabs at stands or by hailing them from any curb not marked with a double yellow line.** Radio cabs are another option though it's often hard to get through to reserve one; it's better to just hail one or take the bus. A driver showing a red disk in the window is returning to his garage and can pick up passengers going only in his direction. Drivers don't expect tips.

Be aware of several surcharges that may apply. A S$3.20 charge is added for taxis booked by phone (there's an additional S$2 surcharge for booking a half hour or more in advance). Trips made between midnight and 6 AM have a 50% surcharge, and rides from, *not to*, the airport carry a S$3 surcharge. Unless a taxi displays a yellow permit, a S$1.50 surcharge is added to fares from the CBD between 4 and 7 PM on weekdays and noon and 3 PM on Saturday. To the CBD, there's a S$3 surcharge for the purchase of an Area License, which is needed to enter the Restricted Zone between 7:30 AM and 6:30 PM Monday–Friday, between 7:30 AM and 2

PM Saturday, and on the eve of five major holidays. You don't pay the fee if the taxi already has the sticker. A S$1 surcharge is added for all trips in London cabs and station wagon taxis; an extra 10% of the fare is charged for payment by credit card. On trips to Sentosa Island there's a S$3 toll in addition to the fare, but only between 7 AM and 10 PM; cabs may drop or collect you only at the three island hotels.

➤ RADIO TAXIS: You can call for a cab (☎ 481–1211) 24 hours a day.

TELEPHONES

To call Singapore from overseas, first dial the country code, 65, then the number (Singapore has no area codes). The country code for Indonesia is 62; the area code for Bintan is 771.

Pay-phone calls within Singapore cost S$.10; insert a coin and dial the seven-digit number. Hotels charge anywhere from S$.10 to S$.50 a call. (Note that there are free public phones at Changi Airport, just past immigration.) Many pay phones only accept cards; the coin-operated phones are smaller and frequently found in shopping malls and at information desks. Phone cards (☞ *below*) in a variety of denominations are available at most kiosks, newsstands, and gift shops. For directory assistance (not yet computerized), simply dial 100.

To make direct overseas calls dial 011 and then the country code and the number; if you'd like operator assistance, dial 104. The top hotels provide direct-dial phones in guest rooms; smaller hotels have switchboards that will place your calls. In either case, check the service charge: it can be substantial. To avoid paying this charge, you **can use the international services at Changi Airport or the Singapore Telecom (SingTel) phone card.** The cards are available in denominations of S$2, S$5, S$10, S$20, and S$50 and permit you to make both local and overseas calls. The price of each call is deducted from the card total, and your balance is roughly indicated by the punched hole in the card. Phone cards are available from post offices, SingTel customer service outlets, and many drugstores.

To save money on calls to North America or the United Kingdom, **use international Home Countries Direct phones** (USA Direct or UK Direct). These put you in touch with either an American or a British operator, who places your call, either charging your phone credit card or making the call collect. You'll find these phones at many post offices around the city center. You can also use pay phones by first depositing the S$.10 and then dialing 8000–111–11 to reach a U.S. operator or 8000–440–440 for a British operator. Note also that some public phones at the airport and many at city post offices accept Diners Club, MasterCard, and Visa.

➤ INFORMATION: SingTel (☎ 288–6633).

CALLING HOME

Before you go, **find out the local access codes** for your destinations. AT&T, MCI, and Sprint long-distance services make calling home relatively convenient, but you may find the local access number blocked in many hotel rooms. First ask the hotel operator to connect you. If the hotel operator balks, ask for an international operator, or dial the international operator yourself. One way to improve your odds of getting connected to your long-distance carrier is to travel with more than one company's calling card (a hotel may block Sprint, for example, but not MCI). If all else fails, call your phone company collect in the United States or call from a pay phone in the hotel lobby.

➤ TO OBTAIN ACCESS CODES: AT&T USADirect (☎ 800/874–4000). MCI Call USA (☎ 800/444–4444). Sprint Express (☎ 800/793–1153).

TIPPING

Tipping isn't customary in Singapore. It's prohibited at the airport and discouraged in hotels (except for bellboys, who generally receive S$1 per bag) or restaurants that levy the 10% service charge. Unlike in other countries, waitstaffs don't receive a percentage of this service charge, except in the more progressive establishments, which need to retain the best waiters and waitresses. Hence, after experiencing some Singapore service you may begin to wish that tipping was the norm. Taxi drivers don't receive tips from Singaporeans, who become upset when they see tourists tip.

TOUR OPERATORS

Buying a prepackaged tour or independent vacation can make your trip to Singapore less expensive and more hassle-free. Because everything is prearranged you'll spend less time planning. Operators that handle several hundred thousand travelers per year can use their purchasing power to give you a good price. Their high volume may also indicate financial stability. But some small companies provide more personalized service; because they tend to specialize, they may also be more knowledgeable about a given area.

A GOOD DEAL?

The more your package or tour includes, the better you can predict the ultimate cost of your vacation. Make sure you know exactly what is covered, and **beware of hidden costs.** Are taxes, tips, and service charges included? Transfers and baggage handling? Entertainment and excursions? These can add up.

If the package or tour you're considering is priced lower than in your wildest dreams, **be skeptical.** Also, **make sure your travel agent knows the accommodations** and other services. Ask about the hotel's location, room size, beds, and whether it has a pool, room service, or programs for children, if you care about these. Has your agent been there in person or sent others you can contact?

BUYER BEWARE

Each year consumers are stranded or lose their money when tour operators—even very large ones with excellent reputations—go out of business. So **check out the operator.** Find out how long the company has been in business, and ask several agents about its reputation. **Don't book unless the firm has a consumer-protection program.**

Members of the National Tour Association and United States Tour Operators Association are required to set aside funds to cover your payments and travel arrangements in case the company defaults. Nonmembers may carry insurance instead. Look for the details, and for the name of an underwriter with a solid reputation, in the operator's brochure. Note: When it comes to tour operators, **don't trust escrow accounts.** Although the Department of Transportation watches over charter-flight operators, no regulatory body prevents tour operators from raiding the till. You may want to protect yourself by buying travel insurance that includes a tour-operator default provision. For more information, *see* Consumer Protection, *above.*

It's also a good idea to choose a company that participates in the American Society of Travel Agent's Tour Operator Program (TOP). This gives you a forum if there are any disputes between you and your tour operator; ASTA will act as mediator.

➤ TOUR-OPERATOR RECOMMENDATIONS: **American Society of Travel Agents** (☞ Travel Agencies, *below*). **National Tour Association** (✉ NTA, 546 E. Main St., Lexington, KY 40508, ☎ 606/226–4444 or 800/755–8687). **United States Tour Operators Association** (✉ USTOA, 342 Madison Ave., Suite 1522, New York, NY 10173, ☎ 212/599–6599, FAX 212/599–6744).

USING AN AGENT

Travel agents are excellent resources. In fact, large operators accept bookings made only through travel agents. But it's a good idea to **collect brochures from several agencies,** because some agents' suggestions may be influenced by relationships with tour and package firms that reward them for volume sales. If you have a special interest, **find an agent with expertise in that area;** ASTA (☞ Travel Agencies, *below*) has a database of specialists worldwide. Do some homework on your own, too: Local tourism boards can provide information about lesser-known and small-niche operators, some of which may sell only direct.

SINGLE TRAVELERS

Prices for packages and tours are usually quoted per person, based on two sharing a room. If traveling solo, you may be required to pay the full double-occupancy rate. Some operators eliminate this surcharge if you agree to be matched with a roommate of the same sex, even if one is not found by departure time.

GROUP TOURS

Among companies that sell tours to Singapore, the following are nationally known, have a proven reputation, and offer plenty of options. The classifications used below represent different price categories, and you'll probably encounter these terms when talking to a travel agent or tour operator. The key difference is usually in accommodations, which run from budget to better, and better-yet to best.

➤ SUPER-DELUXE: **Abercrombie & Kent** (✉ 1520 Kensington Rd., Oak Brook, IL 60521-2141, ☎ 708/954–2944 or 800/323–7308, FAX 708/954–3324) and **Travcoa** (✉ Box 2630, 2350 S.E. Bristol St., Newport Beach, CA 92660, ☎ 714/476–2800 or 800/992–2003, FAX 714/476–2538).

➤ DELUXE: **Globus** (✉ 5301 S. Federal Circle, Littleton, CO 80123, ☎ 303/797–2800 or 800/221–0090, FAX 303/795–0962), **Maupintour** (✉ Box 807, 1515 St. Andrews Dr., Lawrence, KS 66047, ☎ 913/843–1211 or 800/255–4266, FAX 913/843–8351), and **Tauck Tours** (✉ Box 5027, 276 Post Rd. West, Westport, CT 06881, ☎ 203/226–6911 or 800/468–2825, FAX 203/221–6828).

➤ FIRST-CLASS: **Brendan Tours** (✉ 15137 Califa St., Van Nuys, CA 91411, ☎ 818/785–9696 or 800/421–8446, FAX 818/902–9876), **Collette Tours** (✉ 162 Middle St., Pawtucket, RI 02860, ☎ 401/728–3805 or 800/832–4656, FAX 401/728–1380), **DER Tours** (✉ 11933 Wilshire Blvd., Los Angeles, CA 90025, ☎ 310/479–4411 or 800/937–1235), **General Tours** (✉ 53 Summer St., Keene, NH 03431, ☎ 603/357–5033 or 800/221–2216, FAX 603/357–4548), **Orient Flexi-Pax Tours** (✉ 630 3rd Ave., New York, NY 10017, ☎ 212/692–9550 or 800/545–5540), **Pacific Bestour** (✉ 228 Rivervale Rd., River Vale, NJ 07675, ☎ 201/664–8778 or 800/688–3288), and **Pacific Delight**

Tours (✉ 132 Madison Ave., New York, NY 10016, ☎ 212/684–7707 or 800/221–7179).

➤ BUDGET: **Cosmos** (☞ **Globus,** *above*).

PACKAGES

Like group tours, independent vacation packages are available from major tour operators and airlines. The companies listed below offer vacation packages in a broad price range.

Independent vacation packages are available from major airlines and tour operators. Contact **United Vacations** (☎ 800/328–6877). Many of the operators listed under group tours, above, also sell independent tours. Try **DER Tours, Orient Flexi-Pax Tours, Pacific Bestour,** and **Pacific Delight Tours.**

➤ FROM THE U.K.: Tour operators offering packages to Singapore include **Bales Tours** (✉ Bales House, Junction Rd., Dorking, Surrey RH4 3HB, ☎ 01306/876–881 or 01306/885–991), **British Airways Holidays** (✉ Astral Towers, Betts Way, London Rd., Crawley, West Sussex RH10 2XA, ☎ 01293/723171), **Hayes and Jarvis** (✉ Hayes House, 152 King St., London W6 0QU, ☎ 0181/748–5050, and **Kuoni Travel** (✉ Kuoni House, Dorking, Surrey RH5 4AZ, ☎ 01306/740500).

Travel agencies that offer cheap fares to Singapore include **Trailfinders** (✉ 42–50 Earl's Court Rd., London W8 6FT, ☎ 0171/937–5400), **Travel Cuts** (✉ 295 Regent St., London W1R 7YA, ☎ 0171/637–3161), and **Flightfile** (✉ 49 Tottenham Court Rd., London W1P 9RE, ☎ 0171/700–2722).

THEME TRIPS

Customized, deluxe tours of Singapore, tailored to individual interests, are available from **Pacific Experience** (✉ 366 Madison Ave., No. 1203, New York, NY 10017, ☎ 212/661–2604 or 800/279–3639, FAX 212/661–2587).

TRAIN TRAVEL

There are regular trains between Singapore and key cities and towns on the western seaboard of Peninsular Malaysia, including Kuala Lumpur (called "KL") and JB. There are three daily departures to JB; the trip takes about an hour and costs roughly S$3. The air-conditioned express train to KL also leaves three times daily. The trip takes about six hours, and the first-class one-way fare is S$60.

E&OE Services, the company that operates the *Venice Simplon–Orient Express,* runs the deluxe *Eastern & Oriental Express;* it travels between Singapore and Bangkok once a week and stops in Butterworth, Malaysia, permitting an excursion to Penang. The 1,943-km (1,200-mi) journey takes 41 hours and includes two nights and one full day on board. The cabin decor is modeled on the Josef von Sternberg–Marlene Dietrich movie *Shanghai Express.* Fares, which vary according to cabin type and include meals, start at S$2,218 (US$1,300) per person one way.

➤ INFORMATION AND RESERVATIONS: **E&OE Services** (☎ 800/524–2420 in North America; 0171/805–5100 in the U.K.; 3/9699–9766 in Australia; or 9/379–3708 in New Zealand). **Singapore Train Station** (☎ 222–5165).

TRANSPORTATION

Singapore could be considered the transportation hub of Southeast Asia, with its modern and efficient Changi Airport; ferry services from three different terminals; and regular bus and train service. Travel agencies are plentiful, especially in the Orchard Road shopping malls, and all offer three- to seven-day excursions to points outside Singapore. Air travel is usually the fastest way to go, although you must be aware of waits for connecting flights, especially in Malaysia. Buses and trains leave Singapore frequently, and are less expensive than planes. To get a taste of Indonesia, the 45-minute ferry service to Bintan's resort-oriented north coast from Singapore's Tanah Merah Ferry Terminal is the best bet.

TRAVEL AGENCIES

A good travel agent puts your needs first. Look for an agency that has been in business at least five years,

emphasizes customer service, and has someone on staff who specializes in your destination. In addition, **make sure the agency belongs to the American Society of Travel Agents** (ASTA). If your travel agency is also acting as your tour operator, *see* Buyer Beware in Tour Operators, *above*).

➤ LOCAL AGENT REFERRALS: **American Society of Travel Agents** (ASTA, ☎ 800/965–2782 24-hr hot line, FAX 703/684–8319). **Alliance of Canadian Travel Associations** (✉ 1729 Bank St., Suite 201, Ottawa, Ontario K1V 7Z5, ☎ 613/521–0474, FAX 613/521–0805). **Association of British Travel Agents** (✉ 55–57 Newman St., London W1P 4AH, ☎ 0171/637–2444, FAX 0171/637–0713).

TRAVEL GEAR

Travel catalogs specialize in useful items, such as compact alarm clocks and travel irons, that can **save space when packing.** They also offer dual-voltage appliances, currency converters, and foreign-language phrase books.

➤ MAIL-ORDER CATALOGS: **Magellan's** (☎ 800/962–4943, FAX 805/568–5406). **Orvis Travel** (☎ 800/541–3541, FAX 540/343–7053). **TravelSmith** (☎ 800/950–1600, FAX 800/950–1656).

U.S. GOVERNMENT

The U.S. government can be an excellent source of inexpensive travel information. When planning your trip, **find out what government materials are available.**

➤ ADVISORIES: **U.S. Department of State** (✉ Overseas Citizens Services Office, Room 4811 N.S., Washington, DC 20520); enclose a self-addresses, stamped envelope. **Interactive hot line** (☎ 202/647–5225, FAX 202/647–3000). **Computer bulletin board** (☎ 301/946–4400).

➤ PAMPHLETS: **Consumer Information Center** (✉ Consumer Information Catalogue, Pueblo, CO 81009, ☎ 719/948–3334) for a free catalog that includes travel titles.

VISITOR INFORMATION

➤ SINGAPORE TOURISM BOARD (STB): In the U.S.: ✉ 590 5th Ave., 12th floor, New York, NY 10036, ☎ 212/302–4861, FAX 212/302–4801, www.singapore-usa.com; ⊠ Two Prudential Plaza, 180 N. Stetson Ave., Suite 2615, Chicago, IL 60601, ☎ 312/938–1888, FAX 312/938–0086; ⊠ 8484 Wilshire Blvd., Suite 510, Beverly Hills, CA 90211, ☎ 323/852–1901, FAX 323/852–0129. In **Canada:** ⊠ The Standard Life Centre, 121 King St. W, Suite 1000, Toronto, Ontario, M5H 3T9, ☎ 416/363–8898, FAX 416/363–5752, www.singapore-ca.com. In the U.K.: ⊠ Carrington House, 126–130 Regent St., London W1R 5FA, ☎ 0171/437–0033. In **Australia:** ⊠ Level II, AWA Bldg., 47 York St., Sydney, NSW 2000, ☎ 2/9290–2888 or 2/9290–2882, FAX 2/9290–2555; ⊠ 8th floor, St. Georges Ct., 16 St. Georges Terr., Perth, WA 6000, ☎ 9/325–8578 or 325–8511, FAX 9/221–3864. In **New Zealand:** ⊠ 43 High St., 3rd floor, Auckland, ☎ 9/358–1191, FAX 9/358–1196.

➤ IN SINGAPORE: **STB** (⊠ Tourism Court, 1 Orchard Spring La., Singapore 247729, ☎ 736–6622 or 800/738–3778; ⊠ 328 North Bridge Rd., no. 02–34 Raffles Hotel Arcade, 189673, ☎ 800/334–1335 or 800/334–1336). Daily from 8:30 AM to 7 PM, multilingual staff members can answer any questions you have and attend to legitimate complaints.

If you're planning a trip to Bintan Island contact the **Indonesian Tourist Promotion Office** (⊠ No. 15–07 Ocean Bldg., 10 Collyer Quay, Singapore 039192, ☎ 534–2837) for tourist, passport and visa, health, and currency information.

WHEN TO GO

With the equator only 129 km (80 mi) to the south, Singapore is usually either hot or very hot. The average daily temperature is 80°F (26.6°C); it usually reaches 87°F (30.7°C) in the afternoon and drops to a cool 75°F (23.8°C) just before dawn. The months from November through January, during the northeast monsoon, are generally the coolest. The average daily relative humidity is 84.5%, though it drops to 65%–70% on dry afternoons.

Rain falls year-round, but the wettest months are November through January. February is usually the sunniest month; December, the most inclement. Though Singapore has been known to have as much as 512.2 mm (20 inches) of rainfall in one 24-hour period, brief, frequent rainstorms are the norm, and the washed streets soon dry in the sun that follows.

➤ FORECASTS: **Weather Channel Connection** (☎ 900/932–8437), 95¢ per minute from a Touch-Tone phone.

The following are average daily maximum and minimum temperatures for Singapore.

Climate In Singapore

Jan.	86F	30C	May	89F	32C	Sept.	88F	31C
	74	23		75	24		75	24
Feb.	88F	31C	June	88F	31C	Oct.	88F	31C
	74	23		75	24		74	23
Mar.	88F	31C	July	88F	31C	Nov.	88F	31C
	75	24		75	24		74	23
Apr.	88F	31C	Aug.	88F	31C	Dec.	88F	31C
	75	24		75	24		74	23

THE GOLD GUIDE / SMART TRAVEL TIPS

1 Destination: Singapore

A CITY OF MANY FACES

EVER SINCE SINGAPORE BECAME an independent nation in 1965, it has been a standing joke among Singaporeans that if you turn your back for a second, you won't be able to find your way home, the streetscape will have changed so much.

Demolition, development, and renewal rotate in endless cycles on the 646-square-km (249-square-mi) tropical island, contributing to the underlying nervous tension of the place. Singapore's history, pocked with the turbulence of the World War II Japanese Occupation and postwar communist insurgency, has left a residue of anxiety. The vulnerability many feel is heightened by the former British colony's geographical situation as a predominantly Chinese island surrounded by the more traditional and conservative Malayo-Islamic cultures of Malaysia and Indonesia. Hypersensitive to perceived danger and to criticism from without and within, Singapore's government has waged feisty battles with both the foreign press and local liberals.

A real dependence on the global economy and trading system exacerbates this strung-out feeling as the nation darts hither and thither like a nimble shrimp, deftly changing course in response to international currents. But Singapore has always insisted it is a shrimp with a sting in its tail, thanks to a well-equipped army and action-ready citizenry, schooled by military National Service and regular Civil Service drills.

Singapore has a relentless urge to develop and capitalize its limited land resources; the economy has often been primed by massive infrastructural projects, such as the construction of the world's best, most comfortable airport at Changi and also one of the world's most efficient subway systems, the MRT (Mass Rapid Transit System). In addition the government has built blocks of high-rise housing in which more than 80% of Singapore's 2.9 million citizens live as home owners, thanks in part to a government-run compulsory savings fund.

Another local joke (yes, Singaporeans do know how to laugh at themselves, notwithstanding the seeming earnest formality of their public and official personae) has it that all the Singapore girl cares about in Mr. Right is the Five C's—Car, Condo, Cash, Credit Card, and Country Club. That's sexist—those badges of material success are pretty high on the agenda for all Singaporeans, male and female. In a country where you have to bid for the right to own a car before you even begin to buy one and where land sells for about S$5 million and high-rise government-built apartments for half a million, such acquisitions imply serious wealth.

Singapore always has been a social laboratory. Its citizens have taken pride in doing it their way, making up their own rules. Western concepts of liberal democracy, freedoms of the press, speech, and assembly, privacy of information, and the like have often been brushed aside as bothersome brakes on action by a People's Action Party (PAP) government repeatedly re-elected to overwhelming majority power since 1959. Detention without trial for both criminal elements and those deemed political internal security risks is a weapon of state inherited from the British colonial administration and still occasionally used.

There being little real prospect of electoral defeat for the PAP, a certain stability permitting efficient long-term planning has resulted. The populace is largely compliant, give or take a few intellectuals, in return for the government's guarantee of a "full rice bowl": it's an ancient, essentially Confucian, social contract. Stability should not be confused with complacency, however. When faced with an election, the PAP campaigns hard to increase its share of the vote. Likewise, the government is concerned about the declining economic growth rate and strives to recapture the higher rates of the late 1980s and early 1990s.

Singapore is indeed its own nation. When in the late 1970s the government set up an official matchmaking unit, the SDU (Social Development Unit), dedicated initially to getting reluctant or unsuccessful female graduates married off, yet another Singaporean joke scoffed at it as standing for "Single, Desperate, and Ugly." But today it has melted into the mainstream.

That Singapore favors tough laws—hanging for drug trafficking or mere association with firearms carried for a criminal purpose, and caning for various offenses, including immigration visa overstay and vandalism—is well known. Yet it has to be said that the streets of Singapore are among the safest in the world for a woman, or man, to walk alone by night, besides being clean and drug-free.

There is an old saw that Singapore is "a fine city"—S$1,000 fine for littering, S$500 for smoking indoors, S$500 for not flushing the toilet; it's all part of the Singaporean penchant for order, orderliness, and Victorian-style propriety (and, sometimes, hypocrisy to match).

In pursuit of order and decorum, there are now laws banning the importation, sale, purchase, or manufacture (but not the possession or consumption) of chewing gum, backed up by a S$1,000 fine (kids were jamming up the MRT sliding doors with the stuff), and not only nudity in public places but also nudity in private places visible to the public (e.g., your own highrise apartment, as seen from your neighbor's facing window), with a fine of S$2,000, or three months' jail. Another new law holds parents liable for their minor children's delinquency, and yet another allows parents to sue grown children for financial support.

But beneath the orderly surface, tremendous social change is under way. Confronted with its limits to growth, Singapore is externalizing its economy, intentionally creating mini-Singapores abroad, notably in China and India. It is also networking with extensive expatriate and emigrant Singaporean communities in Australia, Canada, and the United States, among other locations. A general broadening of the national mind has been the inevitable result.

With the Five C's becoming ever less affordable, many young Singaporeans are reassessing their culture's fabled work ethic (Saturday morning is still all hands to the deck), wondering if it is worth striving so hard. That's a big change from their parents' attitude.

Barring occasional incidents of censor backlash, the arts scene is becoming more liberal. Reasonably adult films are at last standard cinema fare, in the R(A) or "Restricted (Artistic)" classification category; both local theater and local literature are blooming. Independent voices are more often heard than in the past; among these are fairly vocal green and feminist lobby groups.

In a sense, Singapore wears a reversible costume—Western suit/Mandarin jacket—and swaps Chinese opera masks at will to reflect whatever character it wants to play at any given moment. That makes it a uniquely deceptive place, difficult to know beyond the Western gloss and, in a way, treacherous for the unwary.

Behind the computer terminals sit people who set superstitious store in the power of numbers (unlucky 4 brings death, while lucky 8 wins prosperity) and position their homes and business premises according to the precepts of feng shui, or geomancy; in their leisure hours, some of them may be temple spirit mediums or firewalkers.

Careful background reading, particularly of the country's history, will help you to understand these contradictions, as would study of Singapore's various languages, including that vibrant street-jive creole "Singlish," a potpourri of English, Chinese, and Malay impenetrable to the native English-speaker. (Fortunately, Singaporeans switch easily to "Queen's English.") And don't forget to talk to taxi drivers.

Most foreigners in Singapore (including about 300,000 "guest workers," mostly construction laborers and maids, who do the dirtier work most Singaporeans will not do anymore) are mere birds of passage, but some have found reasons to linger. They find it hard to put their finger on what it is that has made them stay: "It's just a certain something." But when pressed, many point to an underlying gentleness bordering on innocence, or a childlike enjoyment of simple, often material, pleasures that together typify the Singaporean. Others relish the vibrant multicultural street life of a tropical city. Still others cite the energy of the place, the constant sense of being busy and purposeful, of going somewhere.

As in a traditional arranged marriage, you have to *learn* to love Singapore—it's not a love-at-first-sight place. And as the old song goes, to know it is to love it. It only takes time.

— Ilsa Sharp

WHAT'S WHERE

The diamond-shape island of the Republic of Singapore, lying offshore but connected by a causeway to peninsular Malaysia, is only 622 square km, or 240 square mi (646 square km/249 square mi if you include the satellite islands), and yet it has nature reserves, a thriving metropolis, ethnic enclaves, industrial parks, beaches, and entertainment parks. More than 3 million people now live in Singapore, and the majority of their ancestors arrived from all points of the compass within the past 200 years. They brought cultural diversity, which shaped Singapore's evolution into today's vibrant ethnic mix.

Sir Thomas Stamford Raffles chose to develop Singapore as a trading center for the East India Company because of the island's commanding position on the Straits of Malacca and the safe anchorage in the southwestern harbor at the mouth of Singapore River. This was to be the cauldron of sweat and toil that produced Raffles's commercial emporium. Paramount to maintaining a smooth trading operation was the prevention of racial strife, and so Raffles applied his knowledge of 19th-century urban planning. In his perspective, racial harmony was best achieved by geographical segregation: the Chinese, Indians, Malays, and, of course, the Europeans were allotted their separate domains. The vestiges of these racial divisions are still apparent.

Since the most desirable land lay to the east of the river and overlooking the waterfront, Raffles designated it as the domain of the British and their administration. Here, in what has been termed **Colonial Singapore,** is what's left of the work of the Irish architect George Coleman, who with Raffles created one of the major entrepôts in Asia. Coleman's Palladian-style buildings, modified to confront the steaming tropical heat, are impressive monuments to his era and now serve as a buffer zone

between the high-tech glitz of Orchard Road and Chinatown.

The Chinese, on whose backs Singapore's trade depended, were allotted the area south of the Singapore River. Even within **Chinatown,** different ethnic clusters formed. Arriving from China often with no money and in debt to the boat captains who brought them, these immigrants sought shelter with those who came from the same region of China. Crowding was horrendous, with one or more families living in a single room. The only escape was to smoke a pipe in one of the many opium dens, seek company at the corner brothel, or pay tribute to the gods in the hope they'd assist lady luck in the gambling dens. Although Singapore's quest to be a futuristic metropolis caused much of old Chinatown to be bulldozed, there are still a few remnants of the past. Rows of shophouses (two-story buildings with a store or a factory at ground level and living space upstairs); streets specializing in such particularities as herbal medicines or death houses; elaborate temples to the gods of the old country; wet markets; and other structures built by the original immigrants maintain the flavor of Raffles's day.

Land to the east and north of Colonial Singapore beginning at Sungei Road was allotted to the Indian community, whose main street is Serangoon Road. While many Indians came as convict labor and later taught crafts, others came to work as traders, clerks, teachers, and moneylenders. And though they came from all over ethnically diverse India, they melded into their own Singaporean Indian culture. Many of them shared the Hindu religion, and here, in what is known as **Little India,** you'll find several ornate temples. The whole area, especially the streets branching off Serangoon Road, is perfumed with smells of spices and curries, colored by women wearing saris, and crammed with stores brimming with goods brought from the Indian subcontinent.

Slightly to the east of Little India, bordered by Beach and North Bridge roads, is the **Arab District,** sometimes known as Little Araby. Though Malays lived in *kampongs* (small communities) throughout the island, this area was assigned to Malays who wanted to be close to the action. Not only Malays but also other Muslims, especially traders from Indonesia, congregate here.

Streets named Bussorak and Kandahar not only evoke images of the Muslim world, but also provide excellent shopping for imported batiks and Indonesian crafts.

Modern, fashion-conscious Singapore is north and slightly west of Colonial Singapore, the administrative center. **Orchard Road,** its main street, is like New York's Fifth Avenue or London's Regent Street. Here are countless glittering shopping plazas and hotels. At the junction of Orchard and Scotts roads, a central hub, you will see every person who comes to Singapore.

Out of the central city, the **East Coast Parkway** runs toward Changi Airport and the infamous Changi Prison, where the Japanese incarcerated the Europeans captured at the fall of Singapore in 1941. Along this coast are the best, albeit limited, beach areas with facilities for water sports. In the opposite direction, down past the World Trade center and running along the southwest coast, is the **West Coast Highway,** leading to the industrial area of Jurong. Along this route are several theme parks and gardens.

Less than 5% of the island remains forested. However, there is more to Singapore than its concrete buildings and glass skyscrapers. It is not too much of a stretch to call at least the interior of Singapore the **Garden Isle.** Going north and inland from downtown Singapore, you come upon the beautiful Botanic Gardens, said to be second only to those in Bogor on Java for the display of tropical plants. Farther north and slightly to the west is the Bukit Timah Nature Reserve, where trails wind their way through thick forest. To the north of that is the superb Singapore Zoological Garden and the equally fascinating Night Safari park, where nocturnal animals roam in "natural" surrounds. Farther north, you come to the Mandai Orchid Gardens, which have more than 2,000 varieties.

Some 60 small islands lie off the southern coast of the main island of Singapore. The largest is **Sentosa,** now linked by a causeway and a cable car, which has become a full-blown entertainment island with hotels, restaurants, museums, aquariums, and nature parks.

Kusu Island and **St. John's Island,** lying south of Sentosa, are among the outer islands that you can reach via scheduled boat service. They're popular picnic spots for Singaporeans.

Bintan, an Indonesian resort island in the Singapore Strait, is just 45 minutes from Singapore's World Trade Centre by ferry.

PLEASURES AND PASTIMES

Dining

Eating is an all-consuming passion among Singaporeans, and you'll soon discover why. There's a stunning array of cuisine from around the world, particularly from the three major cultures that make up the island nation: Chinese, Malay, and Indian. It also won't take you long to discover that Singaporeans love spices. But spicy doesn't necessarily mean hot. It can also mean tastes that are mellow, as in thick, rich coconut gravies; pungent, as in Indian curries; tart, as in the sour and hot tamarind-, vinegar-, and lime-based gravies of Thailand, Malaysia, Indonesia, and Singapore; or sweet and fragrant, as in Indian desserts and beverages.

Gardens and Parks

You can escape from the concrete and glass that is modern downtown Singapore to visit orchid farms or the wonderfully kept Botanic Gardens. If you have a lot of energy, you can hike the trails of Bukit Timah Nature Reserve—the tigers have long gone, but the sounds and smells of the jungle are still here. If you want to see a tiger or two, as well as animals from as far away as the North Pole, Singapore has a pleasant zoo, designed on the open-moat concept. And because many animals are nocturnal, there's another zoo, the Night Safari, where tigers and rhinoceros wake up at dusk to feed.

Lodging

Although Singapore isn't the same indulgent retreat it once was, it's hard to match the standard of comfort, efficiency of staff, and level of services that Singapore hotels offer. The luxury establishments cater to every whim—and so they should at more than S$300 a night—but you can find good service, freshly decorated rooms, cleanliness, and modern facilities for around S$200. For less money, there are simple, clean hotels (often more personal than the larger ones), with rooms for about S$90. If you're on a tight budget, the youth hostels are spotless, cosmopolitan, and cheap.

Shopping

Once upon a time Singapore, a duty-free republic, was a haven for shoppers. And though shopping is still the major pastime, nowadays the shoppers tend to be rich and sassy. Except for a lucky find in an antiques store, bargains are hard to come by. Still, nowhere else will you find so many shops that carry the latest fashions and electronic equipment. Browsing here is as much a pleasure as shopping.

Theme Parks

No other country of Singapore's size has put so much effort into creating attractions for both its citizens and tourists. Singapore may have spent millions destroying its heritage buildings, but private enterprise has also spent a fortune re-creating the old at theme parks, usually designed to educate and entertain. Haw Par Villa emphasizes Chinese mythology, and the Tang Dynasty Village displays life in ancient China.

NEW AND NOTEWORTHY

Singapore is always adding **new and sparkling hotel rooms** to its already huge inventory—in excess of 30,000. Three of the city's newest hotels—the Ritz-Carlton, the Inter-Continental, and the Four Seasons—are in the luxury category. To accommodate travelers who want convenience, comfort, and efficiency, but who hate high prices, the Shangri-La group recently opened the Traders Hotel; the Raffles Group followed suit with its Merchant Court Hotel.

Singapore's new museums include the **Asian Civilisations Museum, Phase I** (Phase II will open in 2000 at Empress Place) and the **Singapore Philatelic Museum.** Within a few minutes' walking distance from the Singapore Art Mu-

seum, these two are impressive in their respective interests, and are housed in grand colonial buildings.

Despite the economic crisis, **Singapore Airlines** is offering more and better creature comforts. In economy look for personal video monitors (with games or movies), adjustable head and foot rests, gourmet meals (say, terrine of smoked salmon and asparagus), and free champagne. Business class offers wide, plush seats—more like those in first class on other craft—with reading lights, laptop power supplies, sleek video screens, and headphones that eliminate background noise. If the cheese-board hors d'oeuvres and elegant meals don't satisfy you, perhaps the biscotti with your espresso will. First-class minisuites have leather and wood touches, seats that recline all the way (yes, bedding and bedclothes are provided), a retractable working/dining surface, and a 14-inch fold-away video monitor. You choose when you'd like to eat: menus are by seven of the world's most renowned chefs; place settings are by Givenchy.

FODOR'S CHOICE

Sights and Museums

★ **Asian Civilisations Museum.** Here you'll find absolutely top-notch exhibitions, most of which display antiquities from mainland China.

★ **Botanic Gardens.** A trip here offers both an escape from the city's brick and mortar and a chance to appreciate tropical flora.

★ The **Pioneers of Singapore Museum.** At this Sentosa Island establishment you'll find a three-dimensional recounting of Singapore's early days.

★ **Singapore Zoological Gardens and Night Safari.** The open plans place you *in* the animals' habitats.

★ **Sri Mariamman Temple.** This temple brings Hinduism down to earth.

★ The **Sultan Mosque.** With its gold domes and minarets that glisten in the sun, it's really no wonder that this mosque is the focus of the Malay community.

Restaurants

⭐ **Gordon Grill.** Here the best Continental cuisine in town is served in an elegant setting. *$$$$*

⭐ **Jiang Nan-Chun.** The sophisticated presentation is matched by exquisite Cantonese cuisine. *$$$$*

⭐ **Cherry Garden.** In surroundings reminiscent of a Chinese pavilion, you can feast on unusual cuisine from China's Hunan province. *$$$*

⭐ **Club Chinois.** This restaurant's swank surroundings set the tone for "nouvelle Chinoise," a creative fusion of Cantonese and French cuisine. *$$$*

⭐ **Nadaman.** The ultimate in refined Japanese cuisine is served here with the Singapore skyline as a backdrop. *$$$*

⭐ **Tandoor.** A meal in this restaurant makes you feel as if you're dining in a maharaja's palace. It follows that the North Indian dishes are first-rate. *$$$*

⭐ **Café Modestos.** The Mediterranean and traditional-Italian inspired dishes here are all reasonably priced. *$$–$$$*

⭐ **Dragon City.** Many Singaporeans consider this the best place to enjoy the emphatic cuisine of Szechuan. *$$–$$$*

⭐ **Thanying.** Here you'll find refined Thai palace cuisine, produced by Thai chefs under the supervision of a noble Thai family. *$$–$$$*

⭐ **House of Sudanese Food.** Inexpensive delights from west Java are served in this down-to-earth and friendly restaurant. *$–$$*

⭐ **Banana Leaf Apollo.** The South Indian curries, including the famous Singaporean fish-head curry, are served on banana leaves here. *$*

⭐ **Madras New Woodlands Restaurant.** This unpretentious restaurant in the heart of Little India serves the world's most creative vegetarian cuisine. *$*

Hotels

⭐ **The Oriental.** The service here is extraordinary. *$$$$*

⭐ **Raffles Hotel.** Cliché though it may be, this world-famous hotel still oozes tradition and gentility in the midst of its modern, high-rise neighbors. *$$$$*

⭐ **Ritz-Carlton.** When you can see Singapore Harbor from your bathtub, you know you've found a hotel that's truly indulgent. *$$$$*

⭐ **The Duxton.** Intimate, tasteful, and full of character, The Duxton was one of Singapore's first boutique hotels. *$$$*

⭐ **Traders Hotel.** What the Traders lacks in frills it makes up for in basic comforts, efficient service, and reasonable prices. *$$*

⭐ **Ladyhill Hotel.** The comfortable Ladyhill is in a residential neighborhood, making it a pleasant retreat from high-rise and high-tech Singapore. *$*

⭐ **Regalis Court.** At this, another of Singapore's boutique hotels, traditional Asian decor is combined with classical European touches. *$*

⭐ **RELC International House.** This conference center–hostelry may well give you the most bang for your budget bucks. *$*

Nightlife

⭐ **Boat Quay.** With its many indoor and outdoor bars and restaurants, Boat Quay is the best place for people-watching and partying.

⭐ **Que Pasa and Ice Cold Beer.** Next door to each other are these two friendly watering holes, good for meeting old and new friends.

⭐ **Saxophone.** For good jazz, this place is hard to beat.

⭐ **Zouk, Velvet Underground, and Phuture.** At these world-class dance clubs varying music styles and age groups mix effortlessly.

Shopping

⭐ **Ngee Ann City.** This complex has a collection of high-fashion shops anchored by the Takashimaya department store.

⭐ **Chinatown Centre.** For exotic, mouthwatering foods, you'll be hard pressed to find something that beats the wet market here.

⭐ **P. Govindasamy Pillai.** Here you'll find the best-quality Indian silks.

⭐ **China Silk House.** This place has a deservedly high reputation for Chinese silks.

GREAT ITINERARIES

You can do as much or as little as you like in Singapore. If you took in all of the regions explored in this guide without stopping for breath, you would see virtually all of Singapore in five days—and not even have begun to shop! There's plenty to see and do if you have the time.

One way to experience Singapore is to use it as a hub for travel throughout Southeast Asia. From the city-state's airport, Changi, planes travel in all directions, and many flights between countries connect through Singapore. So you may want to see Singapore in installments. After a couple of days spent exploring the city-state, go to another Southeast Asian country, then return to Singapore before continuing to yet another destination. Singapore permits you to catch your breath: it's safe, it's clean, and everything works efficiently.

If You Have 2 Days

On the first morning, you might visit the **Colonial** and **Chinatown** districts, then spend the afternoon shopping and exploring on **Orchard Street.** In the evening, dine at one of the city's many excellent restaurants. The next day have breakfast at the zoo, then return to the city to explore **Little India** and the **Arab District.** In the afternoon, you may want to take the ferry or cable car to **Sentosa Island** to see the **Pioneers of Singapore Museum.** In the evening, try dining at a food center, such as **Newton Circus.**

If You Have 4 Days

In the first two, get to know the city by covering the **Colonial, Chinatown, Little India,** and **Arab districts.** You'll surely spend some time on **Orchard Street** shopping, browsing, and people-watching. One evening soon after dusk, visit the **Night Safari** park, then have dinner at a hawker food center. On the third day, take a trip out to **Kusu** or one of the other islands and spend a few hours exploring. For the afternoon, try one of Singapore's theme parks, perhaps **Haw Par Villa.** In the evening, stroll first around **Clarke Quay** before moving on to **Boat Quay** for drinks, people-watching, and perhaps something to eat. On the fourth day, visit some museums and parks on **Sentosa Island;** try not to miss the **Pioneers of Singapore Museum,** since that gives a good idea of what Singapore was like in the early 1800s. In the evening treat yourself at one of Singapore's gourmet havens.

If You Have 7 or More Days

Use the first three or four days to explore urban Singapore, then head to **Bintan Island, Indonesia,** for a couple of days on the beach. Set aside at least one day for an excursion that takes you to Tanjung Pinang, the island's main town, as well as through a mangrove swamp to a Chinese temple and a traditional Indonesian village.

FESTIVALS AND SEASONAL EVENTS

Singapore is a city of festivals, from the truly exotic (Thaipusam, Festival of the Nine Emperor Gods) to the strictly-for-tourists (International Shopping Festival, Miss Tourism Pageant). Timing your visit to coincide with one of the more colorful celebrations can greatly increase the pleasure of your stay; with so many different cultural and religious groups, you'll find festivals going on almost all the time. There are numerous national holidays and celebrations as well.

Except for the family-oriented festivals and the monthlong fast of Ramadan, these events are as much fun for visitors as they are for the native celebrants. The following is a chronological listing of the major festivals. The dates and seasons of many of them vary from year to year according to the lunar calendar. For a complete listing with current dates, contact the Singapore Tourism Board (STB).

WINTER

LATE DEC.–LATE JAN.➤ **Ramadan** is the month of daytime fasting among the city's Muslim population. Its date is set by the Islamic calendar. Special stalls in Bussorah Street and around the Sultan Mosque sell a variety of dishes, including Malay rice cakes wrapped in banana leaves, fragrant puddings, and mutton

cubes topped with sweet roasted coconut. The best time to visit the food stalls is between 5 and 7:30 PM, when the Muslim community emerges from the day's fast for a binge of snacking. The end of Ramadan is marked with a celebration, **Hari Raya Puasa.** A major feast is undertaken as celebrating Muslims, dressed in traditional garb, visit friends and relatives.

MID-JAN.➤ During **Pongal,** the four-day harvest festival, Tamil Indians from South India offer rice, curries, vegetables, sugarcane, and spices in thanksgiving to the Hindu gods. The Perumal Temple on Serangoon Road is the best place to view these rites. During this holiday, the Tamils give presents and send greeting cards. The cards are sold in most Indian shops and stalls along Serangoon Road.

MID-JAN.–FEB.➤ **Thaipusam** celebrates the victory of the Hindu god Subramaniam over the demon Idumban, who, according to legend, tried to run off with two sacred mountains. After night-long ritual purification and chanting, penitents enter a trance and pierce their flesh—including their tongues and cheeks—with knives, steel rods, and fishhooks, which they wear during the festival's spectacular procession. Mysteriously, the wounds do not bleed or leave scars. The devotees carry *kavadi* (half hoops adorned with peacock feathers) to symbolize the mountains that caused the epic battle. The 8-km (5-mi)

procession begins at the Perumal Temple on Serangoon Road, passes the Sri Mariamman Temple on South Bridge Road, and ends at the Chettiar Temple, where women pour pots of milk over the image of Lord Subramaniam. Thaipusam is not for the squeamish, but it is an extraordinary demonstration of faith.

Chinese New Year is the only time the Chinese stop working. The lunar New Year celebration lasts for 15 days, and most shops and businesses close for about a week. (In 1999 the New Year begins on February 16; in 2000, on February 5.) Employees and children are given *hong bao* (small red envelopes containing money), and hawkers and vendors sell such delicacies as flattened waxed ducks, white mushrooms, red sausages, melon seeds, and other treats. Mandarin oranges, which symbolize gold and the wish for prosperity, are given in even numbers (odd numbers bring bad luck) to friends, relatives, and business associates.

The end of the Chinese New Year is marked by the **Chingay Procession.** Chinese, Malays, and Indians all get into the act for this event. Accompanied by clashing gongs and beating drums, lion dancers lead a procession of stilt-walkers, swordsmen, warriors, acrobats, and characters from Chinese myth and legend. A giant dragon weaves through the dancers in its eternal pursuit of a flaming pearl. The parade route varies from year to year, but all the details are described in local newspapers.

FEB. OR MAR.➤ **The Birthday of the Monkey God** celebrates this character greatly loved by the Chinese (many ask him to be godfather to their children). Among other things, he's believed to cure the sick and absolve sins. Chinese street operas and puppet shows are usually performed in temple courtyards, and processions are held at the temples along Eng Hoon and Cumming streets. Visitors are welcome to take photographs, but stand back: when the medium dressed as the Monkey God leaps from the throne, burning incense flies in all directions.

SPRING

MAR. OR APR.➤ On the **Birthday of the Saint of the Poor,** the image of Guang Ze Zun Wang is carried from the White Cloud Temple on Ganges Avenue around the neighborhood and back to the temple through streets thronged with devotees. Spirit mediums—their cheeks, arms, and tongues pierced with metal skewers—join the procession.

Hari Raya Haji is a holy day for Muslims, commemorating the Haj, or pilgrimage, to Mecca. Prayers are said in the mornings at the mosques. Later in the day, in remembrance of the prophet Ibrahim's willingness to sacrifice his son, animals are ritually slaughtered and their meat distributed among the poor. (The date of this holiday is set by the Islamic calendar.)

During the **Qing Ming Festival,** families honor their ancestors by visiting their graves, cleaning the cemeteries, and making offerings of food and incense. (Note that this isn't a sad event.) The cemeteries where the festival is most often celebrated are along Upper Thomson Road, Lim Chu Kang, and Lornie Road. However, photographers and spectators are not welcome—the Chinese consider Qing Ming a private affair.

Good Friday is a national holiday in Singapore, and Christians celebrate it by attending church services and observing family ceremonies. There's a candlelight procession on the grounds of St. Joseph's Catholic Church on Victoria Street, during which a wax figure of Christ is carried among the congregation. (In 1999, Good Friday is on April 2; in 2000, on April 21.)

Songkran (April 18) is a traditional Thai water festival that marks the beginning of the year's solar cycle. In Singapore's Thai Buddhist temples, images of Buddha are bathed with perfumed holy water, caged birds are set free, and blessings of water are splashed on worshipers and visitors. The liveliest (and wettest) celebrations are at the Ananda Metyrama Thai temple on Silat Road and the Sapthapuchaniyaram Temple on Holland Road. Visitors are welcome. Keep your camera in a waterproof bag—everyone tries to throw as much water as possible on everyone else.

MAY➤ **The Birthday of the Third Prince** celebrates this child god, who carries a magic bracelet in one hand, a spear in the other, and rides on the wheels of wind and fire. The Chinese worship him as a hero and a miracle-worker. A temple in his honor is at the junction of Clarke Street and North Boat Quay, near Chinatown; on his birthday, it's crowded with noisy worshipers who come to watch the flashy Chinese operas, which begin around noon. Offerings of paper cars and houses and imitation money are burned, and in the evening there's a colorful procession.

Vesak Day commemorates the Buddha's birth, Enlightenment, and death. It's the most sacred annual festival in the Buddhist calendar. Throughout the day, starting before dawn, saffron-robed monks chant holy sutras in all the major Buddhist temples. Captive birds are set free. Many temples offer vegetarian feasts, conduct special exhibitions, and offer lectures on the Buddha's teachings. Visitors are permitted at any temple; particularly recommended are the Kong Meng San Phor Kark See temple complex on Bright Hill Drive and the Temple of 1,000 Lights on Race Course Road. Candlelight processions are held around some temples in the evening.

SUMMER

MID-APR.–JUNE➤ **Festival of the Arts** is a new annual international event that features both Asian and Western attractions—musical recitals, concerts, plays, films, Chinese opera. Performances take place throughout the city; the STB will have the schedule.

The **Dragon Boat Festival** commemorates the martyrdom of Qu Yuan, a Chinese poet and minister of state during the Chou Dynasty (4th century BC). Exiled by the court for his protests against injustice and corruption, he wandered from place to place writing poems about his love for his country. Persecuted by officials wherever he went, he finally threw himself into the river. Today, the anniversary of his death is celebrated with a regatta of boats decorated with dragon heads and painted in brilliant colors. The 38-ft-longboats—each manned by up to 24 rowers and a drummer—compete in the sea off East Coast Park. In recent years, the race has attracted crews from Australia, Europe, New Zealand, and the United States.

JULY➤ During the **Birdsong Festival,** owners of tuneful birds hold competitions to see whose chirps best. This is serious business for the bird owners and interesting entertainment for visitors.

AUG. 9➤ **National Day,** the anniversary of the nation's independence, is a day of processions, fireworks, folk and dragon dances, and national pride. The finest view is from the Padang, where the main participants put on their best show. Tickets for special

seating areas are available through the STB.

AUG.–SEPT.➤ For a month each year, during the **Chinese Festival of the Hungry Ghosts,** the Gates of Hell are opened and ghosts are free to wander the earth. It's a busy time. The happy ghosts visit their families, where they're entertained with sumptuous feasts. The unhappy ghosts, those who died without descendants, may cause trouble and must therefore be placated with offerings. Imitation money ("Hell money") and joss sticks are burned, and prayers are said at all Chinese temples and in front of Chinese shops and homes. Noisy auctions are also held, to raise money for the next year's festivities. Street-opera performances begin in the late afternoon and continue until late evening.

SEPT.➤ **The Mooncake Festival,** a traditional Chinese celebration, is named for special cakes—found for the most part only during this festival—that are the subject of legend. One tells of a cruel king of the Hsia Dynasty who discovered an elixir for immortality. Desperate to stop him from drinking it and tyrannizing his subjects eternally, his good-hearted wife swallowed every drop and escaped by leaping to the moon, where she has lived ever since. The festival is held on the night of the year

when the full moon is thought to be at its brightest. There are lantern-making competitions and special entertainments, including lion and dragon dances. (Locations are published in local newspapers.) Mooncakes—sweet pastries filled with red-bean paste, lotus seeds, nuts, and egg yolks—are eaten in abundance.

SEPT.–OCT.➤ During the nine-day **Navarathri Festival,** Hindus pay homage to three goddesses. The first three days are devoted to Parvati, consort of Shiva the Destroyer. The next three are for Lakshmi, goddess of wealth and consort of Vishnu the Protector. The final three are for Sarawathi, goddess of education and consort of Brahma the Creator. On all nights, at the Chettiar Temple on Tank Road, there are performances of classical Indian music, drama, and dancing from 7 to 10 PM. On the last evening the image of a silver horse is taken from its home in the Chettiar Temple and paraded around the streets. Thousands take part in the procession, including women in glittering saris, and the air is heavy with perfumes and incense. The festival is best seen at the Sri Mariamman Temple.

OCT.➤ The Chinese believe that the deities celebrated in the **Festival of the Nine Emperor Gods** can cure illness, bring good luck and wealth, and encourage longevity. Understandably, these deities are very popular! They're honored in most Chinese temples on the ninth day of the ninth lunar month; the celebrations are at their most spectacular in the temples on Upper Serangoon Road (8 km/5 mi, from the city) and at Lorong Tai Seng.

OCT.–NOV.➤ During the **Pilgrimage to Kusu Island,** more than 100,000 Taoist believers travel to the temple of Da Bo Gong, the god of prosperity. They bring offerings of exotic foods, flowers, joss sticks, and candles and pray for good health, prosperity, and obedient children. If you want to join in, take one of the many ferries that leave from Clifford Pier. Be prepared to deal with immense crowds.

In the **Thimithi Festival,** Indian Hindus honor the goddess Duropadai. According to myth, Duropadai proved her chastity by walking over flaming coals. Today worshipers walk barefoot over a bed of red-hot embers. Only the "pure of heart and soul" are said to be able to accomplish this feat—some do walk more quickly than others! See the spectacle at the Sri Mariamman Temple on South Bridge Road. The fire-walking ceremony begins at 4 PM.

Deepavali celebrates the triumph of Krishna over the demon king Nasakasura. All Indian homes and temples are decorated with oil lamps and garlands for the Hindu festival, which marks a time for cleaning house and wearing new clothes. Little India is where the festival is best seen. The streets are brilliantly illuminated, and Indians throng the markets, which do a roaring business selling special greeting cards, gifts, clothes, and food.

NOV.➤ **Merlion Week** is Singapore's version of Carnival, with food fairs, fashion shows, masquerade balls, and fireworks displays. The events start with the crowning of Miss Tourism Singapore and end with the international Singapore Powerboat Grand Prix.

NOV.–DEC.➤ Being a multicultural society, Singapore has taken **Christmas** to heart—and a very commercial heart it is. All the shops are deep in artificial snow, and a Chinese Santa Claus appears every so often to encourage everyone to buy and give presents, which they do with enthusiasm. A lighting ceremony takes place on Orchard Road, the fashionable shopping street, sometime during the last 10 days of November.

2 Exploring Singapore

Away from the glittering hotels of Orchard Road, Singapore's older ethnic neighborhoods offer unexpected backstreet delights. The colonial central business district around the Padang and the legendary Raffles Hotel evoke the era of Joseph Conrad. Beyond downtown, you can explore orchid gardens, zoos, and theme parks. Indonesia's Bintan Island—only 45 minutes away—offers extraordinary beaches, hotels, and golf courses, and still more insight into Asian culture.

THE MAIN ISLAND OF SINGAPORE is shaped like a flattened diamond, 42 km (26 mi) east to west and 23 km (14 mi) north to south. Near the peak is the causeway leading to peninsular Malaysia—Kuala Lumpur is less than four hours away by car. At the foot is Singapore city, with its gleaming office towers and working docks. Offshore are Sentosa and some 59 smaller islands—most of them uninhabited—that serve as bases for oil refining or as playground or beach escape from the city. To the east is Changi International Airport, connected to the city by a parkway lined for miles with amusement centers of one sort or another. To the west are the industrial city of Jurong and several decidedly unindustrial attractions, including gardens and a bird park. At the center of the diamond is Singapore island's "clean and green" heart, with a splendid zoo, an orchid garden, and reservoirs surrounded by luxuriant tropical forest. Of the island's total land area, less than half is built up, with the balance made up of farmland, plantations, swamp areas, and forest. Besides the cities of Singapore and Jurong, there are several suburbs, such as Kallang, an old colonial residential district; Katong, a stronghold of Peranakan culture, with pastel terrace houses and Nonya restaurants; Bedok, once an area of Malay kampongs and now a modern suburb of high-rises; and Ponggal, a fishing village on the northeast shore that's a popular destination with seekers of water sports and seafood restaurants. Well-paved roads connect all parts of the island, and Singapore city has an excellent public transportation system.

No other capital city in Southeast Asia is as easy to explore independently as Singapore. The best way is on foot, wandering the streets to discover small shops, a special house, or a temple, or just to observe the daily scene. It's very difficult to get lost. You can orient yourself in a general way using such landmarks as the financial district's skyscrapers, the new buildings of the Marina Square complex, and Fort Canning Rise—a small hill in the center of town. Also, every street is signposted in English, and most Singaporeans speak English. If you tire of walking, you can easily hop a bus or the subway or hail one of the numerous (except in heavy rain) taxis.

Singapore has been Southeast Asia's most modern city for over a century for a reason. Successive governments have kept it that way through constant change, still in progress. Just since 1994, whole blocks in Singapore's old ethnic neighborhoods have disappeared. Little India's last *dhobi-wallah* (laundryman) house has been converted into office space; an old silver merchant in the Arab District cleared out to make way for a mall; a Chinese shophouse that used to sell traditional engraved ivory chopsticks has been torn down and replaced by a brand new pink-trimmed "refurbished" version of the original.

To get a feel for the vanished Singapore, you'll have to look at old photographs or paintings and read some books. One of the best places to do this is in Antiques of the Orient, an old map and print shop on the second floor of the Tanglin Shopping Centre, where Orchard Road meets Tanglin Road. The shop's owner, Laurence Chua, has an extensive collection of photos and prints of 19th- and early 20th-century Singapore. You can also view the many photo exhibits on the second floor of the shopping malls in Clarke Quay. Comparing the old Singapore with the new makes one question the value of the city's extensive redevelopment.

COLONIAL SINGAPORE

You'll find the heart of Singapore's history and its modern wealth in Colonial Singapore. The area stretches from the skyscrapers in Singapore's financial district to the Raffles Hotel, and from the super-modern convention centers of Marina Square to the National Museum and 19th-century Fort Canning. Although most of old Singapore has been knocked down to make way for the modern city, in Colonial Singapore most of the major landmarks have been preserved, including early 19th-century buildings designed by the Irish architect George Coleman.

Numbers in the text correspond to numbers in the margin and on the Colonial Singapore map.

A Good Walk

A convenient place to start is at **Collyer Quay** ① ("quay" is pronounced "key") and Clifford Pier, where most European colonizers first set foot on the island. Leaving Clifford Pier, walk up the quay—toward the Singapore River—until you come to the **former General Post Office** ②, a proud Victorian building of gray stone that, rumor has it, is slated to become a hotel complex. Walk down the short, narrow, tree-lined street alongside the post office to cross the gracious old iron-link **Cavenagh Bridge** ③. If you walk along the river's south bank before crossing the bridge, you'll find what was once a wide towpath and is now a paved pedestrian street of restaurants and bars—**Boat Quay** ④. The second building on your left houses Harry's Bar, which gained international attention in 1995 as a haunt of derivatives trader Nick Leeson, the young whippersnapper who brought down the venerable Barings Bank.

Once over the Cavenagh Bridge, take a left onto North Boat Quay. Slightly back from the river is **Empress Place** ⑤, a huge white building. A bit farther along the quay is the **statue of Sir Thomas Stamford Raffles** ⑥, who is believed to have landed on this spot in 1819. Turn right onto St. Andrew's Road until you come to **Parliament House** ⑦ on your left, the oldest government building in Singapore, and on your right, **Victoria Memorial Hall** ⑧, built in 1905 as a tribute to Queen Victoria. Across the road is the old **Singapore Cricket Club** ⑨. Just past it, on your right as you continue up St. Andrew's Road, is the **Padang** ⑩, or playing field. To your left are the **Supreme Court** ⑪ and **City Hall** ⑫, two splendidly pretentious, imperial-looking buildings. Continuing northeast on St. Andrew's Road, which runs along the Padang, cross Coleman Street toward the green lawns that surround the Anglican **St. Andrew's Cathedral** ⑬.

Northeast of the cathedral is the huge **Raffles City** ⑭ complex, easily recognized by the towers of the two Westin hotels. Take the MRT underpass north across Stamford Road, and walk through Raffles City to Bras Basah Road. Across the street is the venerable **Raffles Hotel** ⑮. After touring the hotel, continue up Bras Basah Road to Queen Street and make a right to the **Singapore Art Museum** ⑯. After touring the exhibits, cross Bras Basah Road and walk down to Victoria Street, where you'll no doubt find a place to rest and people-watch at the **Chijmes** ⑰ complex. Continue southwest on Victoria Street (it becomes Hill Street after Stamford Road); the **Armenian Church** ⑱ will be on your right just before Coleman Street. From here, stamp collectors should turn left onto Coleman and visit the **Singapore Philatelic Museum** ⑲; culture vultures should go right on Coleman and than right again onto Armenian Street to visit the **Asian Civilisations Museum** ⑳. To see the **National Museum and Art Gallery** ㉑ instead, return to Stamford Road and make a left. You may wish to conclude your tour with a stroll

Singapore City

Orchard Road

Stevens Rd.

NEWTON

Kampong Park

Bukit Timah Rd.

Nassim Rd.

Claymore Hill

Scotts Rd.

Cairnhill Rd.

Clemenceau Ave.

Wilkie Rd.

Tanglin Rd.

ORCHARD

Orchard Rd.

Bideford Rd.

Cavenagh Rd.

Edinburgh Rd.

Orchard Blvd.

Paterson Rd.

One Tree Hill

SOMERSET

Colonial Singa

Grange Rd.

Grange Rd.

Exeter Rd.

Oxley Rise

DHOBY GHAUT

Fort Canning R

Clemenceau

River Valley Rd.

Fort Canning Park

River Valley Rd.

Kim Seng Rd.

Zion Rd.

River Valley Rd.

Singapore River

River Valley Rd.

Coleman Bridge

Alexandra Rd.

Havelock Rd.

Havelock Rd.

Havelock Rd.

Pickering St.

TIONG BAHRU

Tiong Bahru Rd.

Henderson Rd.

New Bridge Rd.

South Bridge Rd.

Outram Park

Jalan Bukit Merah

Outram Rd.

OUTRAM PARK

0   1000 meters

0   1000 yards

Neil Rd.

Craig Rd.

Pagar Rd.

Maxwell Rd.

Cecil St.

N

Cantonment Rd.

TANJONG PAGAR

Bahru Rd.

Spottiswoode Park

Tanjong

Chinatown

Keppel Rd.

South Bridge Rd.

Subway & Rail Lines

North-South MRT line
East-West MRT line
Railroad lines
Subway stop

Keppel Rd.

Empire Dock

South Quay

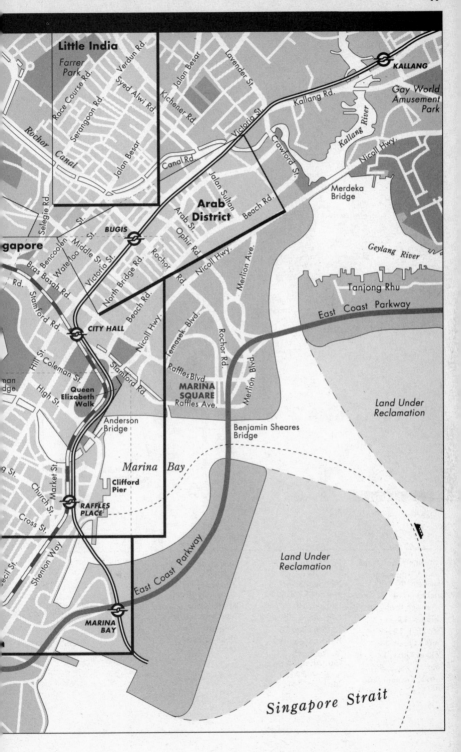

Little India

Farrer Park

Race Course Rd.
Serangoon Rd.
Yerdun Rd.
Syed Alwi Rd.
Jalan Besar

Rochor Canal

Jalan Besar
Kichener Rd.
Lavender St.
Victoria St.

Canal Rd.

KALLANG

Gay World Amusement Park

Kallang Rd.
Kallang River

Crawford St.
Merdeka Bridge
Nicoll Hwy.

Jalan Sultan
Arab District
Beach Rd.

Selegie Rd.
gapore
BUGIS
Bencoolen St.
Middle St.
Waterloo St.
Victoria St.
North Bridge Rd.
Rochor Rd.
Ophir Rd.
Arab St.
Nicoll Hwy.
Merlion Ave.

Geylang River

Bras Basah Rd.
Stamford Rd.
Beach Rd.
Tanjong Rhu

CITY HALL
East Coast Parkway

Hill St.
Coleman St.
High St.
Stamford Rd.
Nicoll Hwy.
Temasek Blvd.
Raffles Blvd.
Rochor Rd.
Merlion Blvd.

Queen Elizabeth Walk

MARINA SQUARE
Raffles Ave.

Anderson Bridge

Land Under Reclamation

Benjamin Sheares Bridge

Marina Bay

Clifford Pier

Market St.
Church St.
RAFFLES PLACE
Cross St.

Shenton Way

East Coast Parkway

Land Under Reclamation

East Coast Parkway

MARINA BAY

Singapore Strait

Colonial Singapore

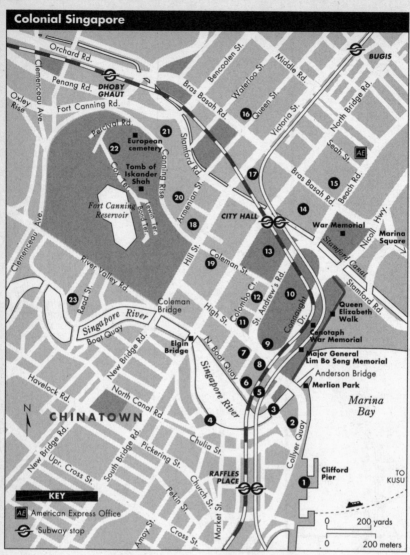

through **Fort Canning Park** ㉒, pausing at the European Cemetery and the Tomb of Iskander Shah, and/or a visit to **Clarke Quay** ㉓, south of the park, with its restaurants and shops.

TIMING

This walking tour, with time factored in to wander through the Raffles Hotel and view the exhibits at one or more of the area's four museums, should take a full day. Allow an hour for the Raffles, including time out for a Singapore sling in the Long Bar. Allow at least an hour to view the exhibits at each museum.

Sights to See

⑱ **Armenian Church.** More correctly, the **Church of St. Gregory the Illuminator** is one of the most endearing buildings in Singapore. It was built in 1835, which makes it the republic's oldest surviving church, and it's still used for regular Armenian Orthodox services. The Armenians were but one of many minority groups that came to Singapore in search of fortune. A dozen wealthy Armenian families supplied the funds for the ubiquitous architect George Coleman to design this church. The main internal circular structure is imposed on a square plan with four projecting porticoes. In the churchyard is the weathered tombstone of Agnes Joaquim, who bred the parent plants of Singapore's national flower. The orchid, with a purplish pink center, was discovered in her garden in the 1890s and still carries her name.

★ ⑳ **Asian Civilisations Museum.** Formerly the Tao Nan School, this grand colonial building reopened in 1997 as the first phase of the Asian Civilisations Museum. (Phase II is slated to open in 2000 at ☞ **Empress Place**.) With a mandate to provide an Asia-wide insight into the legacies of the past and the cultural traditions of the peoples who live in the region, the museum is a fascinating blend of permanent and changing exhibitions. Chinese furniture, ceramics, jade, and a faithfully recreated Chinese scholar's study are on permanent display. ⊠ *39 Armenian St.,* ☎ *338–0000.* ✍ *S$3.* ☉ *Tues.–Sun. 9:30–5:30.*

❹ **Boat Quay.** Right next to the financial district, along the Singapore River, is this popular new restaurant area with both indoor and outdoor dining. Local entrepreneurs have created a mélange of eateries and nightclubs to satisfy diverse tastes. Between 7 PM and midnight, the area swells with people, who stroll along the pleasant quay, stopping to take a meal or refreshment. At the end of Boat Quay and named after Lord Elgin, a governor-general of India, **Elgin Bridge** was built to link Chinatown to the colonial quarter. The original rickety wooden structure was replaced in 1863 with an iron bridge imported from Calcutta; the current ferroconcrete bridge was installed in 1926.

❸ **Cavenagh Bridge.** This gracious old iron-link bridge is named after Major General Orfeur Cavenagh, governor of the Straits Settlements from 1859 to 1867. The bridge, built in 1868 from iron girders imported from Scotland, was once the main route across the river; now Anderson Bridge bears the brunt of the traffic.

⑰ **Chijmes.** Built in 1840 as Caldwell House, the original structure became the Convent of the Holy Infant Jesus—where Catholic nuns housed and schooled abandoned children—in 1852. The church was added between 1901 and 1903. After World War II, both the convent and the church fell into disrepair. The buildings received a S$100 million renovation and were reopened in 1996 as this shopping and entertainment complex. Today the lovingly restored church is rented out for private functions. The new name "Chijmes" (pronounced "chimes") is an acronym of the convent's name, a nod at the complex's noble past.

⑫ **City Hall.** Completed in 1929, this building now houses a number of government ministries, including the Ministry of Foreign Affairs. It was here that the British surrender took place in 1942, followed by the surrender of the Japanese in 1945. Each year on August 9, the building's steps serve as a reviewing stand for the National Day Parade, celebrating Singapore's independence from Great Britain and the birth of the republic.

㉓ **Clarke Quay.** Named in remembrance of Sir Andrew Clarke, the second governor of Singapore, this quay functions as a festival village that offers entertainment, food, and shopping. Here you can observe a tinsmith demonstrating his skill, see a band perform in the central square's small gazebo, and watch stilt-walkers wobble down pedestrian-only streets. Be aware that prices in the shops and restaurants are inflated. The river here is close to being the sleepy waterway it was when Raffles first arrived; cargo vessels are banned from entering. You can board one of the bumboats (small launches) that offer daily 30-minute cruises along the river and into Marina Bay; it's a pleasant ride, and a respite for tired feet.

❶ **Collyer Quay.** Land reclamation in 1933 pushed the seafront back, and Collyer Quay, which now fronts Telok Ayer Street, is three blocks from its original site. In the 19th century, the view from the quay would have included a virtual wall of anchored ships. Today, you look out upon a graceful bridge that carries the East Coast Parkway from one landfill headland to another, enclosing what's now called Marina Bay. **Clifford Pier,** a covered jetty with high, vaulted ceilings, still reveals some of the excitement of the days when European traders arrived by steamship and Chinese immigrants by wind-dependent junks. Now Indonesian sailors sit around smoking clove-scented cigarettes, and seamen from every seafaring nation come ashore to stock up on liquor and duty-free electronics. The atmosphere here is seedy (this is one of the few places in Singapore where women might feel uncomfortable by themselves). Passengers from the ocean liners no longer come ashore here (they now arrive at the World Trade Centre cruise terminal), but it's still possible to set sail from here on a day cruise around Singapore's harbor and to the outlying islands. Bumboats wallow in the bay, waiting to take sailors back to their ships or carry other visitors wherever they want to go for about S$30 an hour. In **Merlion Park,** at the end of the quay near Anderson Bridge, stands a statue of Singapore's tourism symbol, the Merlion—half lion, half fish. In the evening, the statue—on a point of land looking out over the harbor—is floodlit, its eyes are lighted, and its mouth spews water. You can see an even bigger one on Sentosa Island. This creature is based upon the country's national symbol, the lion (from which the name Singapore was derived). The Merlion symbolizes courage, strength, and excellence.

❺ **Empress Place.** This huge, white, neoclassical building was meticulously restored as an exhibition hall but is now closed until the year 2000, when it will reopen as Phase II of the ☞ **Asian Civilisations Museum.** Constructed in the 1860s as the courthouse, the building has since had four major additions and has housed nearly every government body, including the Registry of Births and Deaths and the Immigration Department. Virtually every adult Singaporean has been inside this building at one time or another.

❷ **Former General Post Office.** The post office recently moved to the suburbs from this proud, anachronistic, Victorian building—all gray stone and huge pillars. The government has promised not to knock the structure down to make way for yet another glass-and-steel high-rise. But rumor has it that the building will become yet another hotel and shopping complex. To the left as you face the old post office is **Fullerton Square**, a rest stop for cycle-rickshaw drivers.

☝ ㉒ **Fort Canning Park.** Until recently Fort Canning was hallowed ground, a green sanctuary from the city's mass of concrete commercialism. Alas, like so much in Singapore, the park is undergoing extensive renovations. The government recently added a 19th-century walk, with guideposts pointing you to all the park's 19th-century sites. There are designated picnic areas, and a country club is being built at the park's edge.

What still remains, though, are the tombstones of the **European cemetery**. Once divided into areas for Protestants and for Catholics, the tombstones have been moved to form a wall around an open field. It's hard to read the inscriptions on the weathered plaques, but their brevity suggests the loneliness of the expatriates who had sought fortune far from home.

Seven centuries ago **Fort Canning Rise**, as the park was once called, was home to the royal palaces of the Majapahit rulers, who no doubt chose it for the cool breezes and commanding view of the river. The last five kings of Singa Pura, including the legendary Iskandar Shah, are said to be buried on the hill. Some dispute this, claiming that Iskandar Shah escaped from Singa Pura before its destruction in 1391.

For several hundred years the site was abandoned to the jungle. It was referred to by the Malays as Bukit Larangan, the Forbidden Hill, a place where the spirits of bygone kings roamed on sacred ground. Then Raffles came and, defying the legends, established a government house (headquarters for the colonial governor) on the rise. Later, in 1859, a fort was constructed; its guns were fired to mark dawn, noon, and night.

OFF THE
BEATEN PATH

MARINA SQUARE – A minicity all its own, Marina Square has three malls and five smart atrium hotels—the Pan Pacific, the Marina Mandarin, the Oriental, the Ritz-Carlton, and the Conrad International Centennial (☞ Chapter 4). The mammoth convention center and shopping mall, Suntec City, had its opening in 1995, only to be followed by the opening of an even bigger mall, the Millennia Walk, with its three-story duty-free shop, in late 1996. The Marina Square Shopping Mall provides an eclectic mix of boutique bargain shopping. An arts center, The Esplanade, is slated to open in 2001 across the road from this mall and along the Queen Elizabeth Walk, which opened in 1953 to mark her coronation. The entire Marina Square complex symbolizes much of what Singapore has become: a modern convention city built on landfills and dotted with theme parks and festival malls designed to entertain delegates and their spouses.

㉑ **National Museum and Art Gallery.** Housed in a grand colonial building topped by a silver dome, this museum is also referred to as the Singapore History Museum and was originally opened as the Raffles Museum in 1887. Included in its collection are 20 dioramas that depict the republic's past; the Revere Bell, donated to the original St. Andrew's Church in 1843 by the daughter of American patriot Paul Revere; the 380-piece Haw Par Jade Collection, one of the largest of its kind; ethnographic collections from Southeast Asia; and many historical documents. ⊠ *Stamford Rd.,* ☎ *332–3659.* ▨ *S$3; free guided tour 11 AM Tues.* ⊙ *Tues.–Sun. 9–5:30.*

⑩ **Padang.** Today the Padang, which seemingly constitutes the backyard of the ☞ **Singapore Cricket Club**, is used primarily as a playing field (an appropriate usage, as *padang* is Malay for "field" or "plain"). It has traditionally been a social and political hub. Once called the Esplanade, it was only half its current size until an 1890s land reclamation expanded it, giving colonial gentry still more room to stroll and exchange pleasantries and gossip. Its other uses have not been as polite: during World War II, 2,000 British civilians were gathered here by the Japanese before being marched off to Changi Prison and, in many cases, to their deaths.

Beyond the northeastern edge of the Padang, across Stamford Road and the Stamford Canal, are the four 230-ft, tapering, white columns of the **War Memorial**, known locally as "The Four Chopsticks." The monument honors the thousands of civilians from the four main ethnic groups (Chinese, Malay, Indian, and European) who lost their lives during the Japanese occupation. The highest column represents the Chinese, who were the most persecuted—some 25,000 were immediately executed for being too Western; others were sent to help build the bridge over the River Kwai.

Along the Padang's eastern edge, just across Connaught Drive, are several other monuments. The **Major General Lim Bo Seng Memorial** honors a well-loved freedom fighter of World War II who was tortured and died in a Japanese prison camp in 1944. The imposing **Cenotaph War Memorial** honors the dead of the two world wars.

⑦ Parliament House. George Coleman designed the Parliament House in 1827 for a wealthy merchant, but it went unoccupied until the government bought it for S$15,600 in 1841 to use as a courthouse. It's considered the oldest government building in Singapore. Additions were built, and in the 1870s it became the meeting place for parliament. The bronze elephant in front of the building was a gift from King Chulalongkorn of Siam during his state visit in 1871. ⊠ *Corner of High St. and St. Andrew's Rd.,* ☎ *335–8811.* ▣ *Free.* ⊙ *Daily by appointment.*

⑭ Raffles City. The Raffles City complex of offices and shops contains Asia's tallest hotel, the Westin Stamford, not to be confused with the Westin Plaza, which is in the same building and operates as a semiseparate hotel (☞ Chapter 4). There's a beautiful view of downtown and the harbor from the Compass Rose restaurant atop the Stamford.

⑮ Raffles Hotel. Once a "tiffin house," or tearoom, the Raffles Hotel started life as the home of a British sea captain. In 1887 the Armenian Sarkies brothers took over the building and transformed it into one of Asia's grandest hotels. The Raffles has had many ups and downs, especially during World War II, when it was first a center for British refugees, then quarters for Japanese officers, and then a center for released Allied prisoners of war. There's a delicious irony to the Raffles: viewed as a bastion of colonialism, it was not only the creation of Armenians, but in its 130 years of hosting expatriates, it only once had a British manager. Even so, service has been unfailingly loyal to the colonial heritage. Right before the Japanese arrived, the Chinese waiters took the silverware from the dining rooms and buried it in the Palm Court garden, where it remained safely hidden until the occupiers departed.

After the war the hotel deteriorated, surviving by trading on its heritage rather than its facilities. However, in late 1991, after two years of renovation and expansion, the Raffles reopened as the republic's most expensive hotel. You can no longer just roam around. Instead you're channeled through new colonial-style buildings to take in a free museum of Raffles memorabilia and then, perhaps, to take refreshment in a reproduction of the **Long Bar,** where the famous Singapore Sling was created in 1903 by the bartender Ngiam Tong Boon. The sling here is still regarded as the best in Singapore; note that your S$17.15 tab includes service and tax, but not the glass—that's another S$8. Also note that some consider the new Long Bar a travesty, with manually operated *punkahs* (fans) replaced by those that are electrically powered. Although casual visitors are discouraged from entering the original part of the hotel, if you crave authenticity (and you have few qualms about being persistent) the Tiffin Room and the Bar and Billiard Room are much better bets than the Long Bar. If you aren't feeling brazen, you can simply browse in the arcade's 65 shops, stop by Doc Cheng's restaurant for a taste of its "transethnic" cuisine, or head to the tiny Writers Bar for a drink.

⑬ St. Andrew's Cathedral. This Anglican (Episcopal) church, surrounded by a green lawn, is the second one built on this site. The first was constructed in 1835, but after being struck twice by lightning, it was demolished in 1855. (Locals took the bolts from the heavens as a sign that the site was bedeviled. It was suggested that before another place of worship was built, the spirits should be appeased with the blood from 30 heads; fortunately, the suggestion was ignored.) Indian convicts were brought in to construct a new cathedral in the English Gothic style. The structure, completed in 1862, has bells cast by the firm that made Big Ben's, and it resembles Netley Abbey in Hampshire, England. The British overlords were so impressed by the cathedral that the Indian convict who supplied the working drawings was granted his freedom. The church was expanded once in 1952 and again in 1983. Its lofty interior is white and simple, with stained-glass windows coloring the sunlight as it enters. Around the walls are marble and brass memorial plaques, including one remembering the British who died in a 1915 mutiny of native light infantry and another in memory of 41 Australian army nurses killed in the Japanese invasion. Services are held every Sunday.

⑯ Singapore Art Museum. When this 1852 building—once the all-boys Catholic St. Joseph's Institution—closed in 1987 it did not reopen as a museum until 1996. (Names of school donors still adorn the porch at the entrance.) When Prime Minister Goh Chok Tung opened it, he described a vision of Singapore "reliving, through its museums, its historic role as an entrepôt for art, culture, civilization, and ideas." Collections here include modern art from Singapore and traditional art from other parts of Southeast Asia. The E-Image Gallery has interactive programs that feature 20th-century Southeast Asian art presented on large, high-definition monitors. ⊠ *71 Bras Basah Rd.,* ☎ *332–3222.* 🎟 *S$3.* ☉ *Tues.–Sun. 9–5:30; free guided tours Tues., Fri., and Sat.–Sun. 11 AM.*

NEED A
BREAK?
At the back of the Singapore Art Museum you'll find the **Olio Dome** (☎ 339–0792), a casual breakfast and lunch spot. The Dome, one of several in Singapore, serves a Western menu of soups, salads, and sandwiches—but it really specializes in coffee. A latte goes for S$4.20. You can eat outside on the curving neoclassical porch or inside in a 1920s-style bistro.

⑨ Singapore Cricket Club. Founded during the 1850s, this club became the main center for the social and sporting life of the British community. It now has a multiracial membership of more than 4,000 and offers facilities for various sports, in addition to bars and restaurants. If you're going to be in Singapore for more than a couple of weeks, you can apply, with the support of a member, for a visiting membership. The club isn't open to the general public, but from the Padang you can sneak a quick look at the deep, shaded verandas, from which members still watch cricket, rugby, and tennis matches.

⑲ Singapore Philatelic Museum. Housed in a 92-year-old building, once part of the Anglo Chinese School, is Southeast Asia's first stamp museum. It has a fine collection of local and international stamps as well as an audiovisual theater, a resource center, interactive games, and a souvenir shop. ✉ *23B Coleman St.,* ☎ *337–3888.* ✆ *S$2.* ☺ *Tues.– Sun. 9–4:30.*

❻ Statue of Sir Thomas Stamford Raffles. This statue near Empress Place on North Boat Quay is on the spot where Raffles purportedly landed in Singapore early on the morning of January 29, 1819. Pause here a moment to observe the contrast between the old and the new. Once this river was the organ of bustling commercial life, packed with barges and lighters that ferried goods from cargo ship to dock. There were no cranes—the unloading was done by teams of coolies. Swarms of them tottered under their heavy loads, back and forth between lighter and riverside godowns, amid yells from *compradores* (factotums).

⓫ Supreme Court. In the neoclassical style so beloved by Victorian colonials, the Supreme Court has Corinthian pillars and the look of arrogant certainty. However, it's not as old as it seems. The building was completed in 1939, replacing the famous Hôtel de l'Europe, where Conrad once propped up the bar eavesdropping on sailors' tales that he later used in novels. The pedimental sculptures of the Greek-temple-like facade portray Justice and other allegorical figures. Inside, the echoing hall and staircase are grand and, high above, the vast paneled ceiling is an exercise in showmanship. All of this was completed just in time for the Japanese to use the building as their headquarters.

❽ Victoria Memorial Hall. The Memorial Hall was built in 1905 as a tribute to Queen Victoria. Along with the adjacent **Victoria Theatre,** built in 1862 as the town hall, it's currently the city's main cultural center, offering regular exhibitions, concerts, and theatrical performances of all types (☞ Chapter 5).

CHINATOWN

In a country where 76% of the people are Chinese, it may seem strange to name a small urban area Chinatown. But Chinatown was born some 170 years ago, when the Chinese were a minority (if only for half a century) in the newly formed British settlement. In an attempt to minimize racial tension, Raffles allotted sections of the settlement to different immigrant groups. The Chinese were given the area south of the Singapore River. Today, the river is still the northern boundary of old Chinatown; Maxwell Road marks its southern perimeter and New Bridge Road its western one. Before the 1933 land reclamation, the western perimeter was the sea. The reclaimed area between Telok Ayer Street and Collyer Quay–Shenton Way has become the business district whose expansion has caused Chinese shophouses to be knocked down all the way to Cross Street.

Inside a relatively small rectangle, immigrants—many of them penniless and half-starved—from mainland China were crammed. Within three years of the formation of the Straits Settlement, 3,000 Chinese had arrived; this number increased tenfold over the next decade. The Hokkien people, traders from Fukien Province, made up about a quarter of the community. Other leading groups were the Teochews, from the Swatow region of Guangdong Province, and their mainland neighbors, the Cantonese. In smaller groups, the Hainanese, the nomadic Hakkas, and peoples from Guangxi arrived in tightly packed junks, riding on the northeast monsoon winds.

Most immigrants came with the sole intention of exchanging their rags for riches, then returning to China. They had no allegiance to Singapore or to Chinatown, which was no melting pot but, rather, separate pockets of ethnically diverse groups, each with a different dialect; a different cuisine; and different cultural, social, and religious attitudes. In the shophouses—two-story buildings with shops or small factories on the ground floor and living quarters upstairs—as many as 30 lodgers would share a single room. Life was a fight for space and survival. Crime was rampant. What order existed was maintained by Chinese guilds, clan associations, and secret societies, all of which fought—sometimes savagely—for control of lucrative aspects of community life.

Until recently, all of Chinatown was slated for the bulldozer, to be wiped clean of its past and replaced by uniform concrete structures. The traditional ways of the Chinese groups were to melt away into the modern Singaporean lifestyle. In the name of "progressive social engineering," much of the original community was disassembled and entire blocks were cleared of shophouses. However, the government finally recognized not only the people's desire to maintain Chinese customs and family ties, but also the important role these play in modern society. Chinatown received a stay of execution, and an ambitious plan to restore a large area of shophouses is almost complete. Fortunately, enough of the old remains to permit the imaginative visitor to experience a traditional Chinese community.

Numbers in the text correspond to numbers in the margin and on the Chinatown map.

A Good Walk

Begin at the Elgin Bridge, built to link Chinatown with the colonial administration center. At the south end of the bridge, logically enough, South Bridge Road begins. Off to the right is Upper Circular Road, on the left-hand side of which is **Yeo Swee Huat** ① at No. 13, which sells paper replicas of houses, cars, and other worldly goods intended to be burned at Chinese funerals. (You'll encounter other such shops during your walk.) Circular Road, once home to cloth wholesalers, now has bars and restaurants. Walk down **Lopong Telok Street** ②, with its architecturally interesting shops and clan houses, and take a right onto **North Canal Road.** Here are stores that sell Chinese delicacies—dried foods, turtles for soup, sea cucumbers, sharks' fins, and birds' nests. Trace your steps back along North Canal to Chulia Street. Follow it to Phillip Street and turn right to reach the recently restored **Wak Hai Cheng Bio Temple** ③.

Return to North Canal Road. Continue to New Bridge Road, turn left, and walk past the Furama Singapore Hotel and the People's Park Centre, now home to the Singapore Handicrafts Centre. Cross Upper Cross Street and take a left onto **Mosque Street.** The old shophouses here—now being redeveloped into offices—were originally built as stables. Turn right onto South Bridge Road. The **Jamae Mosque** ④ will be on your right. On the next block is the **Sri Mariamman Temple** ⑤, the oldest Hindu temple in Singapore.

If you take the next right, onto **Temple Street,** you may be fortunate enough to see one of the few remaining scribes in Singapore. At the junction of Trengganu Street, notice the old building on the corner. Reliable sources say this was once a famous **brothel** ⑥. You are now in the core of Chinatown, an area known as **Kreta Ayer.** Trengganu Street leads to the new **Chinatown Centre** ⑦. Leaving the market, walk along **Sago Street** to see more family factories that make paper models to be burned for good fortune at funerals. Parallel to Sago Street is Sago Lane. There's nothing to see here now, but the street was once known for its death houses, where Chinese waited out their last days.

Chinatown

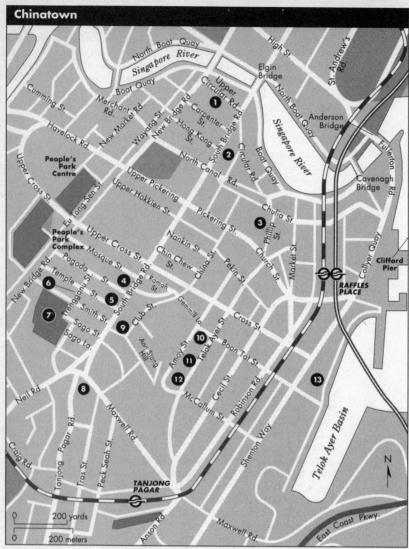

Al Abrar Mosque, **12**
Brothel, **6**
Chinatown Centre, **7**
Guild for Amahs, **9**
Jamae Mosque, **4**
Jinriksha Station, **8**
Lopong Telok
Street, **2**
Nagore Durghe
Shrine, **10**
Sri Mariamman
Temple, **5**
Telok Ayer
Market, **13**

Thian Hock Keng
Temple, **11**
Wak Hai Cheng Bio
Temple, **3**
Yeo Swee Huat, **1**

If you turn right onto South Bridge Road, you'll come to the intersection of **Tanjong Pagar Road** and Neil Road. The **Jinriksha Station** ⑧ was once a rickshaw depot, but it is now a food court. After strolling down Tanjong Pagar Road to see the restored shophouses and trendy restaurants, head back to South Bridge Road. **Smith Street,** on the left, has stores that sell everything from chilies to ground rhinoceros horn. Ann Siang Road, on the other side of South Bridge Road, is full of old shops and is the site of the **Guild for Amahs** ⑨. From Ann Siang Road, turn left onto Club Street, and then right at Gemmill Lane. When you get to Telok Ayer Street, turn right, and you'll find the **Nagore Durghe Shrine** ⑩—an odd mix of minarets and Greek columns decorated with Christmas lights—built by South Indian Muslims in the early 19th century. Continue down the road to the interesting **Thian Hock Keng Temple** ⑪, which, at press time, was undergoing renovation as part of a new housing-shopping complex on Telok Ayer Street. Across from the temple is the China Square Food Centre, home of the unusual House of Mao (☞ Chapter 3) restaurant. A little farther down the street is the **Al Abrar Mosque** ⑫, built in 1827. Walk east along McCallum Street toward the bay and take a left onto Shenton Way. At Boon Tat Street, you'll see the **Telok Ayer Market** ⑬, the largest Victorian cast-iron structure in Southeast Asia. Here you can refresh yourself at the food court, then take the subway back to Raffles Place on Collyer Quay.

TIMING

Allow two to three hours for this walk, and factor in a half an hour each for the Wak Hai Cheng Bio, Thian Hock Keng, and Sri Mariamman temples. Owing to all the construction and restoration projects in this area, you may need a little more patience than usual to get around.

Sights to See

⑫ **Al Abrar Mosque.** Also known as Kuchu Palli (the Tamil word for "small mosque"), this structure dates from 1850. The original mosque, built in 1827, was one of the first for Singapore's Indian Muslims.

OFF THE
BEATEN PATH

BIRD-SINGING CAFÉS – A special Sunday-morning treat is to take breakfast with the birds. Bird fanciers bring their prize specimens, in intricate bamboo cages, to coffee shops and hang the cages outside for training sessions: by listening to their feathered friends, the birds learn how to warble. Bird-singing enthusiasts take their hobby seriously and, incidentally, pay handsomely for it. For you, it costs only the price of a cup of coffee to sit at a table and listen. One place to try is the Seng Poh Coffee Shop on the corner of Tiong Bahru and Seng Poh roads, west of Tanjong Pagar; arrive at around 9 AM.

⑥ **Brothel.** Reliable sources say this was a famous brothel. Opium dens and brothels played important roles in the lives of Chinese immigrants, who usually arrived alone and worked long days, with little time for relaxation or pleasure. Many immigrants took to soothing their aching minds and bodies at opium dens; as only 12% of the community were women, men often sought female companionship from professionals. Gambling was another popular pastime. (Except for the state lottery and the official horse-race-betting system, gambling is now outlawed by the government. But you can be sure that when you hear the slap of mah-jongg in a coffeehouse, a wager or two has been made.) Raffles tried to ban gambling, but to no avail—the habit was too firmly entrenched. One legendary figure, Tan Che Seng, who had amassed a fortune subsidizing junks bringing immigrants to work in the warehouses, resolved to give up gambling. As a reminder of his resolution, he cut off half of his little finger. Still, he continued to gamble!

⑦ Chinatown Centre. This market is mobbed inside and out with jostling shoppers. At the open-air vegetable and fruit stands, women—toothless and wrinkled with age—sell their wares. Inside, on the first floor, hawker stalls sell a variety of cooked foods, but it's the basement floor that fascinates: here you'll find a wet market—so called because water is continually sloshed over the floors—where an amazing array of meats, fowl, and fish are bought and sold. Some of the sights may spoil your appetite; at the far left corner, for example, live pigeons, furry white rabbits, and sleepy turtles are crammed into cages, awaiting hungry buyers.

⑨ Guild for Amahs. Club Street is full of old buildings that continue to house clan associations, including the professional guild for *amahs*. Though their numbers are few today, these female servants were once an integral part of European households in Singapore. Like the *samsui* (women who vowed never to marry)—a few of whom can still be observed in their traditional red headdresses passing bricks or carrying buckets at construction sites—the amahs choose to earn an independent living, however hard the work, rather than submit to the servitude of marriage. (In traditional Chinese society, a daughter-in-law is the lowest-ranking member of the family.) In the past, when a woman decided to become an amah or samsui, she went through a ritual—a sort of substitute for marriage. Family and friends gathered and even brought gifts. The woman then tied up her hair—to indicate she wasn't available for marriage—and moved to a *gongxi,* or communal house, where she shared expenses and household duties and cared for her sisters.

④ Jamae Mosque. Popularly called Masjid Chulia, the simple, almost austere mosque was built in the 1830s by Chulia Muslims from India's Coromandel Coast. So long as it isn't prayer time and the doors are open, you're welcome to step inside for a look (you must be dressed conservatively and take your shoes off before entering; women may need shawls or scarves to cover their heads).

⑧ Jinriksha Station. This station was once the bustling central depot for Singapore's rickshaws, which numbered more than 9,000 in 1919. Now there's nary a one, and the station has been converted into a food market on one side and an office block on the other. This is a good place to sit down with a cool drink.

Kreta Ayer. Named after the bullock carts that carried water for cleaning the streets, this is the core of Chinatown.

② Lopong Telok Street. Nos. 27, 28, and 29 on this architecturally interesting street have intricately carved panels above the shop doorways. Across the street are old clan houses whose stonework facades appear to have a Portuguese influence—possibly by way of Malacca, a Portuguese trading post in the 17th century until the Dutch, and then the British, took possession of it.

Mosque Street. The old shophouses here—mercifully spared demolition—were originally built as stables. Now they house Hakka families selling second- or, more likely, thirdhand wares, from clothes to old medicine bottles.

⑩ Nagore Durghe Shrine. This odd mix of minarets and Greek columns was built by South Indian Muslims between 1828 and 1830. Inside it's now decorated with Christmas tree lights.

Sago Street. At No. 20, Fong Moon Kee, the best tikar mats—used by the older Chinese instead of soft mattresses—are sold. They're easy to carry and excellent for picnics, although prices begin at S$60. A cake shop at No. 34 is extremely popular for fresh baked goods, especially during the Mooncake Festival. Nearby, at **No. 26,** is Ban Yoo Foh Medical Hall, a store that sells dried snakes and lizards, for increasing fertility, and powdered antelope horn, for curing headaches and cooling the body.

Smith Street. Stores here sell chilies, teas, and soybeans. A medicine hall offers ground rhinoceros horn (a controversial product owing to wildlife protection issues) to help overcome impotency and pearl dust to help ladies' complexions.

★ ❺ **Sri Mariamman Temple.** The oldest Hindu temple in Singapore, the building has a pagodalike entrance topped by one of the most ornate *gopurams* (pyramidal gateway towers) you are ever likely to see. Hundreds of brightly colored statues of deities and mythical animals line the tiers of this towering porch; glazed cement cows sit, seemingly in great contentment, atop the surrounding walls. The story of this Hindu temple smack in the heart of Chinatown begins with Naraina Pillay, who came to Singapore on the same ship as Raffles in 1819 and started work as a clerk. Within a short time, he had set up his own construction business, often using convicts sent over to Singapore from India, and quickly made a fortune. He obtained this site to build a temple on, so that devotees could pray on the way to and from work at the harbor. This first temple, built in 1827 of wood and *atap* (wattle and daub), was replaced in 1843 by the current brick structure. The gopuram was added in 1936. Inside are some spectacular paintings that have been recently restored by Tamil craftsmen brought over from South India.

Tanjong Pagar Road. The center of an area of redevelopment in Chinatown, the area has 220 shophouses restored to their 19th-century appearance—or rather a sanitized, dollhouselike version of it. They now contain teahouses, calligraphers, mah-jongg makers, and other shops. More shophouses are presently being restored and, at current rents, will probably be occupied by upscale boutiques and restaurants.

⓭ **Telok Ayer Market.** This market, which looks a lot like a chicken coop, is the largest Victorian cast-iron structure left in Southeast Asia. Already a thriving fish market in 1822, it was redesigned as an octagon by George Coleman in 1894. It has been transformed into a planned food court, with hawker stalls offering all types of Asian fare. By day it's busy with office workers. After 7 PM Boon Tat Street is closed to traffic and the mood turns festive: hawkers wheel out their carts, and street musicians perform.

Temple Street. Here you may be fortunate enough to see one of the few remaining practitioners of a dying profession. Sometimes found sitting on a stool here is a scribe, an old man to whom other elderly Chinese who have not perfected the art of writing come to have their letters written. The street is slated to become a pedestrian street in the near future.

⓫ **Thian Hock Keng Temple.** Though at press time this—the Temple of Heavenly Happiness—was closed for renovations and it was unclear when the work would be finished, you should at least pass by to see the exterior. The temple was completed in 1841 to replace a simple shrine built 20 years earlier. It's one of Singapore's oldest and largest Chinese temples, built on the spot where, prior to land reclamation, immigrants stepped ashore after a hazardous journey across the China Sea. In gratitude for their safe passage, the Hokkien people dedicated the temple to Ma Chu P'oh, the goddess of the sea. Thian Hock Keng is richly decorated with gilded carvings, sculptures, tiled roofs topped with dragons, and fine carved stone pillars. The pillars and sculptures were brought over from China, the exterior cast-iron railings were made in

Glasgow, and the blue porcelain tiles on an outer building came from Holland. On either side of the entrance are two stone lions. The one on the left is female and holds a cup, symbolizing fertility; the other, a male, holds a ball, a symbol of wealth. If the temple is open, note that as you enter you must step over a high threshold board. This serves a dual function. First, it forces devotees to look downward, as they should, when entering the temple. Second, it keeps out wandering ghosts—ghosts tend to shuffle their feet, so if they try to enter, the threshold board will trip them.

Inside, a statue of a maternal Ma Chu P'oh, surrounded by masses of burning incense and candles, dominates the room. On either side of her are the deities of health (on the left if your back is to the entrance) and of wealth. The two tall figures you'll notice are her sentinels: one can see for 1,000 miles, the other can hear for 1,000 miles. The gluey black substance on their lips—placed there by devotees in days past—is opium, to heighten their senses. While the main temple is Taoist, the temple at the back is Buddhist and dedicated to Kuan Yin, the goddess of mercy. Her many arms represent how she reaches out to all those who suffer on earth. This is a good place to learn your fortune. Choose a number out of the box, then pick up two small, stenciled pieces of wood at the back of the altar and let them fall to the ground. If they land showing opposite faces, then the number you have picked is valid. If they land same-side up, try again. From a valid number, the person in the nearby booth will tell you your fate, and whether you like it or not, you pay for the information. Leave the grounds by the alley that runs alongside the main temple. The two statues to the left are the gambling brothers. They will help you choose a lucky number for your next betting session; if you win, you must return and place lighted cigarettes in their hands.

③ Wak Hai Cheng Bio Temple. Built between 1852 and 1855 by Teochew Chinese from Guangdong Province and dedicated to the goddess of the sea, restoration of this temple was completed in 1998. Its wonderfully ornate roof is covered with decorations—including miniature pagodas and human figures—depicting ancient Chinese villages and scenes from opera. Chinese temples, incidentally, are invariably dusty, thick with incense, and packed with offerings and statuary—evidence of devotees asking for favors and offering thanks for favors granted. To a Chinese, a sparkling clean, spartan temple would suggest unsympathetic deities with few followers. Where burning joss sticks have left a layer of dust and continue to fill the air with scent, the gods are willing to hear requests and grant wishes. If word spreads that many wishes have been realized by people visiting a particular temple, it can, virtually overnight, become the most popular temple in town.

④ Yeo Swee Huat. At No. 13 Upper Circular Road, you'll see a cottage industry designed to help Chinese take care of one obligation to their ancestors: making sure they have everything they need in the afterlife. Here, paper models of the paraphernalia of life—horses, cars, boats, planes, even fake money—are made, to be purchased by relatives of the deceased (you can buy them, too) and ritually burned so that their essence passes through to the spirit world in flames and smoke. Note that although the items may elicit chuckles, this custom is a very serious part of Chinese beliefs; try not to offend the proprietors.

LITTLE INDIA

Indians have been part of Singapore's development from the beginning. While Singapore was administered by the East India Company, headquartered in Calcutta, Indian convicts were sent here to serve their time.

These convicts left an indelible mark on Singapore, reclaiming land from swampy marshes and constructing a great deal of the city's infrastructure, including public buildings, St. Andrew's Cathedral, and many Hindu temples. The enlightened penal program permitted convicts to study a trade of their choice in the evenings. Many, on gaining their freedom, chose to stay in Singapore.

Other Indians came freely to seek their fortunes as clerks, traders, teachers, and moneylenders. The vast majority came from the south of India—both Hindu Tamils and Muslims from the Coromandel and Malabar coasts—but there were also Gujaratis, Sindhis, Sikhs, Parsis, and Bengalis. Each group brought its own language, cuisine, religion, and customs, and these divisions remain evident today. The Indians also brought their love of colorful festivals, which they now celebrate more frequently and more spectacularly than is done in India itself. The gory Thaipusam is among the most fascinating (☞ Chapter 1).

The area Raffles allotted to the Indian immigrants was north of the British colonial district. The heart of this area—known today as Little India—is Serangoon Road and the streets east and west of it between Bukit Timah and Sungei roads to the south and Perumal Road to the north. Although new buildings have replaced many of the old, the sights, sounds, and smells will make you believe you're in an Indian town.

Numbers in the text correspond to numbers in the margin and on the Little India map.

A Good Walk

Try to plan your walk for a weekday morning when crowds are at their thinnest and temperatures are at their lowest. Avoid Sunday afternoons, when the neighborhood teems with people. A good starting point is the junction of Serangoon and Sungei roads. As you walk along Serangoon, your senses will be sharpened by the fragrances of curry powders and perfumes, by tapes of high-pitched Indian music, by jewelry shops selling gold and stands selling garlands of flowers. (Indian women delight in wearing flowers and glittering arm bangles, but once their husbands die, they never do so again.) Other shops supply the colorful dyes used to mark the *tilak*—the dot seen on the forehead of Indian women. Traditionally, a Tamil woman wears a red dot to signify that she's married; a North Indian woman conveys the same message with a red streak down the part of her hair. However, the modern trend is for an Indian girl or woman to choose a dye color to match her sari or Western dress. Occasionally you'll see an unmarried woman with a black dot on her forehead: this is intended to counter the effects of the evil eye.

The first block on the left is **Zhujiao Centre** ①, one of the largest wet markets in the city. The streets to the right off Serangoon Road—Campbell Lane (home of **P. Govindasamy Pillai** ②, famous for its beautiful silk saris) and Dunlop Street—as well as **Clive Street,** which runs parallel to Serangoon, are filled with shops that sell such utilitarian items as pots and pans as well as rice, spices, brown cakes of palm sugar, and every other type of Indian grocery imaginable. You'll also see open-air barbershops and tailors working old-fashioned treadle sewing machines, and everywhere you go you'll hear sugar-sweet love songs from Indian movies. Along **Buffalo Road,** to the left off Serangoon, are shops specializing in saris, flower garlands, and electronic equipment. Above the doorways are strings of dried mango leaves, a customary Indian sign of blessing and good fortune. (If you detour down Dunlop Street, to the right off Serangoon Road, you'll come to the **Abdul Gaffoor Mosque** ③, with its detailed facade of green and gold.)

32

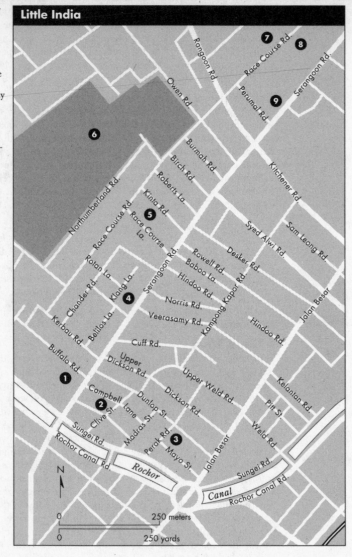

Little India

A little farther down Serangoon Road on the left (opposite Veerasamy Road), you'll notice the elaborate gopuram of the **Sri Veeramakaliamman Temple** ④, built in 1881 by indentured Bengali laborers working the lime pits nearby. Take Kinta Road to the **Burmese Buddhist Temple** ⑤ with its 11-ft-tall white marble Buddha. Turn right on Race Course Road to **Farrer Park** ⑥, site of Singapore's original racecourse. Farther along Race Course Road is the charming **Long San Chee Temple** ⑦, dedicated to Kuan Yin. Across the road is Sakya Muni Buddha Gaya Temple, more commonly referred to as the **Temple of 1,000 Lights** ⑧. Backtrack on Race Course Road to Perumal Road; to the left is the **Sri Srinivasa Perumal Temple** ⑨. Dedicated to Vishnu the Preserver, the temple is easy to recognize by the 59-ft-high monumental gopuram, depicting Vishnu in nine forms. If you continue along Race Course Road, you'll come to the Banana Leaf Apollo, an excellent place for a drink and a curry (☞ Chapter 3).

TIMING

This whole Race Course Road area has been under construction for a new MRT (subway) line and may require a couple of detours while walking. Even so, you should be able to do this tour in three to four hours. Factor in a half an hour extra for the temples.

Sights to See

❸ Abdul Gaffoor Mosque. This small, personable temple at No. 41 Dunlop Street has none of the exotic, multicolor statuary of the Hindu temples. But it still woos you with an intricately detailed facade in the Muslim colors of green and gold. When entering, make sure your legs are covered to the ankles, and remember to take off your shoes. Note that only worshippers are allowed into the prayer hall. Out of respect you shouldn't enter during evening prayer sessions or at any time on Friday.

Buffalo Road. Shops here specialize in saris, flower garlands, and electronic equipment. Also along this short street are a number of moneylenders from the Chettiar caste—the only caste that continues to pursue in Singapore the role prescribed to them in India. You'll find them seated on the floor before decrepit desks, but don't let the simplicity of their style fool you: some of them are very, very rich.

❺ Burmese Buddhist Temple. Built in 1878, this temple houses an 11-ft Buddha carved from a 10-ton block of white marble from Mandalay. The other, smaller Buddhas were placed here by Rama V, the king of Siam, and high priests from Rangoon, Burma (now called Yangon, Myanmar).

Clive Street. On this byway off Sungei Road, you'll find shops that purvey sugar, prawn crackers, rice, and dried beans. The older Indian women you'll notice with red lips and stained teeth are betel-nut chewers. If you want to try the stuff, you can buy a mouthful from street vendors.

❻ Farrer Park. This is the site of Singapore's original racetrack. It's also where the first aircraft to land in Singapore came to rest en route from England to Australia in 1919.

❼ Long San Chee Temple. Its main altar is dedicated to Kuan Yin—also known as Bodhisattva Avalokitesvara—and framed by beautiful, ornate carvings of flowers, a phoenix, and other birds.

❷ P. Govindasamy Pillai. This shop is famous for Indian textiles, especially saris. It sits on Campbell Lane amid other shops that sell spices, nuts, flower garlands, plastic flowers, and plastic statues.

❾ Sri Srinivasa Perumal Temple. Dedicated to Vishnu the Preserver, the temple is easy to recognize by the 60-ft-high monumental gopuram, with tiers of intricate sculptures depicting Vishnu in the nine forms in which he has appeared on earth. Especially vivid are the depictions of Vishnu's manifestations as Rama, on his seventh visit, and as Krishna, on his eighth. Rama is thought to be the personification of the ideal man; Krishna was brought up with peasants and, therefore, was a manifestation popular with laborers in the early days of Singapore. Sri Srinivasa Perumal is very much a people's temple. Inside you'll find devotees making offerings of fruit to one of the manifestations of Vishnu. This is done either by handing the coconuts or bananas, along with a slip of paper with one's name on it, to a temple official, who will chant the appropriate prayers to the deity and place holy ash on your head, or by walking and praying, coconut in hand, around one of the shrines a certain number of times, then breaking the coconut (a successful break symbolizes that Vishnu has been receptive to the incantation). The Temple is open from 6:30 AM to noon and 6 PM to 9 PM. Dress conservatively, and don't wear shoes inside.

❹ Sri Veeramakaliamman Temple. Built in 1881 by indentured Bengali laborers working the lime pits nearby, this temple is dedicated to Kali the Courageous, a ferocious incarnation of Shiva's wife, Parvati the Beautiful. Inside is a jet-black statue of Kali, the fiercest of the Hindu deities, who demands sacrifices and is often depicted with a garland of skulls. More cheerful is the shrine to Ganesh, the elephant-headed god of wisdom and prosperity. Perhaps the most popular Hindu deity, Ganesh is the child of Shiva and Parvati. (He was not born with an elephant head but received it in the following way: Shiva came back from a long absence to find his wife in a room with a young man. In a blind rage, he lopped off the man's head, not realizing that it was his now-grown-up son. The only way to bring Ganesh back to life was with the head of the first living thing Shiva saw; he saw an elephant.) Unlike some of Singapore's temples, which are open all day, this one is only open 8 AM–noon and 5:30–8:30 PM. During these times, you will see Hindus going in to receive blessings: the priest streaks devotees' foreheads with *vibhuti*, the white ash from burned cow dung.

❽ Temple of 1,000 Lights. The Sakya Muni Buddha Gaya is better known by its popular name because, for a small donation, you can pull a switch that lights countless bulbs around a 50-ft Buddha. The entire temple, as well as the Buddha statue, was built by the Thai monk Vutthisasala, who, until he died at the age of 94, was always in the temple, ready to explain Buddhist philosophy to anyone who wanted to listen. The monk also managed to procure relics for the temple: a mother-of-pearl-inlaid cast of the Buddha's footprint and a piece of bark from the bodhi tree under which the Buddha received Enlightenment. Around the pedestal supporting the great Buddha statue is a series of scenes depicting the story of his search for Enlightenment; inside a hollow chamber at the back is a re-creation of the scene of the Buddha's last sermon.

❶ Zhujiao Centre. One of the largest wet markets in the city, it has a staggering array of fruits, vegetables, fish, herbs, and spices. On the Sungei Road side of the ground floor are food stalls that offer Chinese, Indian, Malay, and Western foods. Upstairs are shops selling brass goods, "antiques," porcelains, and textiles.

THE ARAB DISTRICT

Long before the Europeans arrived, Arab traders plied the coastlines of the Malay Peninsula and Indonesia, bringing with them the teachings of Islam. By the time Raffles came to Singapore in 1819, to be a Malay was also to be a Muslim. Traditionally, Malays' lives have centered on their religion and their villages, known as kampongs. These consisted of a number of wood houses, with steep roofs of corrugated iron or thatch, gathered around a communal center, where chickens fed and children played under the watchful eye of mothers and the village elders while the younger men tended the fields or took to the sea in fishing boats. The houses were usually built on stilts above marshes and reached by narrow planks serving as bridges. If the kampong was on dry land, flowers and fruit trees would surround the houses.

Except for a Malay community on Pulau Sakeng (reachable only by private boat), all traditional kampongs have fallen to the might of the bulldozer in the name of urban renewal. Though all ethnic groups have had their social fabrics undermined by the demolition of their old communities, the Malays have suffered the most, since social life centered on the kampong.

The area known as the Arab District, or Little Araby, while not a true kampong, remains a Malay enclave, held firmly together by strict observance of the tenets of Islam. At the heart of the community is the Sultan Mosque, or Masjid Sultan, originally built with a grant from the East India Company to the Sultan of Jahore. Around it are streets whose very names—Bussorah, Baghdad, Kandahar—evoke the fragrances of the Muslim world. The pace of life is slower here: there are few cars, people gossip in doorways, and closet-size shops are crammed with such wares as *songkok* hats (the white skullcaps presented to hajji, those who have made the hajj, as the pilgrimage to Mecca is called) as well as Indonesian batiks, leather bags, and herbs whose packages promise youth and beauty, or many children.

The Arab District is a small area, bounded by Beach and North Bridge roads to the south and north and spreading a couple of blocks to either side of Arab Street. It's a place to meander, taking time to browse through shops or enjoy Muslim food at a simple café. Much of this neighborhood has undergone extensive renovation since 1996, but this only seems to be adding to the area's quiet charm.

Numbers in the text correspond to numbers in the margin and on The Arab District map.

A Good Walk

This walk begins at the foot of **Arab Street,** a street of specialty shops just off **North Bridge Road.** Wander past the shops and take a right onto Baghdad Street; watch for the dramatic view of the **Sultan Mosque** ① where **Bussorah Street** opens to your left. Leaving the mosque, return to Arab Street and take the first left onto Muscat Street, turn right onto Kandahar Street, and then left onto Baghdad Street. At Sultan Gate, you'll find **Istana Kampong Glam** ②, the sultan's Malay-style palace, built in the 1840s. Baghdad Street becomes Pahang Street at Sultan Gate, where traditional Chinese stonemasons create statues curbside. At the junction of Pahang Street and Jalan Sultan, turn right and, at Beach Road, left, to visit the endearing **Hajjah Fatimah Mosque** ③, built in 1845. It leans at a 6° angle. Return to Jalan Sultan and take a right. Past Minto Road is the **Sultan Plaza** ④, which houses fabric stores. Continue along Jalan Sultan, crossing **North Bridge Road,** to the junction of Victoria Street and the **Malabar Jama-Ath Mosque** ⑤.

Follow Victoria Street down to **Bugis Street** ⑥. Three blocks beyond where Bugis Street becomes Albert Street—between the Fu Lu Shou shopping complex (whose shops mostly sell clothes) and the food-oriented Albert Complex—is Waterloo Street. Near the corner is the **Kuan Yin Temple** ⑦, one of the most popular Chinese temples in Singapore.

TIMING

This walking tour shouldn't take more than two hours, including stops to look around the temples and mosques. But take your time. This is one of the friendliest places in Singapore.

Sights to See

Arab Street. On this street of specialty shops, you'll find baskets of every description—stacked on the floor or suspended from the ceiling. Farther along shops that sell fabrics—batiks, embroidered table linens, rich silks and velvets—dominate.

⑥ **Bugis Street.** Until recently Bugis Street was the epitome of Singapore's seedy but colorful nightlife; locals and visitors delighted in its red lights and bars. The government wasn't delighted, though, and the area was razed to make way for a new MRT station. So strong was the outcry that Bugis Street has been re-created, just steps from its original site, between Victoria and Queen streets, Rochor Road, and Cheng

36

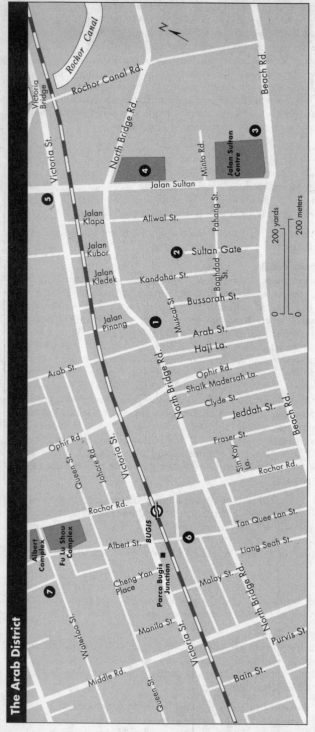

The Arab District

N

Rochor Canal

Rochor Canal Rd.

Victoria Bridge

North Bridge Rd.

Beach Rd.

3

Minto Rd.

4 Jalan Sultan Centre

Jalan Sultan

Victoria St.

5

Jalan Klapa

Aliwal St.

Pahang St.

Jalan Kubor

2 Sultan Gate

Jalan Kledek

Kandahar St.

Baghdad St.

Bussorah St.

Jalan Pinang

1

Muscat St.

Arab St.

Haji La.

Arab St.

Ophir Rd.

Shaik Madersah La.

Clyde St.

Jeddah St.

Ophir Rd.

Fraser St.

Victoria St.

Johore Rd.

Queen St.

Sin Koy La.

Rochor Rd.

Rochor Rd.

BUGIS

Tan Quee Lan St.

Albert Complex

Fu Lu Shou Complex

Albert St.

Liang Seah St.

7

6

Cheng Yan Place

Parco Bugis Junction

Malay St.

North Bridge Rd.

Waterloo St.

Manila St.

Purvis St.

Middle Rd.

Queen St.

Victoria St.

Bain St.

200 yards

200 meters

Bugis Street, **6**
Hajjah Fatimah Mosque, **3**
Istana Kampong Glam, **2**
Kuan Yin Temple, **7**

Malabar Jama-Ath Mosque, **5**
Sultan Mosque, **1**
Sultan Plaza, **4**

Yan Place. The shophouses have been resurrected; hawker food stands compete with open-fronted restaurants (Kentucky Fried Chicken has a prominent spot on a corner). Closed to traffic, the streets in the center of the block are the places to find bargain watches and CDs; you'll also find the Parco Bugis Junction, an upscale shopping center that's quite a contrast to all the area's dollar stores and souvenir shops.

❸ Hajjah Fatimah Mosque. In 1845 Hajjah Fatimah, a wealthy Muslim woman married to a Bugis trader, commissioned a British architect to build this mosque. (Hajjah is the title given to a woman who has made the pilgrimage to Mecca.) The minaret is reputedly modeled on the spire of the original St. Andrew's Church in colonial Singapore, but it leans at a 6° angle. No one knows whether this was intentional or accidental, and engineers brought in to see if the minaret could be straightened have walked away shaking their heads. Islam forbids carved images of Allah. The only decorative element usually employed is the beautiful flowing Arabic script in which quotations from the Qur'an (Koran) are written across the walls. This relatively small mosque is an intimate oasis amid all the bustle. It's extremely relaxing to enter the prayer hall (remember to take your shoes off) and sit in the shade of its dome. French contractors and Malay artisans rebuilt the mosque in the 1930s. Hajjah Fatimah, her daughter, and her son-in-law are buried in an enclosure behind the mosque.

❷ Istana Kampong Glam. The sultan's Malay-style palace, rebuilt in the 1840s on a design by George Coleman, has been refurbished, and next door is another grand royal bungalow: the home of the sultan's first minister. Notice its gateposts surmounted by green eagles. Neither building is open to the public, but through the gates you can get a glimpse of the past.

❼ Kuan Yin Temple. The dusty, incense-filled interior of this popular temple, its altars heaped with hundreds of small statues of gods from the Chinese pantheon, transports you into the world of Chinese mythology. Of the hundreds of Chinese deities, Kuan Yin is perhaps most dear to the hearts of Singaporeans. Legend has it that just as she was about to enter Nirvana, she heard a plaintive cry from Earth. Filled with compassion, she gave up her place in Paradise to devote herself to alleviating the pain of those on Earth; thereupon, she took the name Kuan Yin, meaning "to see and hear all." People in search of advice on anything from an auspicious date for a marriage to possible solutions for domestic or work crises come to her temple, shake *cham si* (bamboo fortune sticks), and wait for an answer. The gods are the most receptive on days of a new or full moon.

For more immediate advice, you can speak to any of the fortune-tellers who sit under umbrellas outside the temple. They'll pore over ancient scrolls of the Chinese almanac and, for a few dollars, tell you your future. If the news isn't good, you may want to buy some of the flowers sold nearby and add them to your bathwater. They're said to help wash away bad luck. A small vegetarian restaurant next to the temple serves Chinese pastries.

❺ Malabar Jama-Ath Mosque. The land on which this mosque sits was originally granted to the Muslim Kling community (Muslims from either Malaysia or the Philippines) in 1848 by Sultan Ally Iskander Shah as a burial ground. The mosque they erected here was abandoned and later taken over by the Malabar Muslims (those with ancestors from India or Ceylon, now Sri Lanka), who rebuilt it in 1963.

North Bridge Road. North Bridge Road is full of fascinating stores that sell costumes and headdresses for Muslim weddings, clothes for traditional Malay dances, prayer beads, scarves, perfumes, and much more. Interspersed among the shops are small, simple restaurants that serve Muslim food. Toward the Sultan Mosque, the shops tend to concentrate on Muslim religious items, including *bareng haji,* the clothing and other requisites for a pilgrimage to Mecca.

★ ❶ **Sultan Mosque.** The first mosque on this site was built early in the 1820s with a S$3,000 grant from the East India Company. The current structure, built in 1928 by Denis Santry—the architect who designed the Victoria Memorial Hall—is a dramatic building with golden domes and minarets that glisten in the sun. The walls of the vast prayer hall are adorned with green and gold mosaic tiles on which passages from the Qur'an (Koran) are written in decorative Arab script. The main dome has an odd architectural feature: hundreds of brown bottles, stacked five or more rows deep, are seemingly jammed in neck first between the dome and base. No one seems to know why. Five times a day—at dawn, 12:30 PM, 4 PM, sunset, and 8:15 PM—the sound of the muezzin, or crier, calls the faithful to prayer. At midday on Friday, the Islamic sabbath, seemingly every Malay in Singapore enters through one of the Sultan Mosque's 14 portals to recite the Qur'an. During Ramadan, the month of fasting, the nearby streets, especially Bussorah, and the square before the mosque are lined with hundreds of stalls selling curries, cakes, and candy; at dusk, Muslims break their day's fast in this square. Non-Muslims, too, come to enjoy the rich array of Muslim foods and the party atmosphere.

❹ **Sultan Plaza.** Inside, dozens of traders offer batiks and other fabrics in traditional Indonesian and Malay designs.

ORCHARD ROAD

If "downtown" is defined as where the action is, then Singapore's downtown is Orchard Road. Here are some of the city's most fashionable shops, hotels (which often, like the Hilton, for example, have expensive, upscale malls all their own), restaurants, and nightclubs. The street has been dubbed the Fifth Avenue or Bond Street of Singapore but, air of luxury aside, it has little in common with either of those older, relatively understated marketplaces for the wealthy. Orchard Road is an ultra-high-rent district that's very modern and very, very flashy—especially at night, when millions of lightbulbs, flashing from seemingly every building, assault the senses. In addition to all those glittering lights and windows, Orchard Road offers a number of sights with which to break up a shopping trip. Still, if the urge to splurge has overtaken the need to sightsee, you'll find additional information on the malls and stores mentioned in this tour *in* Chapter 7.

Numbers in the text correspond to numbers in the margin and on the Orchard Road map.

A Good Walk

Start at the bottom of Orchard Road and head toward the junction with Scotts Road, the hub of downtown. You'll see the enormous **Istana** ①, once the official residence of the colonial governor and now that of the president of the republic. Senior Minister Lee Kuan Yew also keeps his office here. On the other side of Orchard Road, and a few steps down Cleamenceau Avenue, is the lovely old **Tan Yeok Nee House** ②. Built in 1815 for a wealthy Chinese merchant, the house used to be a museum, but now it's being redeveloped. Turn on Tank Road and continue to the **Chettiar Temple** ③, which houses the image of Lord Subramaniam. Return to Orchard Road and turn left. On the right is Cuppage Road, with a market (open every morning) known for imported and unusual fruit and a row of antiques shops.

Returning once more to Orchard Road, you'll pass the block-long **Centrepoint**; immediately after it is **Peranakan Place** ④, a celebration of Peranakan culture. A bit farther along and on the other side of Orchard Road is the **Mandarin Singapore** ⑤ hotel, which has an interesting art collection. Cross back to the other side of Orchard Road and follow it to the intersection of Scotts Road, where you'll find **Shaw House** ⑥, which has Isetan as its major anchor. A detour up Scotts Road leads to the landmark **Goodwood Park Hotel,** which offers one of the most civilized high teas in town. Farther up Scotts Road is the **Newton Circus** ⑦ food hawker center.

Retrace your steps to the intersection of Scotts and Orchard roads. Walk up the left side of Orchard Road, past the Lane Crawford building. Taxi drivers call it "the rocket," and you'll see why. **Planet Hollywood** opened at the Liat Towers on Orchard Road in early 1997 and still gets its share of visiting celebrities. As you continue up Orchard Road, the **Palais Renaissance** will be on your right. Where Orchard turns into Tanglin, you'll find the **Tanglin Shopping Centre.** The second floor has some of the best antiques shops in town.

TIMING

Orchard Road has so many shopping diversions that you should allow three to four hours for the walk. Allow half an hour for the Chettiar Temple and, if you are an antiques fan, at least an hour for the Tanglin Shopping Centre.

Sights to See

Centrepoint. One of the liveliest shopping complexes, spacious and impressive Centrepoint has the **Robinsons** department store as its largest tenant. It also has **Marks & Spencer;** leading watch retailer **The Hour Glass;** jewelry, silverware, and fashion clothing shops; furniture stores that sell Philippine bamboo and Korean chests; and a large basement supermarket. For those craving a Big Mac, a popular **McDonald's** is also here.

❸ **Chettiar Temple.** This southern Indian temple, home to numerous shrines, is a recent (1984) replacement of the original, which was built in the 19th century. The 70-ft-high gopuram, with its many colorful sculptures of godly manifestations, is astounding. The chandelier-lit interior is lavishly decorated; 48 painted-glass panels are inset in the ceiling and angled to reflect the sunrise and sunset. The temple's daily hours are more limited than those at most Singapore temples; it's open from 8 AM to noon and then again from 5:30 to 8:30.

Goodwood Park Hotel. Though not as well known as the Raffles and 30 years younger, this hotel (☞ *also* Chapter 4) is just as much a landmark. Partaking of an elegant afternoon tea here—accompanied by live piano music—is the perfect way to take a break from all that shopping. Tea is served from 2:30 to 6 and costs about S$21.

❶ **Istana.** Once the official residence of the colonial governor and now that of the president of the republic, the building is open to the public only on National Day. On the first Sunday of each month, there's a changing-of-the-guard ceremony: the new guards leave Bideford Road at 5:30 PM and march along Orchard Road to the Istana, reaching the entrance gate punctually at 6. Former prime minister and senior minister Lee Kuan Yew has his office here.

❺ **Mandarin Singapore.** In the main lobby of this hotel is an exquisite mural delineated by real gold etched into white marble. The 70-ft-long work, by Yuy Tang, is called *87 Taoist Immortals* and is based on an 8th-century Tang scroll. It depicts 87 mythical figures paying homage

Orchard Road

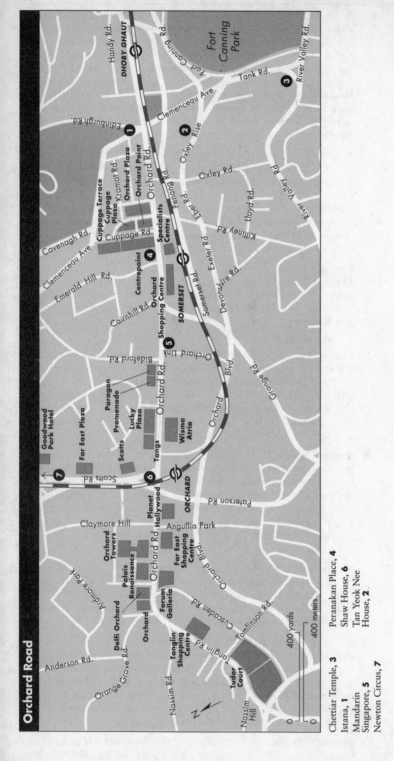

Handy Rd.

DHOBY GHAUT

Fort Canning Park

Fort Canning Rd.

Clemenceau Rd.

Tank Rd.

River Valley Rd.

3

Edinburgh Rd.

Clemenceau Ave.

1

2

Oxley Rise

Oxley Rd.

River Valley Rd.

Kramat Rd.

Orchard Plaza

Orchard Point

Orchard Rd.

Penang Rd.

Eber Rd.

Lloyd Rd.

Killiney Rd.

Cuppage Terrace

Cuppage Plaza

Specialists Centre

Cavenagh Rd.

Cuppage Rd.

4

Exeter Rd.

Clemenceau Ave.

Centrepoint

Somerset Rd.

Devonshire Rd.

Emerald Hill Rd.

Orchard Shopping Centre

SOMERSET

Cairnhill Rd.

5

Orchard Link

Bideford Rd.

Orchard Rd.

Orchard Blvd.

Grange Rd.

Goodwood Park Hotel

Paragon

Far East Plaza

Promenade

Lucky Plaza

Orchard Rd.

Scotts

Wisma Atria

Orchard

Tangs

7

Scotts Rd.

6

ORCHARD

Paterson Rd.

Claymore Hill

Planet Hollywood

Angullia Park

Orchard Rd.

Orchard Towers

Far East Shopping Centre

Orchard Blvd.

Ardmore Park

Palais Renaissance

Cuscaden Rd.

Delfi Orchard

Orchard

Forum Galleria

Anderson Rd.

Tanglin Shopping Centre

Tanglin Rd.

Tomlinson Rd.

Orange Grove Rd.

Nassim Rd.

Tudor Court

Nassim Hill

N

400 yards

400 meters

0

0

Chettiar Temple, **3**

Istana, **1**

Mandarin Singapore, **5**

Newton Circus, **7**

Peranakan Place, **4**

Shaw House, **6**

Tan Yeok Nee House, **2**

to Xi Wangmu, Mother of God, on her birthday. While in the Mandarin, you may want to wander around to see the other works of art displayed. In the Mezzanine Lounge is Gerard Henderson's floor-to-ceiling mural *Gift to Singapore*. Henderson, half Chinese and half Irish, also created a powerful series of eight canvases titled *Riders of the World*. Five of these vibrant paintings dominate the wall adjoining the lobby. They depict the untamed and unconquered, including a 13th-century Japanese samurai, a Mandarin of the Ming Dynasty, a 9th-century Moor, and a 20th-century cossack. Don't miss the huge abstract batik mural by Seah Kim Joo, one of Singapore's best-known contemporary artists, that adorns three walls of the Mandarin's upstairs gallery.

7 Newton Circus. This is one of the best-known hawker centers in town. (The "circus" refers to the rotary, as in Piccadilly Circus.) Some of the stalls are open all day, but the best times to go are either around 9 AM, when a few stalls serve Chinese breakfasts, or after 7 PM, when all the stores are open and the Circus is humming with the hungry.

Palais Renaissance. The Palais Renaissance complex is chic, opulent, and overpriced but a delight to wander through. Boutiques such as **Ralph Lauren, Dunhill, Chanel,** and **Gucci** are for the shopper seeking status labels at high prices.

4 Peranakan Place. A celebration of Peranakan (also called straits-born Chinese, Baba, or Nonya) culture, an innovative blending of Chinese and Malay cultures that emerged in the 19th century as Chinese born in the straits settlements adopted (and often adapted) Malay fashions, cuisine, and architecture. At Peranakan Place, six old wooden shophouses, with fretted woodwork and painted in pastel colors, have been beautifully restored. Notice the typical Peranakan touches, such as the use of decorative tiles and the unusual fence doors.

☾ Planet Hollywood. The Liat Towers, formerly home to Galleries Lafayette, the French department store, was transformed into a branch of the now ubiquitous Planet Hollywood. With leopard-print sofas, California cuisine, and film memorabilia adorning the walls, Planet Hollywood remains popular. Teenagers sit across from the entrance waiting for a glimpse of their favorite North American celebrities, who often sign autographs here when in town.

6 Shaw House. Japan's large **Isetan** department store is the major anchor in this shopping complex at the corner of Scotts and Orchard roads. **Kinokuniya** bookstore, in the older Shaw Centre, is especially good for publications about Japan, but also carries English-language books.

Tanglin Shopping Centre. At the corner of Napier and Tanglin roads, this suburban mall was built to cater to the surrounding wealthy neighborhood. It has an excellent food court in its basement.

2 Tan Yeok Nee House. The house was built around 1885 for Tan Yeok Nee (1827–1902), a merchant from China who started out here as a cloth peddler and became a very wealthy man through trade in opium, gambier, and pepper. Whereas most homes built in Singapore at that time followed European styles, this town house was designed in a style popular in South China—notice the keyhole gables, terra-cotta tiles, and massive granite pillars. After the railway was laid along Tank Road in 1901, the house became the stationmaster's. In 1912, St. Mary's Home and School for Girls took it over. Since 1940 the Salvation Army has made the place its local headquarters. The house is now being redeveloped.

SIDE TRIPS AROUND
SINGAPORE AND BEYOND

Although there's a great deal to see and do in Singapore, you may want
to escape to areas just outside the city or to small islands just off the
coast. A jaunt to the nearby Indonesian island of Bintan—with its pristine shores, mangrove swamps, and hideaway resorts—will no doubt
add still more dimension to your Southeast Asia journey.

The East Coast

Two decades ago, Singapore's eastern coastal area contained only coconut plantations, rural Malay villages, and a few undeveloped beaches.
Today, however, it is totally different. At the extreme northeastern tip
of the island is Changi International Airport, one of the finest in the
world. Between the airport and the city, numerous satellite residential
developments have sprung up, and vast land-reclamation projects
along the seashore have created a park 8 km (5 mi) long, with plenty
of recreational facilities.

*Numbers in the text correspond to numbers in the margin and on The
East and West Coasts and the Green Interior map.*

A Good Tour

A trip to the east coast is a relaxing way to spend a morning or afternoon. This two- to three-hour tour is best done by taxi, which will cost
you roughly S$8–S$15 each way. Catch a cab at the junction of Nicoll
Highway and Bras Basah Road, near the Raffles Hotel and Marina
Square.

Nicoll Highway leads onto East Coast Road, and heading east along
it, you come to the Kallang area. Cross the Rochar and Kallang rivers
by the Merdeka (Independent) Bridge and you'll see, to the left and
right, an estuary that was once the haunt of pirates and smugglers. A
few shipyards are visible to the left, where the old Bugis trading
schooners once anchored. (The Bugis, a seafaring people from the
Celebes—now Sulawesi—Indonesia, have a long history as great traders;
their schooners, called *prahus,* still ply Indonesian waters.) To the
right is the huge National Stadium, where international sporting events
are held. Just past the stadium, Mountbatten Road crosses Old Airport Road, once the runway of Singapore's first airfield. One of the
old British colonial residential districts, this area is still home to the
wealthy, as attested by the splendid houses in both traditional and modern architectural styles.

Ask the driver to take you up East Coast Parkway, so that you can visit
the **Crocodilarium** ① (for still more reptile fun you can head up to the
Singapore Crocodile Farm) or the **East Coast Park** ②. Stop to eat at the
East Coast Park Food Centre or the **UDMC Seafood Centre.** Catch another taxi to take you farther east to the infamous **Changi Prison** ③.

Sights to See

❸ **Changi Prison.** This home to Nick Leeson, the young Englishman who
broke the Barings Bank, is well worth a visit. The sprawling, squat,
sinister-looking place, built in 1927 by the British, was used by the Japanese in World War II to intern some 70,000 prisoners of war, who
endured terrible hardships here. Today it houses some 2,000 convicts,
many of whom are here owing to Singapore's strict drug laws. This is
where serious offenders are hanged at dawn on Friday.

If you're not part of an organized tour (☞ Tour Operators *in* the Gold
Guide section), you can really only visit the **Changi Prison Chapel and**

Museum, whose walls hold poignant memorial plaques to those interned here during the war. It's a replica of one of 14 chapels where 85,000 Allied POWs and civilians gained the faith and courage to overcome the degradation and deprivation inflicted upon them by the Japanese. The museum contains drawings, sketches, and photographs by POWs depicting their wartime experiences. ⊠ *Upper Changi Rd.,* ☎ *471–9955 or 471–9937 (ranger's office).* ⌨ *Donations accepted.* ☉ *Chapel and museum: Mon.–Sat. 9:30–4:30; visitors welcome at 5:30 PM Sun. service.*

Organized guided tours may take you through the old British barracks areas to the former RAF camp. Here, in **Block 151**—a prisoners' hospital during the war—you'll see the simple but striking murals painted by a British POW, bombardier Stanley Warren. (Fax the prison's public affairs department at 764–6119 for approval to view the murals if you're visiting on your own.) The scale of military spending in the 1930s by the British—who put up these well-designed barracks to accommodate tens of thousands of men—is amazing. You can clearly see why the British believed Singapore was impregnable! This is still a military area; most of the barracks are used by Singapore's servicemen during their 2½-year compulsory duty.

❶ Crocodilarium. More than 1,000 of the jaw-snapping crocodiles here are bred to be skinned. You can watch crocodile wrestling Tuesday through Sunday at 1:15 and 4:15 PM; a definite feeding time is Tuesday at 11 AM. Naturally, there's a place to buy crocodile-skin bags and belts—at inflated prices. ☎ *447–3722.* ⌨ *S$2.* ☉ *Daily 9–5.*

❷ East Coast Park. Between the highway and the sea, this park has a wide variety of water sports and other recreational facilities. A cool sea breeze makes it the best place in town for running (☞ Chapter 6).

East Coast Park Food Centre. Next to the Europa Sailing Club, this alfresco center has many food stalls and a view of the harbor.

<table>
<tr><td>OFF THE
BEATEN PATH</td><td>**SINGAPORE CROCODILE FARM** – Yet more of these popular creatures—plus alligators, snakes, and lizards—are on view at a 1-acre breeding farm 6½ km (4 mi) northwest of the Crocodilarium. Feeding time is 11 AM Tuesday through Sunday. At the factory, observe the process of turning hides into accessories that—along with imported eel-skin products—are sold at the farm shop. ⊠ *790 Upper Serangoon Rd.,* ☎ *288-9385.* ⌨ *Free.* ☉ *Daily 8:30–5:30.*</td></tr>
</table>

UDMC Seafood Centre. This gathering of eight outdoor restaurants is a popular evening destination (☞ Chapter 3).

The West Coast

The satellite city of Jurong is Singapore's main industrial area. It's estimated that more than 70% of the nation's manufacturing workforce is employed here by more than 3,000 companies. Though this may seem an unlikely vacation destination, there are actually several interesting attractions in or around Jurong. A garden environment exists here, demonstrating that an industrial area doesn't have to be ugly.

A Good Tour

West Coast attractions are far from the center of town and far from one another. Allow a half day for each sight (except the Crocodile Paradise, which deserves an hour at most). You can arrange a tour through your hotel or take taxis alone or in combination with the MRT. A cab ride from the center of town to Jurong will cost about S$15. **Haw Par Villa** ④ amusement park is much closer to town than the other sights.

The East and West Coasts and the Green Interior

Johore Bahru

Johore Straits

Causeway

Admiralty Rd. W.

WOODLANDS

Sarimbun Reservoir

Woodlands Rd.

Kranji War Memorial

Kranji Reservoir

YISHUN

Mandai Rd.

Seletar Reservoir

Lim Chu Kang Rd.

Murai Reservoir

Singapore Zoological Gardens ⑪ ⑫

⑬

Mandai Orchid Garden

Night Safari

Sembawang Rd.

Yishun Ave. 2

Poyan Reservoir

BUKIT PANJANG

Jalan Behar

Choa Chu Kang Rd.

Upper Bukit Timah Rd.

Bukit Timah

Bukit Timah Expwy.

Upper Peirce Reservoir

Lower Peirce Reservoir

Upper Thomson Rd.

Kong M San Ph Kark S Temple

JURONG WEST

Pan Island Expwy.

Bukit Timah Nature Reserve ⑭

MacRitchie Reservoir ⑮

Upper Jurong Rd.

Chinese Garden ⑦

Japanese Garden ⑧

⑨ **Singapore Science Centre**

Tang Dynasty City ⑩

Bukit Timah Rd.

Holland Rd.

Queensway

Farrer Rd.

Jalan Ahmad Ibrahim

Upper Ayah Rajah Rd.

Jurong Bird Park

⑤ ⑥ **Jurong Crocodile Paradise**

Jalan Buroh

Singapore Mint Coin Gallery

West Coast Rd.

Botanic Gardens ⑯

Tanglin Rd.

Orchard Rd.

Pandan Reservoir

New Ming Village

West Coast Hwy.

Ayah Rajah Rd.

P. Pesek

P. Merlimau

Terumbu Retan Laut

Mt. Faber

Haw Par Villa ④

Telok Blangah Rd.

World Trade Centre Ferry Terminal

P. Ayer Chawan

P. Seraya

P. Ayer Merbau

Sentosa Island

P. Br

P. Sakra

P. Bakau

P. Busing

P. Bukum

P. Te

P. Ular

P. Hantu

TO
P. SAKENG,
P. SENANG

Sister's Islands

0 ——— 4 miles
0 ——— 6 km

WEST
MALAYSIA

P. Seletar

Johore Straits

TO DESARU,
MALAYSIA

S. Seletar

P. Serangoon

P. Ubin

Punggol Rd.

TO P.
TEKONG

P. Ketam

PUNGGOL

S. Serangoon

Serangoon Harbour

Yio Chu Kang Rd.

SERANGOON

CHANGI

Loyang Ave.

U. Chang Rd.

Changi
Airport

ong Meng
an Phor
ark See
mple

Upper Serangoon Rd.

Tampines Rd.

Changi
Prison

③

■ Singapore
Crocodile Farm

Central Expwy

Paya Lebar Rd.

Airport Blvd.

Siong Lim
Temple and
Gardens
■

Pan Island Expressway

BEDOK

New Upper Changi

Changi Coast Rd.

Serangoon Rd.

Sims Ave.

New Upper Changi
Rd.

Geylang Rd.

East Coast Rd.

N

Kallang Rd.

KATONG

Mountbatten Rd.

National
Stadium ■

East Coast Parkway

■ East Coast
Park Food Centre

d Rd.

Nicoll Hwy.

Crocodilarium

Recreational
Centre

UDMC
Seafood
Centre

② ■ East Coast
Park

①

Strait of Singapore

P. Brani

*Buran
Darat*

P. Tekukor

P. Renggit

Kusu Island

Lazarus Island

St. John's Island

Subway & Rail Lines

- - - - North-South MRT line
——— East-West MRT line
——— Railroad lines
⊘ Subway stop

The nearest MRT station is Buona Vista Station, from which you must transfer to Bus 200 (though air-conditioned express coach service is available from hotels along Orchard Road). Haw Par Villa is also near one of the main jumping-off points to Sentosa Island, a short ride away, so consider pairing a visit to the villa with one to the island (☞ Sentosa Island, *below*).

On another day, you might start with a visit to **Jurong Bird Park** ⑤. An MRT ride to Clementi will cost about S$1.50, depending on where you start your journey, and a taxi from here to the park itself will cost another S$5 or so. If take a taxi the whole way, plan to spend S$30 round-trip. Exploring the park is tiring, so take a break (or two) in one of the on-site restaurants. If you haven't tired of all the fauna, check out the **Jurong Crocodile Paradise** ⑥, directly across the parking lot from the bird park. If, however, you're ready to view some flora, spend your afternoon at the **Chinese Garden** ⑦ and the **Japanese Garden** ⑧ (take the MRT to the Chinese Garden Station to get here).

Alternatively, you could spend your afternoon at the **Singapore Science Centre** ⑨ or the **Tang Dynasty City** ⑩. If you don't want to spring for a taxi from Orchard Road (about a 20-minute ride), you can take the westbound MRT to the Jurong East Station, and then transfer to Bus 335 or make the 10-minute walk to the Science Centre's Omni-Theatre. To reach Tang Dynasty City, simply take the MRT to the Lakeside Station. Other area sights include the **Singapore Mint Coin Gallery**, where coins are made and displayed, and pottery demonstrations at **New Ming Village**.

Sights to See

🐾 ⑦ **Chinese Garden.** This 34.6-acre reconstruction of a Chinese imperial garden (one inspiration for it was the garden of the Beijing Summer Palace) has pagodas, temples, courtyards, and bridges. Lotus-filled lakes and placid streams are overhung by groves of willows. Rental rowboats allow a swan's-eye view of the grounds, and there are refreshment facilities. Within the main garden you'll find the **Ixora Garden,** with several varieties of the showy flowering ixora shrub; the **Herb Garden,** showcasing plants used in herbal medicines; and the **Garden of Fragrance,** where many newlyweds have their photographs taken against stone plaques with auspicious Chinese engravings. If you're coming directly from Singapore, take the MRT to the Chinese Garden stop; it's only a short walk to the garden itself. ⊠ *Off Yuan Ching Rd.,* ☎ *264–3455.* ☜ *S$4.50 (includes admission to Japanese Garden).* ☉ *Mon.–Sat., 9–7, Sun. 8:30–7. Last admission at 6 PM daily.*

🐾 ④ **Haw Par Villa.** Also known as the Tiger Balm Gardens, the villa presents Chinese folklore in theme-park fashion. Part of an estate owned by two eccentric brothers in the 1930s, after World War II the gardens were opened to the public. They fell into disarray and were sold to a soft-drink-bottling company that spent S$85 million on their transformation. Haw Par Villa was reopened in late 1990 and today it has both traditional amusements and multimedia presentations. The most popular attractions are a boat ride ("Tales of China") through the inside of a dragon whose entrails have scenes from the 10 courts of hell; a slide presentation ("Legends and Heroes") of Chinese mythology that explains why we have only one sun; a 3-D movie ("Creation of the World"); and a water roller coaster ("Wrath of the Water Gods"). These and seven other attractions will keep your child's interest, though you will be either bored or amused by the corniness of the sanitized production sets. The best time to start your visit is at 9:30 AM, before the crowds and long lines. ⊠ *262 Pasir Panjang Rd.,* ☎ *774–0300.* ☜ *S$16.50 (includes all attractions).* ☉ *Daily 9–6.*

🖑 **8** **Japanese Garden.** Adjacent to the Chinese Garden, this delightful formal garden is one of the largest of its kind outside Japan. Its classic simplicity, serenity, and harmonious arrangement of plants, stones, bridges, and trees induce tranquility. (Indeed, the garden's Japanese name, Seiwaen, means "Garden of Tranquility.") A miniature waterfall spills into a pond full of water lilies and lotus. ⊠ *Off Yuan Ching Rd., Jurong,* ☎ *264–3455.* 🎟 *S$4.50 (includes admission to Chinese Garden).* ⊙ *Mon.–Sat. 9–7, Sun. 8:30–7; last admission at 6.*

🖑 **5** **Jurong Bird Park.** Built on 50 landscaped acres, the world's largest walk-in aviary includes a 100-ft man-made waterfall that cascades into a stream. More than 3,600 birds from 365 species are here, including the colorful, the rare, and the noisy. It's a shock to stand atop Jurong Hill, amid the twittering birds and lush vegetation, and look down on factories that crank out Singapore's economic success. For an overview of the park with sweeping vistas, consider taking the 10-minute ride on the Panorail, an air-conditioned monorail train.

If you arrive here early, try the breakfast buffet from 9 to 11 at the **Song Bird Terrace,** where birds in bamboo cages tunefully trill as you help yourself to sausages, eggs, and toast. From here you can walk over to the **Penguin Feeding** (held at 10:30). In the afternoon (at 3), you might catch the JBP All Star BirdShow, at the **Pools Amphitheatre.** The nocturnal-bird house allows a glimpse of owls, night herons, frogsmouth, kiwi, and others usually cloaked in darkness. The bee-eaters and starlings are fed at 10:30 AM, 11:30 AM, and 4:30 PM; you can be fed throughout the day at the **Waterfront Cafe** or **Burger King.** ⊠ *2 Jurong Hill, Jalan Ahmad Ibrahim,* ☎ *265–0022.* 🎟 *S$10.30, Panorail S$2.* ⊙ *Daily 9–6.*

🖑 **6** **Jurong Crocodile Paradise.** Singaporeans seem to be fascinated with crocs, and at this 5-acre park you'll find 2,500 of them in landscaped streams, at a feeding platform, or in a breeding lake. You can feed the crocodiles, watch muscle-bound showmen (and a showlady) wrestle with them, or buy crocodile-skin products at the shop. You can also watch the beasts through glass, in an underwater viewing gallery. A seafood restaurant and fast-food outlets provide refreshments, and there are rides for children. ⊠ *241 Jalan Ahmad Ibrahim,* ☎ *261–8866.* 🎟 *S$7.* ⊙ *Daily 9–6; wrestling at 11:45, 2, and 4.*

New Ming Village. At this small complex of buildings not far from the Jurong Bird Park, demonstrations of the art of Chinese pottery making are given, and copies of Ming Dynasty blue and white porcelain are produced and sold. ⊠ *32 Pandam Rd.,* ☎ *265–7711.* 🎟 *Free.* ⊙ *Daily 9–5:30.*

Singapore Mint Coin Gallery. Close to the ☞ Singapore Science Centre and just east of the Boon Lay MRT station, you can watch minting operations. There are also displays of coins, medals, and medallions from Singapore and around the world. ⊠ *20 Teban Garden Crescent,* ☎ *566–2626.* 🎟 *Free.* ⊙ *Weekdays 9:30–4:30.*

🖑 **9** **Singapore Science Centre.** Here, subjects such as aviation, nuclear science, robotics, astronomy, and space technology are entertainingly explored through audiovisual and interactive exhibits. You can walk into a "human body" for a closer look at vital organs or test yourself on computer quiz games. You'll also find a flight simulator of a Boeing 747 and the Omni Theatre, which presents two programs: "Oasis in Space" travels to the beginning of the universe and "To Fly" simulates the feel of space travel. Children of any age are sure to get a thrill from the brave new world of science presented here. ⊠ *Science Centre Rd., off Jurong Town Hall Rd.,* ☎ *560–3316.* 🎟 *S$3; Omni Theatre S$9.* ⊙ *Tues.–Sun. 10–6.*

Tang Dynasty City. This theme park re-creates the 7th-century Chinese village of Chang'an (present-day Xian) with pagodas, gilded imperial courts, and an underground palace of the royal dead guarded by 1,000 terra-cotta warriors. The Imperial Palace is really a cluster of six palaces built to scale. Restaurants and entertainment facilities are modern intrusions, but artisans make and sell traditional wares, and acrobats, rickshaws, and oxcarts add to the authenticity. A tram takes you around. ⊠ *2 Yuan Ching Rd.,* ☎ *251–1116.* 🎫 *S$15.45 (including tram ride).* ☉ *Daily 10–6:30.*

Into the Garden Isle

Singapore is called the Garden Isle, and with good reason. Although the government seems obsessed with reinforced concrete, it has also established nature reserves, gardens, and a zoo. This excursion from downtown takes you into the center of the island to enjoy some of its greenery. If you have only a little time to spare, at least visit the zoo—it's truly exceptional. If you want to learn more about Singapore's natural habitats and plant life, contact the nature society (☎ 253–2179).

A Good Tour

Much of Singapore's natural world is miles from the center of the city. Because of the heat, walking through nature here is tiring, so you probably won't be able to see all the sights in one day. Taxis or hotel tours are the favored ways of getting to the orchid garden, the zoo, and the Night Safari—all of which you can tour in the space of an afternoon and an evening. The **Mandai Orchid Garden** ⑪ is a must for flower-lovers; a taxi here from the center of town will cost about S$16, or you can take SBS Bus 138 from the Ang Mo Kio MRT station. Spend about an hour here, then visit the **Singapore Zoological Gardens** ⑫. The taxi ride here from the orchid garden will cost about S$6 (though you can also take Bus 138). If you arrive by 3 PM sharp, you'll be in time for tea with an orangutan. You can then get a good look at the zoo before it closes at 6 and head over to **Night Safari** ⑬ for dinner in the restaurant at its entrance (the grounds don't open till 7:30).

To reach the **Bukit Timah Nature Reserve** ⑭ take Bus 171, which departs from the Newton MRT station. From the Orchard MRT station to **MacRitchie Reservoir** ⑮ it's about a S$6.50 taxi ride. Plan to spend about S$4 on a cab to reach the **Botanic Gardens** ⑯ from the city center or you can catch Bus 7, 105, 106, 123, or 174 from the Orchard MRT station. Allow two hours for the Botanic Gardens and another two for the reservoir. Allow about three hours for the nature reserve.

On a trip to this area, culture vultures can work in visits to the **Kong Meng San Phor Kark See Temple** and the **Siong Lim Temple and Gardens**; nature lovers can check out the **Selatar Reservoir**; and history buffs can stop by the **Kranji War Memorial.**

Sights to See

 Botanic Gardens. The gardens were begun in the days of Queen Victoria as a collection of tropical trees and plants (indeed, the 19th-century bandstand perpetuates the image of carefully conceived British gardens). Later, botanist Henry Ridley experimented here with rubber-tree seeds from South America; his work led to the development of the region's huge rubber industry and to the decline of the Amazon basin's importance as a source of the commodity.

Spread over some 74 acres, the grounds contain a large lake, masses of shrubs and flowers, and magnificent examples of many tree species, including fan palms more than 90 ft high. Locals come here to stroll along nature walks, jog, practice tai chi, feed geese, or just enjoy the serenity. The combined fragrance of frangipani, hibiscus, and aromatic herbs that pervades is delightful. ⊠ *Corner of Napier and Cluny Rds.,* ☎ *800/467–1540.* ☒ *Free.* ☉ *Daily 5 AM–midnight.*

Inside the Botanic Gardens, the 7.4-acre **Singapore Orchid Garden** was opened in 1995 by Senior Minister Lee Kuan Yew, the former prime minister. Here you can see more than 3,000 orchids in all their glory. ☒ *S$2.* ☉ *Daily 8:30–6.*

⑭ Bukit Timah Nature Reserve. If you like your nature a little wilder than what's found in manicured urban parks, then this is the place for you. In these 148 acres around Singapore's highest hill (574 ft), the tropical forest runs riot, giving you a feel for how things might have been when tigers roamed the island. Wandering along structured, well-marked paths, you may be startled by flying lemurs, civet cats, or—if you're really lucky—a troupe of long-tailed macaques. The view from the hilltop is superb. Wear good walking shoes—the trails are rocky, sometimes muddy, paths. You can buy trail maps from the visitor center. ⊠ *177 Hindhede Dr.,* ☎ *800/468–5736.* ☒ *Free.* ☉ *Daily 8:30–6:30.*

Kong Meng San Phor Kark See Temple. The Bright Hill Temple, as it's commonly known, is a relatively modern complex of Buddhist temples typical of the ornate Chinese style, with much gilded carving. ⊠ *88 Bright Hill Dr., 1½ km (1 mi) west of Bishan MRT station.*

Kranji War Memorial. This cemetery, a tribute to the forces who fought to defend Singapore in World War II, is in the north of the island, near the causeway off Woodlands Road. Rows of Allied dead are grouped with their countrymen in plots on a peaceful, well-manicured hill. This is a touching experience, a reminder of the greatness of the loss in this and all wars.

⑮ MacRitchie Reservoir. This 30-acre park has a jogging track with exercise areas, a playground, and a tea kiosk. The path around the reservoir is peaceful, with only the warbling of birds and chatter of monkeys to break your reverie. Crocodile spotting became a favorite pastime after baby crocs were found in the reservoir in early 1996. Don't go in the water. ⊠ *Lornie Rd., near Thomson Rd., no phone.* ☒ *Free.* ☉ *Daily dawn–dusk.*

⑪ Mandai Orchid Garden. Less than a kilometer down the road from the zoo (TIBS Bus 171 links the two) is a commercial orchid farm. The hillside is covered with the exotic blooms, cultivated for domestic sale and export. There are many varieties to admire, some quite spectacular. However, unless you are an orchid enthusiast, and since it is a good 30-minute taxi ride from downtown, a visit here is worth it only when combined with a visit to the zoo. The ☞ **Botanic Gardens** are closer to downtown and also have orchids. ⊠ *Mandai Lake Rd.,* ☎ *269–0136.* ☒ *S$2 (refunded if you make a purchase).* ☉ *Weekdays 8:30–5:30.*

⑬ Night Safari. Right next to the ☞ **Singapore Zoological gardens,** the safari claims to be the world's first nighttime wildlife park. Here 80 acres of secondary jungle provide a home to 100 species of wildlife that are more active at night than during the day. Some 90% of tropical animals are, in fact, nocturnal, and to see them active—instead of snoozing—gives their behavior a new dimension. Night Safari, like the zoo, uses a moat concept to create open, natural habitats; areas are floodlit with enough light to see the animals' colors, but not enough to limit their normal activity. You're taken on a 45-minute tram ride along 3 km (2 mi) of road, stopping frequently to admire the beasts and their antics. On another kilometer or so of walking trails you can observe some of the small cat families, primates (such as the slow loris and tarsier), and the pangolin (scaly anteater). Larger animals include the Nepalese rhino (the largest of rhinos, with a single, mammoth horn) and the beautifully marked royal Bengal tigers—which are somewhat intimidating to the nearby mouse deer, babirusa (pig deer with curled tusks that protrude through the upper lip), *gorals* (wild mountain goats), and bharals (mountain sheep). ⊠ *80 Mandai Lake Rd.,* ☎ *269–3411.* ⊡ *S$15.45.* ☉ *Daily 7:30 PM–midnight.*

Seletar Reservoir. Larger and wilder than the MacRitchie Reservoir, the Seletar is the largest and least developed natural area on the island. ⊠ *Mandai Rd., near the zoo,* ☎ *no phone.* ⊡ *Free.* ☉ *Daily dawn–dusk.*

★ ℭ ⑫ **Singapore Zoological Gardens.** You get the impression that animals come here for a vacation and not, as is often the case elsewhere, to serve a prison sentence. The Singapore zoo has an open-moat concept, wherein a wet or dry moat separates the animals from the people. (Interestingly, a mere 3-ft-deep moat will keep humans and giraffes apart, for a giraffe's gait makes even a shallow trench impossible to negotiate. A narrow water-filled moat prevents spider monkeys from leaving their home turf for a closer inspection of visitors.) Few zoos have have been able to afford the huge cost of employing this system, which was developed by Carl Hagenbeck, who created the Hamburg, Germany, zoo at the turn of the century. The Singapore zoo has managed by starting small and expanding gradually. It now sprawls over 69 acres of a 220-acre forested area.

Try to arrive at the zoo in time for the buffet breakfast. The food itself isn't special, but the company is. At 9:30 AM, Ah Meng, a 24-year-old orangutan, comes by for her repast. She weighs about 250 pounds, so she starts by taking a table by herself, but you're welcome to join her for a snack. (Ah Meng also takes tea promptly at 3.) Afterward, from glass windows that look into a watery grotto, you can watch polar bears dive for their own fishy breakfast. At the reptile house, be sure to check out the Komodo dragon lizards, which can grow to 10 ft in length. Then it will be time for the primate-and-reptile show, in which monkeys, gibbons, and chimpanzees have humans perform tricks, and snakes embrace volunteers from the audience.

There are performances by fur seals, elephants, free-flying storks, and other zoo inhabitants at various times throughout the day. In numerous miniparks that re-create different environments, giraffes, Celebese apes, bearded pigs, tigers, lions, and other of the zoo's 1,700 animals from among 160 species take life easy. ⊠ *80 Mandai Lake Rd.,* ☎ *269–3411.* ⊡ *S$10.30; breakfast or tea with Ah Meng S$15.* ☉ *Daily 8:30–6; breakfast with Ah Meng Tues.–Sat. 9–10 AM; high tea at 3.*

Siong Lim Temple and Gardens. The largest Buddhist temple complex in Singapore was built by two wealthy Hokkien merchants between 1868 and 1908. Set among groves of bamboo, the temple is guarded by the giant Four Kings of Heaven, in full armor. There are a number of shrines and halls, with many ornate features and statues of the Lord Buddha. The goddess of mercy, Kuan Yin, has her shrine behind the main hall; another hall houses a number of fine Thai Buddha images. The oldest building in the complex is a small wood shrine containing antique murals of the favorite Chinese legend "Pilgrimage to the West." ⊠ *184 E. Jalan Toa Payoh, about 1 km (½ mi) east of the Toa Payoh MRT station.*

Sentosa Island

In 1968 the government decided that Sentosa, the Isle of Tranquillity, would be transformed from the military area it was into a resort playground, with museums, parks, golf courses, restaurants, and hotels (☞ Chapter 4). A lot of money has been spent on development, and some Singaporeans find Sentosa an enjoyable getaway. However, this "pleasure park" is likely to hold little interest for travelers who have come 10,000 miles to visit Asia, a fact lost on the Singapore government. That said, there are two good reasons to visit the island: the visual drama of reaching it—particularly via cable car—and its fascinating wax museum.

In addition to all its historical and scientific exhibitions, Sentosa has a nature walk through secondary jungle; a *pasar malam* (night market) with 40 stalls, open Friday–Sunday 10–6 PM; campsites by the lagoon and tent rentals; and a wide range of recreational activities. You can swim in the lagoon and at a small ocean beach, though owing to all the cargo ships—you'll see hundreds of them anchored off the coast—the waters leave a lot to be desired. If golf is your game, consider a few rounds at the Sentosa Golf Club (☞ Chapter 6) or putt away on one of WonderGolf's 45 uniquely landscaped greens.

The best way to make the 2-km (1-mi) trip to Sentosa is by cable car (small gondolas that hold four passengers each). Other options include a shuttle bus or taxi via the causeway or a ferry ride (☞ Bus Travel or Boat Travel *in* the Gold Guide section). The island's S$5 admission price will get you into many attractions, though some have separate entrance fees. Sentosa has Southeast Asia's first monorail, which operates daily from 9 AM to 10 PM. It has stations close to the major attractions (a recording discusses each sight as you pass it), and unlimited rides are included in the price of the island admission. A free bus can also take you to most of the sights; it runs daily from 9–7:30 with night service from 7:30 to 10:30 at 10-minute intervals. A small train runs along the south coast for about 3 km (2 mi); bicycles are available for rent at kiosks throughout the island; and, of course, you always have your own two feet. For more information about Sentosa and its facilities, call the **Sentosa Development Corporation**'s Sales Department (☎ 275–0388).

Numbers in the text correspond to numbers in the margin and on the Sentosa Island map.

A Good Tour

This tour will take three to four hours; longer if you linger at the beach or visit VolcanoLand or WonderGolf. Start at the World Trade Centre, where you'll take a ferry or cable car (from the nearby station) to Sentosa. Between the ferry terminal and the cable car station on the Sentosa side is **WonderGolf** and **Asian Village & Adventure Asia** ①, a mini-theme park (the **Fountain Gardens** and **Sentosa Orchid Garden** are also nearby). From Asian Village you can follow the signs to the **Pioneers of Singapore/Surrender Chambers** ②, a wax museum that gives you an idea of what Singapore was like 100 years ago. Close by is the **Butterfly Park and World Insectarium** ③. After seeing all the bugs, board the monorail for a trip to **Underwater World** ④, a popular aquarium. Next to that, you will find **Ft. Siloso** ⑤, an old British fort whose cannons were pointed the wrong way during World War II. From here, take the monorail again to the swimming lagoon.

After a drink at the **Sunset Bar,** where you can sit on the wooden deck, gaze out at the view, and watch the nonstop volleyball, head up the hill behind the bar to the **Merlion** ⑥, Singapore's 10-story mascot. The view from the top is good—the city and the container port on one side, the harbor, the refineries, and the Indonesian islands of Bintan and Bataam on the other. Such watery scenery gets you in the mood for the **Maritime Museum** ⑦, which is due east from the Merlion. On the way there, you can stop at **VolcanoLand** or **Fantasy Island.**

Sights to See

🐾 ❶ **Asian Village & Adventure Asia.** Adjacent to the ferry terminal, this village contains three independent "communes" representing East Asia, South Asia, and Southeast Asia. In each village, street performances, demonstrations, merchandise, and food stalls do what they can to add life to an eclectic mix that, for example, combines Thai and north Sumatran architecture in one village and a Japanese torii gate and a Chinese teahouse in another. At Adventure Asia you can go on as many amusement rides as you like for one price. ✉ *Asian Village: free. Adventure Asia: S$10.* ☉ *Daily 10–9.*

🐾 ❸ **Butterfly Park and World Insectarium.** This park has a collection of 2,500 live butterflies from 50 species, 4,000 mounted butterflies and insects, plus lots of other insects—like tree-horn rhino beetles, scorpions, and tarantulas—that still creep, crawl, or fly. The park has an Asian landscape with a moon gate, streams, and bridges. ✉ *S$5.* ☉ *Daily 9–6:30.*

🐾 **Fantasy Island.** This is a great place to escape Singapore's heat. Among other attractions, you'll find a water slide and an action river with whitewater rapids. ✉ *S$20.* ☉ *Fri.–Tues. 10–7.*

NEED A BREAK?	You may want to enjoy high tea or an early dinner at the **Rasa Sentosa Food Centre,** open daily 10 AM–10:30 PM, next to the ferry terminal. More than 40 stalls offer a variety of foods for alfresco dining in groomed tropical surroundings.

🐾 ❺ **Ft. Siloso.** The fort covers 10 acres of gun emplacements and tunnels created by the British to fend off invasions by the Japanese. Unfortunately, the Japanese arrived by land (through Malaysia) instead of by sea, so the huge guns were pointed in the wrong direction. (The guns could have been redirected, but they were designed to fire shells that pierced ships' armor, not to deal with land forces.) Gun buffs will enjoy the range of artillery pieces. Photographs document the war in the Pacific, and dioramas depict the life of POWs during the Japanese occupation. ✉ *S$3.* ☉ *Daily 9–6.*

Fountain Gardens. Several times each evening, visitors to the gardens, conveniently close to the ferry terminal, are invited to dance along with the illuminated sprays from the fountains to classical or pop music. This activity is not for introverts. Performances by traditional-dance groups are sometimes held.

🐾 ❼ **Maritime Museum.** A small but interesting collection of ship models, pictures, and other items show Singapore's involvement with the sea in business and in war. A fishing gallery displays nets, traps, and spears used in the area throughout the centuries; a collection of full-size native watercraft traces the development of local boatbuilding from dugout canoes to Indonesian prahus. ✉ *S$2.* ☉ *Daily 10–7.*

🐾 ❻ **Merlion.** This monument, which some find to be in questionable taste, is Singapore's tourism mascot—a 10-story, off-white "lion fish" creature that emits laser beams from its eyes and smoke from its nostrils. It even glows in the dark. To get to the observation tower, you walk through a pirate cave exhibition. The walls are covered with TV screens, some showing "The Legend of the Merlion," others showing advertisements for the rest of Sentosa. The ride up to the 10th story is by elevator, then you climb two stories to the top where there's a view of Singapore and the Indonesian islands of Bataam and Bintan. ✉ *S$3.* ☉ *Daily 9–10.*

★ 🐾 ❷ **Pioneers of Singapore/Surrender Chambers.** This wax museum stands out from all the rest of Sentosa's attractions. Galleries trace the de-

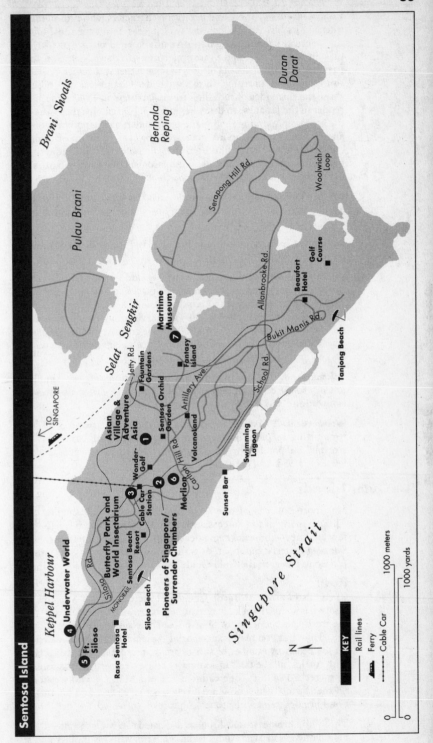

velopment of Singapore and depict the characters who profoundly influenced its history. Though the wax figures aren't the most lifelike, the scenes and the running narrative offer a vivid picture of 19th-century life in Singapore and a rare opportunity, in the modern Singapore, to ponder the diversity of cultures that were thrust together in the pursuit of trade and fortune. In the Surrender Chambers, wax tableaux show the surrender of the Allies to the Japanese in 1942 and the surrender of the Japanese to the Allies in 1945. (Originally, there was only the scene representing the Japanese surrender; as the numbers of Japanese visitors to Singapore increased, however, museum officials decided to show both.) Photographs, documents, and audiovisuals highlight events in the Japanese occupation and the various battles that led to their defeat. 🎫 *S$5.* ⊗ *Daily 9–9.*

Ⓒ **Sentosa Orchid Garden.** This exotic garden is filled with orchids from around the world. You'll also find a flower clock, a carp pond, and a Japanese teahouse. 🎫 *S$2.50.* ⊗ *Daily 9–7.*

Sunset Bar. Expatriates hang out here to play volleyball and other beach games to the beat of rap music.

Ⓒ ➍ **Underwater World.** Completed in 1991, Underwater World reverses the traditional aquarium experience by placing you right in the water. Two gigantic tanks house thousands of Asian Pacific fish and other marine life; you walk through a 100-yard acrylic tunnel that curves along the bottom. In total, there are 6,000 marine creatures from 350 species. The latest inhabitants (acquired in 1998) are a giant octopus, wolf eels, and giant spider crabs. 🎫 *S$13.* ⊗ *Daily 9–9.*

Ⓒ **VolcanoLand.** This multisensory theme attraction creates a simulated journey to the center of the earth. There are also exhibits on the Maya civilization. 🎫 *S$10.* ⊗ *Daily 10–8.*

Ⓒ **WonderGolf.** A first for southeast Asia, this course features 45 holes for putting in picturesque surroundings, including caves, ravines, streams, and ponds. Three greens deliver different experiences and challenges. 🎫 *S$8.* ⊗ *Daily 9–9.*

The Outer Islands

Singapore consists of one large island and some 60 smaller ones. Though many of the outer islands are still off the beaten track—with few facilities—some are being developed as beach destinations. Island hopping by ferry, bumboat, or water taxi is relatively easy to arrange. (☞ Boat Travel *in* the Gold Guide section).

Kusu

Kusu, also known as Turtle Island and sacred to both Muslims and Taoists, is an ideal weekday retreat (it gets crowded on weekends) from the traffic and concrete of Singapore. There's a small coffee shop on the island, but you may want to bring a picnic lunch to enjoy in peace on the beach. A number of stories attempt to explain the association with turtles; all the tales in some way relate to a turtle that saved two shipwrecked sailors—one Chinese and one Malay—who washed up on the shore. Turtles now are given sanctuary here, and an artificial pond honors them with stone sculptures.

The hilltop **kramat kusu** (shrine) is dedicated to a Malay saint—a pious man named Haji Syed Abdul Rahman, who, with his mother and sister, is said to have disappeared supernaturally from the island in the 19th century. To reach the shrine, you climb the 122 steps that snake up through a forest. Plastic bags containing stones have been hung on the trees by devotees who have come to the shrine to pray for forgiveness of sins and the correction of wayward children. If their wishes are granted, believers must return the following year to remove their bags and give thanks.

Tua Pekong, a small, open-fronted Chinese temple, was built by Hoe Beng Watt in gratitude for the birth of his child. The temple is dedicated to Da Bo Gong, the god of prosperity, and the ever-popular Kuan Yin, goddess of mercy. Here she's also known by her Chinese surname, Sung Tzu Niang ("Giver of Sons"), and is associated with longevity, love of virtue, and fulfillment of destiny. Sung Tzu had a difficult childhood. She was determined to become a nun, but her father forbade it. When she ran away to join an order, he tried to have her killed. In the nick of time she was saved by a tiger and fulfilled her destiny. In gratitude, she cut off her arm as a sacrifice. This so impressed the gods that she was then blessed with many arms. Hence, when you see her statue in many of the Chinese temples in Singapore, she is depicted with six or eight arms. This temple has become the site of an annual pilgrimage. From late October to early November (or in the ninth lunar month), some 100,000 Taoists bring exotic foods, flowers, joss sticks, and candles, and pray for prosperity and healthy children.

Pulau Ubin

Here amid the *kelongs* (fishing huts) and duck and prawn farms the lifestyle hasn't changed much in 30 years. The island is a natural haven for plants, birds and insects found in its mangrove and forest areas. There are colorful Thai *Ma Chor* temples along the seashore.

St. John's

St. John's was first a leper colony, then a prison camp. Later it became a place to intern political enemies of the republic, and now it has become an island for picnicking and overnight camping. Without any temples or particular sights, it is quieter than Kusu. There are plans to develop camping facilities, which will surely take away some of the peaceful solitude one can experience here now.

Sister's Island

One of the most beautiful of the southern islands is also one of the best for snorkeling and diving. To get there, you'll have to hire a water taxi (S$50 per hour) at the Jardine Steps or Clifford Pier or take an organized day cruise (check with your hotel). Some of the boatmen know where to find the best coral reefs. If you plan to dive, be advised that the currents can be very strong.

Bintan Island, Indonesia

From the tallest building in Singapore you can see the nearby islands of Indonesia's Riau Archipelago. In 45 minutes, you can cross the straits on a ferry south (☞ *also* Boat Travel *in* the Gold Guide section) to the Bataam Islands. Bataam itself is undergoing a vast development project that includes a duty-free industrial zone and a tourist complex. However, Bataam and its resorts have been overshadowed by the more interesting island of Bintan.

Today the *orang laut* (sea people; island inhabitants who are descendants of pirates and traders) still live in houses on stilts over the sea— an interesting contrast to the six modern beach resorts here. Overnight trips to Bintan, more than twice the size of Singapore, can include a stay at a five-star hotel with your own private pool or a more adventurous jaunt in a sampan to the 16th-century palace of a Malaysian sultan. Make hotel reservations as far in advance as possible (☞ Chapter 4). You may also want to consider booking a guided tour of the island (☞ Tour Operators *in* the Gold Guide section). Note that citizens of Canada, the United Kingdom, and the United States need only passports for stays in Indonesia of less than one month.

Sights to See

Bintan's main town is **Tanjung Pinang,** where the primary activity is shopping at **Pasar Pelantar Dua.** Tanjung Pinang is a jumping-off point for some interesting nearby sites.

You can take a tour from Tanjung Pinang's Pelentar Pier up the **Snake River** through the mangrove swamps to the oldest **Chinese temple** in Riau. As the boatman poles his way up the small tributary choked with mangroves, the sudden view of the isolated 300-year-old temple with its murals of hell will send chills down your spine. Have the boatman take you back down the river to **Tanjung Berakit,** where tiny huts perch on stilts. Friendly villagers live in spartan homes without electricity or water—this only an hour and a half from Singapore.

Another good stop by motorboat is **Pulau Penyengat** (Wasp Island), once the heart of the Riau sultanate and the cultural hub of the Malay empire. In the 16th century, the Malay sultanate fled here after being defeated by the Portuguese in Malacca. The island is just 15 minutes by motorboat from Tanjung Pinang's Pelentar Pier. Sites include royal graves, the banyan-shrouded ruins of the palace, and the **Mesjid Raya** (Sultan's Mosque)—a bright yellow building that was plastered together with egg yolks.

3 Dining

In Singapore, eating is a national pastime, and you'll soon discover why. From breakfast in Chinatown to high tea in your hotel to a late-night snack in a hawker center, you can sample the international array of cuisines virtually around the clock.

SINGAPORE OFFERS THE BEST feast in the East. You'll find restaurants that serve home-grown Nonya (or Peranakan) fare; others that specialize in cuisine from all parts of Asia; and still others that offer European and American dishes. Some cultures consider atmosphere, decor, and service more important than food. In Singapore, however, the food's the thing: you're as likely to find gourmet cooking (and high standards of cleanliness) in unpretentious food stalls as you are in elegant eateries.

Many of the poshest restaurants are in hotels. Such establishments offer fine dining, complete with the freshest ingredients, displays of roses and orchids, polished silver and gleaming crystal, waiters dressed in tuxedos, and impeccable service. Several hotels also offer high tea (generally served 3 PM–6 PM at a cost of about S$20 per person without tax or service charge). The Singapore version of this British tradition is usually served buffet style and includes dim sum (called *dian xin* here) and fried noodles as well as finger sandwiches and scones. Standout teas include those at the Oriental, Goodwood Park, the Raffles, the Four Seasons, and the Ritz-Carlton.

If you prefer coffee and a casual setting to tea in formal surroundings, you'll be pleased to note that alfresco coffeehouses have taken Singapore by storm. Starbucks, Spinellis, and Delifrance have locations everywhere and are very popular despite the humidity. In addition, widespread building restoration has given rise to several chic dining addresses. Boat Quay—a riverside strip of cafés, restaurants, and bars—may well be the busiest place in town at night. Restaurants to look for here include Kinara (North Indian) and Warung Wayan (Indonesian). At Clarke Quay, another massive restoration project, you can dine on a moored *tongkang,* a type of boat that once plied the river; sample the horrible-to-smell, good-to-eat durian fruit at Durian House; or try seafood at Key Largo, Thai cuisine at Thanying Restaurant, or Mediterranean fare at Bastiani's. Other dining areas include Chinatown's Tanjong Pagar—with such trendy restaurants as Da Paolo (Italian) and L'Aigle d'Or (French)—and Robertson Quay.

Food is a route to cultural empathy, especially if it's consumed at a stir-fry stall (fondly called "wok-and-roll" stalls) or at a vendor's stall in an open-air hawker center. You'll find many stir-fry stalls—most are half restaurant and half parking lot—on East Coast Road. They open at about 5 PM and serve such simple, freshly cooked dishes as deep-fried baby squid and steamed prawns—accompanied, of course, by fried noodles.

The hawker centers have quite a history. At one time, food vendors moved through the streets, each one serving a single dish (often made using a secret family recipe). A hawker advertised by sounding a horn, knocking bamboo sticks together, or simply shouting. Hearing the sound, people dashed from their houses to place orders. After everyone had eaten, the hawker collected and washed the crockery and utensils and continued up the road. Many hawkers might have passed a house in a day. Several years ago, the government gathered the hawkers into large centers for reasons of hygiene (and rest assured that everything is *very* clean; health authorities are strict). Today, these centers enable you to see the raw materials and watch the cooking methods in stall after stall. Then you simply find a seat at a table, note the table number, relate your order and this number to the vendor, and sit down to wait for your food. (Someone will come to your table to take a drink order.) Though you sometimes pay at the end of the meal, paying when you place your order is more the norm. Most dishes cost S$4 or slightly more; for S$12, you can get a meal that includes a drink and fresh fruit for dessert.

The sheltered hawker center at Marina South has hundreds of stalls. The most touristy open-air center is the raucous, festive Newton Circus. Come here for the experience, but avoid the seafood stalls, which are known to fleece tourists. Feast instead at stalls that offer traditional one-dish meals and that have prices displayed prominently. (When you place an order, specify whether you want a S$2, S$3, or S$4 portion.) Other open-air centers include the historic Lau Pa Sat Festival Market in the downtown financial district, Telok Ayer Transit Food Centre on Shenton Way, and Bugis Square at Eminent Plaza. Indoor, air-conditioned food centers are a great way to beat the midday heat. Those in the Orchard Road area include Picnic in the basement of Scotts Centre and the Food Chain in the basement of Orchard Emerald (opposite and just down from the Mandarin Singapore hotel). The following are dishes and food names that you'll often encounter at hawker centers:

char kway teow—flat rice noodles mixed with soy sauce, chili paste, fish cakes, and bean sprouts and fried in lard.

Hokkien prawn mee—fresh wheat noodles in a prawn-and-pork broth served with freshly boiled prawns.

laksa—a one-dish meal of round rice noodles in coconut gravy spiced with lemongrass, chilies, turmeric, shrimp paste, and shallots. It's served with a garnish of steamed prawns, rice cakes, and bean sprouts.

mee rebus—a Malay version of Chinese wheat noodles with a spicy gravy. The dish is garnished with sliced eggs, pieces of fried bean curd, and bean sprouts.

rojak—a Malay word for "salad." Chinese rojak consists of cucumber, lettuce, pineapple, *bangkwang* (jicama), and deep-fried bean curd— tossed with a dressing made from salty shrimp paste, ground toasted peanuts, sugar, and rice vinegar. Indian rojak consists of deep-fried lentil and prawn patties, boiled potatoes, and deep-fried bean curd, all served with a spicy dip sweetened with mashed sweet potatoes.

roti prata—an Indian pancake made by tossing a piece of wheat-flour dough into the air until it's paper-thin and then folding it to form many layers. The dough is fried until crisp on a cast-iron griddle, then served with curry powder or sugar. An ideal breakfast dish.

satay—small strips of meat marinated in fresh spices and threaded onto short skewers. A Malay dish, satay is barbecued over charcoal and eaten with a spiced peanut sauce, sliced cucumbers, raw onions, and pressed rice cakes.

thosai—an Indian rice-flour pancake that's a popular breakfast dish, eaten with either curry powder or brown sugar.

In sit-down restaurants, plan on small servings of four to five dishes for four people or three dishes for two people. Food is either served family-style—placed all at once at the center of the table so everyone can dig in—or, for more formal meals, served a course at a time, again with diners sharing from a single dish at the center of the table. Each diner is given a plate or bowl of rice. Most Chinese restaurants automatically add a charge of about S$2 per person for tea, peanuts, pickles, and rice.

Most restaurants are open from noon to 2:30 or 3 for lunch and from 7 to 10:30 PM (last order) for dinner. Some hotel coffee shops (and the Indian coffee shops along Changi Road) are open 24 hours a day; others close between 2 and 6 AM. At hawker centers, some stalls are open for breakfast and lunch while others are open for lunch and dinner. Late-night food centers such as Eminent Plaza in Jalan Bešar are in full swing until 3 AM.

Competition among Singapore's restaurants has kept the overall meal prices low, but liquor has remained expensive. A cocktail or a glass of wine costs S$8–S$12; a bottle of wine is a minimum of S$50. Seafood is inexpensive (though expensive delicacies such as shark's fin, dried abalone, and lobster are served in some Chinese restaurants). Dishes marked "market price" on the menu are premium items. Before ordering, find out exactly how much each dish will cost, and don't be surprised if you're charged for the napkins and cashew nuts that arrive at the start of your meal. Note that smoking is banned in air-conditioned restaurants and banquet/meeting rooms, though many establishments now offer outdoor patios with a seating area for smokers.

What to Wear

Except at the fancier hotel dining rooms, Singaporeans don't dress up to eat out. The weather calls for lighter wear than a jacket and tie. (Some restaurants tried to enforce a dress code for men but found that their customers went elsewhere to eat. Now an open-neck shirt and a jacket represent the upper limit of formality.) Generally, though, shorts, sleeveless cotton T-shirts, and track suits aren't appropriate. If you're sensitive to cold, bring a sweater—many restaurants are air-conditioned to subarctic temperatures.

Chinese

$$$$ ✗ **Chang Jiang.** Meals in this Goodwood Park hotel (☞ Chapter 4)
★   Shanghainese restaurant are served Western-style (portions are presented on dinner plates, and you don't serve yourself from a central platter). The kitchen staff was trained by the chef of Shanghai's leading restaurant, Yang Zhou. Recommended dishes are the chicken and goose surprise, fresh crabmeat in a yam basket, baby kale with scallops, and sliced beef stir-fried and served with leeks. Presentation is an art here. Even the chopsticks are gold-plated. The service and surroundings are very formal. ☒ *22 Scotts Rd.,* ☎ *734–7188. AE, DC, MC, V.*

$$$$ ✗ **Hai Tien Lo.** Sit in the right place at this 37th-floor restaurant and you'll get a view of the sea, the Padang, and City Hall. The Cantonese cuisine, the decor, and the service are all extremely elegant: plates are changed with every course, waitresses wear *cheongsams* (Chinese dresses with high collars and side slits) with black with gold trim, and the delicate white china is hand-painted with cherry blossoms. For lunch, opt for the dim sum, priced at a premium because of the top-quality ingredients. Other specialties include roast chicken with crispy golden-brown skin and tender, juicy flesh; beef cubes fried with black pepper and oyster sauce; and deep-fried fresh scallops stuffed with minced prawns and tossed in a salty black-bean sauce. The pièce de résistance is Monk Jumps over the Wall—dried abalone, whole chicken, ham, fish stomach lining, dried scallops, and shark's fin steamed together for hours. At S$100 per serving, it's one of the most expensive dishes in town, but the broth is the best in the world—the really rich simply drink it and leave the rest. ☒ *Pan Pacific Hotel Singapore, Marina Square, 6 Raffles Blvd.,* ☎ *336–8111. AE, DC, MC, V.*

$$$$ ✗ **Jiang Nan-Chun.** On the second floor of the Four Seasons hotel (☞
★   Chapter 4), this dining room is home to the innovative creations of one of the youngest master chefs in Singapore, Sam Leong. His delicious Cantonese food has Thai and Japanese influences. Although a set menu is offered, the restaurant's regular customers often request the chef's favorites, which may include deep-fried scallops with pear sauce, baked oysters with bok choy, or fried prawns with sesame and lime mayonnaise. The presentation is unusual and artistic (the double-boiled seafood soup, for example, is served in a hollowed coconut),

BONUS MILES MAKE GREAT SOUVENIRS.

Earn Miles With Your MCI Card.

Take the MCI Card along on this trip and start earning miles for the next one. You'll earn frequent flyer miles on all your calls and save with the low rates you've come to expect from MCI. Before you know it, you'll be on your way to some other international destination.

Sign up for MCI by calling 1-800-FLY-FREE

Earn Frequent Flyer Miles.

Is this a great time, or what? :-)

Easy To Call Home.

1. To use your MCI Card, just dial the WorldPhone access number of the country you're calling from.
2. Dial or give the operator your MCI Card number.
3. Dial or give the number you're calling.

American Samoa	633-2MCI (633-2624)
# Antigua	1-800-888-8000
(Available from public card phones only)	#2
# Argentina (CC)	0-800-5-1002
# Aruba ÷	800-888-8
# Bahamas	1-800-888-8000
# Barbados	1-800-888-8000
# Belize	557 from hotels
	815 from pay phones
# Bermuda ÷	1-800-888-8000
# Bolivia ♦ (CC)	0-800-2222
# Brazil (CC)	000-8012
# British Virgin Islands ÷	1-800-888-8000
# Cayman Islands	1-800-888-8000
# Chile (CC)	
To call using CTC ■	800-207-300
To call using ENTEL ■	800-360-180
# Colombia (CC) ♦	980-16-0001
Collect Access in Spanish	980-16-1000
# Costa Rica ♦	0800-012-2222
# Dominica	1-800-888-8000
# Dominican Republic (CC) ÷	1-800-888-8000
Collect Access in Spanish	1121
# Ecuador (CC) ÷	999-170
El Salvador	800-1767
# Grenada ÷	1-800-888-8000
Guatemala (CC) ♦	9999-189
Guyana	177
# Haiti ÷ Collect Access	193
Collect Access in French/Creole	190
Honduras ÷	8000-122
# Jamaica ÷ Collect Access	1-800-888-8000
(From Special Hotels only)	873
From payphones	★2
# Mexico (CC)	
Avantel	01-800-021-8000
Telmex ▲	001-800-674-7000
Mexico Access in Spanish	01-800-021-1000
# Netherlands Antilles (CC) ÷	001-800-888-8000
Nicaragua (CC)	166
(Outside of Managua, dial 02 first)	
Collect Access in Spanish from any public payphone	★2
# Panama	108
Military Bases	2810-108
# Paraguay ÷	00-812-800
# Peru	0-800-500-10
# Puerto Rico (CC)	1-800-888-8000
# St. Lucia ÷	1-800-888-8000
# Trinidad & Tobago ÷	1-800-888-8000
# Turks & Caicos ÷	1-800-888-8000
# Uruguay	000-412
# U.S. Virgin Islands (CC)	1-800-888-8000
# Venezuela (CC) ÷ ♦	800-1114-0

Automation available from most locations. (CC) Country-to-country calling available to/from most international locations. ÷ Limited availability. ♦ Public phones may require deposit of coin or phone card for dial tone. ■ International communications carrier. ▲ When calling from public phones, use phones marked LADATEL. Limit one bonus program per MCI account. Terms and conditions apply. All airline program rules and conditions apply. ©1998 MCI Telecommunications Corporation. All rights reserved. Is this a great time, or what? is a service mark of MCI.

MCI Calling Card
123 456 7891 2345
J. D. SMITH
WorldPhone

Earn Miles With Your MCI Card.

Take the MCI Card along on this trip and start earning miles for the next one. You'll earn frequent flyer miles on all your calls and save with the low rates you've come to expect from MCI. Before you know it, you'll be on your way to some other international destination.

Sign up for MCI by calling 1-800-FLY-FREE

Earn Frequent Flyer Miles.

AmericanAirlines
AAdvantage

Continental Airlines
OnePass

▲ Delta Air Lines
SkyMiles

NORTHWEST
AIRLINES
WORLDPERKS

MILEAGE PLUS.
United Airlines

US AIRWAYS
DIVIDEND MILES

Is this a great time, or what? :-)

MCI

Easy To Call Home.

1. To use your MCI Card, just dial the WorldPhone access number of the country you're calling from.
2. Dial or give the operator your MCI Card number.
3. Dial or give the number you're calling.

# Bahrain	800-002
# Brunei	800-011
# China ❖	108-12
For a Mandarin-speaking operator	108-17
# Cyprus ♦	080-90000
# Egypt (CC) ♦ (Outside of Cairo, dial 02 first)	355-5770
# Federated States of Micronesia	624
# Fiji	004-890-1002
# Guam (CC)	1-800-888-8000
# Hong Kong (CC)	800-96-1121
# India (CC) ❖	000-127
# Indonesia (CC) ♦	001-801-11
Iran ⁚⁚	(Special Phones Only)
# Israel (CC)	1-800-940-2727
# Japan (CC) ♦	
To call using KDD ■	00539-121▶
To call using IDC ■	0066-55-121
To call using ITJ ■	0044-11-121
# Jordan	18-800-001
# Korea (CC)	
To call using KT ■	009-14
To call using DACOM ■	00309-12
Phone Booths ⁚⁚ Red Button 03, then press ★	
Military Bases	550-2255
# Kuwait	800-MCI (800-624)
Lebanon ⁚⁚ Collect Access	600-MCI (600-624)
# Macao	0800-131
# Malaysia (CC) ♦	1-800-80-0012
# Philippines (CC) ♦	
To call using PLDT ■	105-14
Collect access via PLDT in Filipino ■	105-15
Collect access via ICC in Filipino ■	1237-77
# Qatar ★	0800-012-77
# Saipan (CC) ⁚⁚	950-1022
# Saudi Arabia (CC) ⁚⁚	1-800-11
# Singapore	8000-112-112
# Sri Lanka (Outside of Colombo, dial 01 first)	440-100
# Syria	0800
# Taiwan (CC) ♦	0080-13-4567
# Thailand ★	001-999-1-2001
# United Arab Emirates ♦	800-111
Vietnam ●	1201-1022
Yemen	008-00-102

Automation available from most locations. ❖ Available from most major cities. ♦ Public phones may require deposit of coin or phone card for dial tone. (CC) Country-to-country calling available to/from most international locations. ⁚⁚ Limited availability. ■ International communications carrier. ▶ Regulation does not permit intra-Japan calls. ★ Not available from public pay phones. ● Local service fee in U.S. currency required to complete call. Limit one bonus program per MCI account. Terms and conditions apply. All airline program rules and conditions apply. © 1998 MCI Telecommunications Corporation. All rights reserved. Is this a great time, or what? is a service mark of MCI.

the service is attentive, and the ambience is understated and relaxed. ⊠ *190 Orchard Blvd.,* ☏ *734–1110. Reservations essential. AE, DC, MC, V.*

$$$$ ✕ **Shang Palace.** Locals and expats alike frequent this elegant Cantonese dining room in the Shangri-La hotel (☞ Chapter 4). Large and decorated in brilliant red and gold, the room can be noisy during a full house, but the delicious food more than compensates. The staff is very knowledgeable about the menu, prepared by Hong Kong–born chef Lo Ka Cheung. Try the prawns deep fried with minced shrimp and sesame seeds, or the steamed asparagus served with a poached egg and caviar. For connoisseurs, there are more than 11 Chinese teas from which to choose. ⊠ *22 Orange Grove Rd.,* ☏ *737–3644. Reservations essential. AE, DC, MC, V.*

$$$–$$$$ ✕ **Li Bai.** The dining room in the Sheraton Towers hotel (☞ Chapter
★ 4) evokes richness without overindulgence—deep maroon wall panels edged with black and backlighted, elaborate floral displays, jade table settings, ivory chopsticks. The service is very fine, as is the cooking, which is modern and innovative, yet deeply rooted in the Cantonese tradition. The chef's unusual creations include deep-fried diamonds of egg noodles in a rich stock with crabmeat and mustard greens; fried lobster in black-bean paste; and double-boiled shark's fin with Chinese wine and *jinhua* ham. The restaurant is small, seating fewer than 100 people. ⊠ *39 Scotts Rd.,* ☏ *737–6888. AE, DC, MC, V.*

$$$ ✕ **Cherry Garden.** At the Oriental hotel (☞ Chapter 4), a wooden-roof
★ pavilion with walls of antique Chinese brick encloses a landscaped courtyard that makes a fine setting for a meal. The artwork is tastefully chosen and displayed, the service is impeccable, and the Hunanese food is a welcome change from the usual Cantonese fare. Try the minced-pigeon broth with dried scallops steamed in a bamboo tube or, in season, served in a fragrant baby melon; the superior Yunnan honey-glazed ham served between thin slices of steamed bread; or the camphor-smoked duck in a savory bean-curd crust. ⊠ *Marina Square, 6 Raffles Blvd.,* ☏ *331–0538. AE, DC, MC, V.*

$$$ ✕ **Golden Peony.** "Refined" is the word that best describes everything—from the service and the table settings to the decor and ambience—in the Cantonese dining room at the Conrad International Centennial hotel (☞ Chapter 4). All dishes are exquisitely prepared and ultrafresh. Specialties include deboned crispy chicken with bean curd skin and Yunnan ham (eaten like a sandwich); steamed crab claw in Hua Tiao wine and ginger juice; and steamed Canadian bass and salmon with mushrooms. ⊠ *2 Temasek Blvd.,* ☏ *334–8888 ext. 7482. AE, DC, MC, V.*

$$$ ✕ **Min Jiang.** Housed in a Chinese pavilion on the grounds of the Goodwood Park hotel (☞ Chapter 4), Min Jiang is always packed, thanks to its delicious Szechuan food, fast service, and longtime manageress, the friendly Shirley Neow. The decor is attractive—a restrained and elegant interpretation of Chinese style. The camphor-smoked duck and the long beans fried with minced pork are favorites. ⊠ *22 Scotts Rd.,* ☏ *737–7411. AE, DC, MC, V.*

$$$ ✕ **Pine Court.** Baked tench, marinated lamb, and fried dry scallops are just a few of the dishes that distinguish the Pekingese cooking at this restaurant in the Mandarin Singapore hotel (☞ Chapter 4). The restaurant's Peking duck is famed for its crisp, melt-in-your-mouth skin and delicate pancake wrapping. Dinner here is the best meal; the more economical lunch (frequently a buffet) is less inspired. The carved-wood wall panels will make you feel as if you're in a Chinese mansion; the award-winning service is fine and caring. ⊠ *333 Orchard Rd.,* ☏ *737–4411. AE, DC, MC, V.*

Singapore Dining

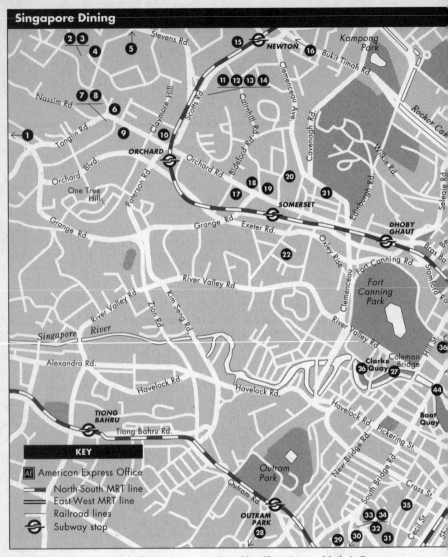

L'Aigle d'Or, **29**
Alkaff Mansion, **28**
Annalakshmi, **36**
Aziza's, **20**
Banana Leaf Apollo, **24**
Bastiani's, **26**
Beng Hiang, **34**
Blue Ginger, **19, 32**
Café Modestos, **7**
Chang Jiang, **11**
Cherry Garden, **43**

Club Chinois, **8**
Compass Rose Restaurant, **38**
Dragon City, **5**
Golden Peony, **51**
Gordon Grill, **13**
Hai Tien Lo, **48**
House of Mao, **35**
House of Sudenese Food, **44, 50**
Imperial Herbal Restaurant, **40**
Ivin's Restaurant, **16**

Jiang Nan-Chun, **9**
Keyaki, **49**
Latour, **2**
Lee Kui (Ah Hoi), **31**
Lei Garden, **37**
Li Bai, **15**
Long Jiang, **18**
Madras New Woodlands Restaurant, **25**
Min Jiang, **12**
Moi Kong, **33**

Muthu's Curry Restaurant, **23**
Nadaman, **4**
Our Village, **46**
Palm Beach Seafood, **53**
Paolo & Ping's, **10**
Pine Court, **17**
Rajah Inn, **22**
Ristorante Bologna, **42**
Samy's Curry Restaurant, **1**

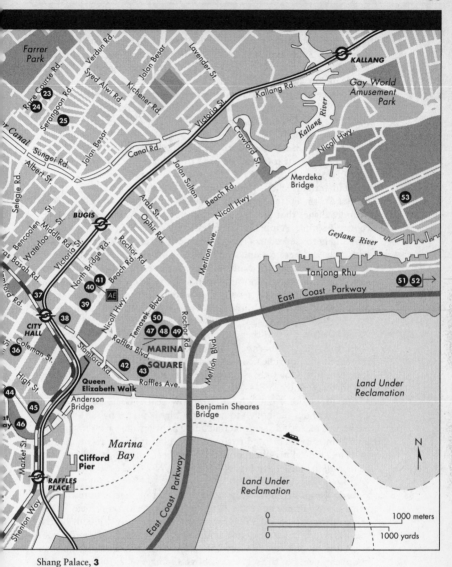

Shang Palace, **3**
Shima, **14**
Suntory, **6**
Tandoor, **21**
Thanying, **27, 30**
Tiffin Room, **39**
Tsui Hang Village, **47**
UDMC Seafood
Centre, **52**
Warung Wayan, **45**
Yhingthai Palace, **41**

$$-$$$ ✕ **Dragon City.** Many Singaporeans consider Dragon City the best place
★   for Szechuan food. Set in a courtyard and entered through a flamboyant,
red, moon-gate door, the large dining room looks Chinese but is not
particularly appealing. All artistry is reserved for the food. Choose from
such delicious staples as kung po chicken, minced-pork soup in a
whole melon, steamed red fish with soybean crumbs, or smoked duck.
The service is fast. If you don't quite know how to order your meal,
ask for Wang Ban Say, the restaurant's manager and one of the owners. ✉ *Novotel Orchid Inn, Plymouth Wing, 214 Dunearn Rd.,* ☎ *250–
3322. AE, DC, MC, V.*

$$-$$$ ✕ **Imperial Herbal Restaurant.** The Chinese believe that "you are what
you eat" and that food can be used to maintain or restore health. In
the Metropole Hotel's (☞ Chapter 4) unique restaurant, an herbal-
ist—rather than a chef—runs the kitchen, and there's a traditional phar-
macy near the entrance where herbs are stored (and sold). The menu
includes dishes that are decidedly exotic as well as those that are de-
ceptively simple. A must is the delicate quick-fried egg white with scallops and herbs served in a crunchy nest of potato threads. The eel fried
with garlic and fresh coriander and the eggplant with pine nuts are equally
delicious; the crispy fried ants on prawn toast are not only a conversation piece but totally inoffensive. It's nice to know that that the food
that's satisfying your taste buds is also doing you good. Beer and wine
are available, as are restorative tonics and teas. ✉ *41 Seah St., 3rd floor,*
☎ *337–0491. AE, MC, V.*

$$-$$$ ✕ **Lei Garden.** This aesthetically pleasing restaurant has built up a de-
voted following with branches in Hong Kong and Kowloon. The food
represents the nouvelle Cantonese style with its pristine tastes and delicate textures. One old-fashioned item is the soup of the day, cooked
just the way mother did—assuming that mother had the time to stew
a soup lovingly for many hours over low heat. The menu also offers
a long list of double-boiled tonic soups (highly prized by the Chinese),
barbecued meats, and seafood (including a variety of shark's fin dishes).
Dim sum is available and extremely popular at lunch; recommendations include Peking duck, grilled rib-eye beef, and fresh scallops with
bean curd in black-bean sauce. ✉ *Chijmes, No. 01-24, 30 Victoria St.,*
☎ *339–3822. AE, DC, MC, V.*

$$-$$$ ✕ **Long Jiang.** Perhaps the greatest draw of this Szechuan restaurant
in the Crown Prince Hotel (☞ Chapter 4) is the "all-you-can-eat" offer.
For a set price (around S$24), you can sample nearly 40 items on the
menu, including hot-and-sour soup, shark's fin soup, smoked duck,
and kung po chicken. It's not unlike most other Chinese restaurants
in appearance, but the service is above average. ✉ *270 Orchard Rd.,*
☎ *732–1111. AE, DC, MC, V.*

$$-$$$ ✕ **Tsui Hang Village.** The decor of this well-regarded Cantonese restau-
rant includes green tiles, brick walls, and rooflike overhangs that give
it a courtyard ambience. The seafood is fresh and flown in from Hong
Kong (the superior braised shark's fin is among the best in town). At
lunch, try the inexpensive dim sum or one of the set menus. The deep-
fried roast chicken pleases most palates. ✉ *Marina Square, No. 02–
142, 6 Raffles Blvd.,* ☎ *338–6668. AE, DC, MC, V.*

$$ ✕ **Beng Hiang.** At this restaurant in a restored shophouse just outside
the financial district, you'll find peasant-style Hokkien cooking: hearty,
rough, and delicious. *Kwa huay* (liver rolls) and *ngo hiang* (pork-and-
prawn rolls) are very popular and are eaten dipped in sweet plum sauce.
Hay cho (deep-fried prawn dumplings) are another Hokkien staple.
Beng Hiang also serves *khong bak* (braised pig's feet) and what is re-
putedly the best roast suckling pig in Singapore. ✉ *112–116 Amoy
St.,* ☎ *221–6695. Reservations not accepted. No credit cards.*

$$ ✕ **House of Mao.** Opened in the spring of 1998 to great fanfare, this kitschy, pop-art homage to the late dictator is an amalgamation of Warhol meets Julia Child's favorite Chinese (specifically, Hunanese) dishes. The memorabilia and the staff's Red Army uniforms are only two of the reasons to come; the tasty, contemporary Hunanese food is the third. The service can be uneven due to the crowds that have been flocking here since its opening.   ✉ *No. 03-02 China Square Food Centre, 51 Telok Ayer St.,* ☎ *533–0660. Reservations not accepted. AE, DC, MC, V.*

$$ ✕ **Lee Kui (Ah Hoi) Restaurant.** This unassuming storefront restaurant in the heart of Chinatown serves you at large tables (if your party is small, you may have to share a table with others); it's busy, noisy, and often crowded. The distinctive flavors of Teochew cuisine are evident: try the cold crab as a starter, followed by winter melon soup, prawns with young chives and *ngohiang* (minced pork rolls). Your glass of tea will be constantly replenished. It may be helpful to go with a Mandarin-speaking person, as the staff speaks little English. ✉ *46 Mosque St.,* ☎ *222–3654. Reservations not accepted. No credit cards.*

$$ ✕ **Moi Kong.** At this unpretentious Chinese (Hakka) eatery, try the prawns fried with red-wine lees, the steamed chicken with wine, or the *khong bak mui choy* (braised pork in dark soy sauce with a preserved salted green vegetable), delicious with rice. ✉ *22 Murray St.,* ☎ *221–7758. Reservations not accepted. AE, DC, V.*

Continental

$$$$ ✕ **Gordon Grill.** The Scottish country/hunting lodge look here is light-
★ ened with celadon and apple greens, light-wood chairs, and glass panels etched with delicate drawings of Scottish lairds. Tradition is served up here—not surprising for a Goodwood Park hotel (☞ Chapter 4) restaurant—so you won't find any trendy "fusion" cooking, only Continental dining at its best. Specialties include excellent roast beef, perfect steaks, and the best sherry trifle in town. The service is very good. ✉ *22 Scotts Rd.,* ☎ *737–7411. AE, DC, MC, V.*

$$$$ ✕ **Latour.** At press time, the very highly regarded Latour was—owing
★ to renovations—being moved from one part of the Shangri-La hotel (☞ Chapter 4) to another. It was slated to reopen on the 24th floor, with a "less stuffy" atmosphere, according to the mâitre d'. When it does open, the wine list will no doubt still be one of the best in town, and diners will still be able to order such popular dishes as the panfried duck liver and the seasonal salad flavored with a truffle sauce. ✉ *22 Orange Grove Rd.,* ☎ *737–3644. Reservations essential. AE, DC, MC, V.*

Eclectic

$$$ ✕ **Bastiani's.** Mediterranean food with New World accents stars at this
★ restaurant in a restored riverside warehouse. Downstairs there's a comfortable bar and a patio; upstairs the spacious dining room has a terrace (where renegade smokers can indulge in their habit). With its Asian rugs on polished wood floors, eclectic furniture, and open kitchen—hung with garlic, salamis, and the like—Bastiani's has a casual elegance. The menu changes every two months, but it always emphasizes fresh vegetables and herbs; grains such as couscous and polenta; and grilled or baked poultry, red meat, and fish. Pizza is cooked in a wood-fired oven. The more than 4,000 bottles in the wine cellar should satisfy the most fastidious wine buff. ✉ *Clarke Quay,* ☎ *433–0156. AE, DC, MC, V.*

$$$ ✕ **Compass Rose Restaurant.** This elegant restaurant is spread out over three floors of the Westin Stamford hotel (☞ Chapter 4); on a clear day, the view from the 70th floor includes Malaysia and some Indonesian islands. Indulge in the luxurious lounge (where high tea and drinks are served) or in the more formal dining room, where artistically presented meals preside. "East meets West" is the theme in such dishes as sautéed veal tenderloin and grilled goose liver, lobster bisque, and broiled king prawns topped with coriander and macadamia pesto. Lunches are considerably less expensive than dinners, and the noontime seafood buffet (S$42) has an amazing variety of dishes. There's always a line at night for seats in the lounge. ⊠ *2 Stamford Rd.,* ☎ *431–6156. AE, DC, MC, V.*

$$–$$$ ✗ **Club Chinois.** When Tan Zhuan Qing opened the prestigious Club
   ★   Chinois in Shanghai in 1925, he couldn't have imagined that a Singaporean restaurateur, Andrew Tjioe, would model another restaurant on it more than 70 years later. Here, in the Orchard Parade Hotel (☞ Chapter 4) you'll find a delectable fusion of Cantonese and French cuisine, aptly directed by famed Canadian chef Susar Lee. The decor is swank and breezy: cream-color tablecloths are accented by turquoise monogrammed napkins and Wedgwood china. Mandarin cha-cha music from the '20s and '30s fills the room as the Armani-clad staff serves delightful dishes. Try the olive-oil-blanched tuna and lobster salad; the soybean bisque with morels; and a chili-marinated rack of lamb with tamarind, orange, and onion marmalade and soft pumpkin cake. ⊠ *No. 02-18, 1 Tanglin Rd.,* ☎ *834–0660. AE, DC, MC, V.*

$$ ✗ **Paolo & Ping's.** Though the mix of Chinese and Italian dishes may seem odd, this place has been very popular since its opening in the Royal Crowne Plaza Singapore hotel (☞ Chapter 4) in mid-1997. Though the turquoise and yellow-ocher interior is a bit noisy (owing to an open-kitchen layout) for intimate dinners, you can request a seat in the quieter Ping's Tea Room and Paolo's Tables section or on the outdoor terrace. Try the spaghetti *con aragosta* (with lobster, tomato, and fresh herbs) or the wok-fried beef with garlic on potato dumplings. For dessert, the deep-fried bittersweet chocolate "wontons" are a decadent treat. The restaurant has live entertainment most evenings until 1 AM. ⊠ *25 Scotts Rd.,* ☎ *731–7985. AE, DC, MC, V.*

French

$$$ ✗ **L'Aigle d'Or.** Glittering crystal contrasts with gaily decorated floral plates at this small, cheerful restaurant in the Duxton Hotel (☞ Chapter 4). A five-course *menu dégustation* (sampling menu) for about S$100 may include lobster consommé, sautéed fresh foie gras, baked John Dory fillets, and roast rack of lamb. Desserts come in pairs; you'll rave about the hot lemon soufflé in a chocolate shell. A set lunch menu changes daily and costs about S$36 per person. ⊠ *83 Duxton Rd.,* ☎ *227–7678. AE, DC, MC, V.*

Indian

$$$ ✗ **Tandoor.** The food has a distinctly Kashmiri flavor at this luxuri-
   ★   ous restaurant, where Indian paintings, rust and terra-cotta colors, and Indian musicians (at night) create the ambience of the Moghul court. The tandoor oven, which you can see through glass across a lotus pond, dominates the room. After you order tandoori chicken, lobster, fish, or shrimp—marinated in yogurt and spices, then roasted in the oven— sit back and watch the chef work. Also cooked in the oven is the northern Indian leavened bread called *naan*; the garlic naan is justifiably famous. The tender, spice-marinated roast leg of lamb is a favorite with regulars. Spiced *masala* tea is a perfect ending to the meal. Service is exceptionally attentive. ⊠ *Holiday Inn Park View, 11 Cavenagh Rd.,* ☎ *733–8333. AE, DC, MC, V.*

$$-$$$ ✕ **Annalakshmi.** Run by a Hindu cultural organization, this restaurant in the Excelsior Hotel (☞ Chapter 4) is considerably more elegant and more expensive than the average vegetarian eatery. The lunch buffet is very popular with Indian businessmen. At night, the paper-thin *dosai* pancakes are delicious in the special Sampoorna dinner. The selection often includes cabbage curry, *channa dhal* (chickpea stew), *kurma* (a mild vegetable curry cooked with yogurt or cream), *poori* (puffy, deep-fried bread), *samosa* (deep-fried, vegetable-stuffed patties), and *jangri* (a cold dessert). The flavors are delicate; spices are judiciously employed to enhance—rather than mask—the taste. ⊠ *5 Coleman St.,* ☎ *339–9993. AE, DC, MC, V. Closed Sun.*

$$ ✕ **Our Village.** There are considerably more attractive—and expensive—
★ Indian restaurants along Boat Quay, but aficionados swear that the food here is superior. Look for the narrow corridor that leads to the restaurant's elevator, which will take you to the fifth floor and a rooftop terrace that's delightfully cool and has excellent views. The menu contains all the usual North Indian favorites, yet the food, cooked home-style rather than prepared hours in advance, has a particular freshness and intensity of flavor. The *sag paneer* (spinach with homemade cheese) and *bhindi bhartha* (okra) are very good; so are the naan and any of the dishes cooked in the tandoor. ⊠ *46 Boat Quay, 4th and 5th floors,* ☎ *538–3058. AE, MC, V.*

$ ✕ **Banana Leaf Apollo.** Along Race Course Road are a host of South
★ Indian restaurants that serve meals on fresh rectangles of banana leaf. This down-home cafeteria-style spot was recently transformed into a stylish restaurant that specializes in fish-head curry (S$18–S$25, depending on the size). The food is fabulous, though it's often so hot that you may wind up with tears streaming down your face. Each person is given a large piece of banana leaf; steaming-hot rice is spooned into the center; then two *papadam* (deep-fried lentil crackers) and two vegetables, with delicious spiced sauces, are arranged neatly around the rice. Optional extras such as the fish-head curry or spicy mutton may be added. ⊠ *54–58 Race Course Rd.,* ☎ *293–8682. AE, MC, V.*

$ ✕ **Madras New Woodlands Restaurant.** Many locals have quite an al-
★ legiance to this simple restaurant in the heart of Little India. The zesty food is vegetarian, combining northern and southern styles. For a full meal, order a *thali:* a large platter of dosai pancakes served with three spiced vegetables, curd, dhal, *rasam* (hot and sour soup), *sambar* (spicy sauce), sweet *raita* (chopped vegetables with yogurt), and papadam. Ask for the paper dosai, which is particularly crisp and comes in an enormous roll; it's served with two spiced coconut sauces and a rasam and is wonderful enough to make a meal on its own. The milk-based sweetmeats are irresistible. ⊠ *14 Upper Dickson Rd.,* ☎ *297–1594. Reservations not accepted. No credit cards.*

$ ✕ **Muthu's Curry Restaurant.** Curry aficionados argue endlessly over which sibling serves the better food, Muthu or his brother, who owns the Banana Leaf Apollo (☞ *above*) down the street. The decor is similar, and Muthu's also has air-conditioning. ⊠ *78 Race Course Rd.,* ☎ *293–7029. Reservations not accepted. AE, MC, V.*

$ ✕ **Samy's Curry Restaurant.** It's *très* chic to lunch at this restaurant on the grounds that used to be home to the Ministry of Defense, not least because there's no way you can stumble upon it by chance—you have to be in the know. The old, no-fuss, civil-service clubhouse is a legacy of the British rule. The decor and service are equally no-fuss. The food—spicy-hot South Indian curries that are served on banana leaves—is excellent. There's no air-conditioning, which means that you sweat it out in true colonial fashion. It's cooler in the evening, but arrive no later than 7 PM for the best dishes. ⊠ *Singapore Civil Service*

Club House, Block 25, Dempsey Rd., ☎ *472–2080 or 296–9391. Reservations not accepted. AE, DC, V. No dinner Thurs.*

Italian

$$$ ✕ **Ristorante Bologna.** The Bologna, in the Marina Mandarin hotel (☞ Chapter 4) insists on making pastas fresh and on using fresh herbs in such dishes as *agnello al dragoncello* (roast rack of lamb stuffed with snow peas and tarragon). Ingredients are flown in from Italy to ensure authenticity. Waiters in vests provide impeccable service. The decor is light, airy, and luxurious; Renaissance-inspired murals adorn the walls, Carrera marble tiles the floor, and a cascading waterfall tops off the view. ⌧ *Marina Square, 6 Raffles Blvd.,* ☎ *845–1113. Reservations not accepted. AE, DC, MC, V.*

$$–$$$ ✕ **Café Modestos.** Blessed with an unbeatable location on the ground
★ floor of the Orchard Parade Hotel (☞ Chapter 4), at the corner of Orchard and Tanglin roads, Café Modestos does more than just wait for folks to wander in. It *draws* them in with its reasonably priced menu of Italian favorites and live entertainment. You can feast on chef Frederico's creative pizza and pasta on the outdoor patio, in the semi-outdoor area (which smokers appreciate), or in the air-conditioned main dining room. There's also a cigar lounge and a wine cellar. Try the carpaccio *di manzo ai funghi misti* (with mushrooms and Parmesan), the linguine *alla modesto* (with assorted seafood), or the *branzino patate e capperi* (sea bass with roasted potatoes in a caper and white-wine sauce). The best pizza has to be the *nera ai frutti di mare* (a squid-ink crust topped with tomatoes and seafood). ⌧ *1 Tanglin Rd.,* ☎ *235–7808. AE, DC, MC, V.*

Japanese

$$$–$$$$ ✕ **Suntory.** Owned by a Japanese beer company, this is reputedly the most expensive Japanese restaurant in town. You'll find a *teppanyaki* room (you're seated at large tables around a large griddle where fish, meat, vegetables, and rice are lightly seared), a sushi counter, tables for *shabu-shabu* (a kind of fondue meal where seafood and meats are lightly swished in boiling stock, then dipped in a variety of sauces), tatami rooms, and a very attractive lounge. The decor is exquisite, the staff well trained, and the food excellent. ⌧ *Delfi Orchard, No. 06–01/02, 402 Orchard Rd.,* ☎ *732–5111. AE, DC, MC, V.*

$$$ ✕ **Keyaki.** A Japanese farmhouse has been re-created in a formal Japanese garden with a golden-carp pond on the rooftop of the Pan Pacific Hotel (☞ Chapter 4). The waitresses in kimonos, the waiters in *happi* coats, and the Japanese lacquerware and porcelain make you feel as if you're in Japan (despite the European-looking wood chairs). The teppanyaki may be the best in Singapore, with a distinctive garlic fried rice and excellent beef, scallops, salmon, and shrimp. ⌧ *Marina Square, 7 Raffles Blvd.,* ☎ *336–8111. AE, DC, V.*

$$$ ✕ **Nadaman.** There's nothing quite so exciting as watching a teppa-
★ nyaki chef perform his culinary calisthenics. The Nadaman, in the Shangri-La hotel (☞ Chapter 4) offers sushi, sashimi (the fresh lobster sashimi is excellent), teppanyaki, tempura, and *kaiseki* (a formal Japanese banquet). Try one of the *bento* lunches—fixed-price meals (around S$35) beautifully decorated in the Japanese manner and served in lacquer trays and boxes. The decor is distinctly Japanese, and the service is discreetly attentive. ⌧ *22 Orange Grove Rd.,* ☎ *737–3644. AE, DC, MC, V.*

$$–$$$ ✕ **Shima.** Strangely, "German baronial" is perhaps the best way to describe the look of this Japanese restaurant in the Goodwood Park hotel (☞ Chapter 4). Teppanyaki, shabu-shabu, and *yakiniku* (grill-it-yourself slices of beef, chicken, or fish) are the only items on the menu. You sit around a teppanyaki grill, watching the chef at work, or at the shabu-shabu and yakiniku tables cooking for yourself. Copper chimneys remove the smoke and smell. ☒ *22 Scotts Rd.,* ☏ *734–6281/2. AE, DC, MC, V.*

Malay and Indonesian

$$$ ✕ **Alkaff Mansion.** Once the estate of wealthy merchants, this 19th-century house on Mt. Faber Ridge, a short distance southwest of the city center, opened as a restaurant in 1991. You can sit inside under twirling fans inside or out on a veranda decorated to reflect the diverse tastes of the old Arab traders. Downstairs there's a huge Malay-Indonesian dinner buffet; on the balconies upstairs, 10 sarong-clad waitresses serve a multicourse rijsttafel. Western food—from steaks to seafood bordelaise—is also offered on a three-course luncheon menu and a more elaborate à la carte dinner menu. Overall, the delightful turn-of-the-century ambience and the presentation are more rewarding than the food. ☒ *10 Telok Blangah Green,* ☏ *278–6979. AE, DC, MC, V.*

$$$ ✕ **Tiffin Room.** For a taste of nostalgia and of a typical British "curry tiffin," part of the Malay colonial tradition, a visit to the Tiffin Room in the landmark Raffles Hotel (☞ Chapter 4) is a must. Despite its popularity with tour groups, the light, airy restaurant with its marble floors is still gracious; the service is courteous if a fraction slow during busy lunches. The lunch and dinner buffets are tempting spreads of largely Indian dishes. Forget that concession to modern tastes, the salad bar, and head straight for the mulligatawny, a spicy curry soup. There's a large array of spicy (but not necessarily chili-hot) vegetable, meat, poultry, and seafood dishes, and far more pickles, chutneys, and other condiments than a genuine Indian meal would provide. If you've still got room, you can choose from one or two local desserts as well as Indian and international favorites. ☒ *1 Beach Rd.,* ☏ *331–1612. AE, DC, MC, V.*

$$ ✕ **Aziza's.** It's the spicy cooking of the Malay Peninsula you get here— lots of lemongrass, shallots, pepper, coriander, cloves, and cinnamon. Try the *rendang* (beef simmered for hours in a mixture of spices and coconut milk), *gado gado* (a light salad with a spiced peanut sauce), or *bergedel* (Dutch-influenced potato cutlets). The oxtail soup is especially delicious. Ask for *nasi ambang,* and you'll get festive rice with a sampling of dishes from the menu. The friendly setting makes this an easy place to experiment with Malay food. ☒ *180 Albert St.,* ☏ *235–1130. AE, DC, MC, V.*

$$ ✕ **Rajah Inn.** In the lobby of the charming Regalis Court boutique hotel (☞ Chapter 4), this surprisingly large Indonesian restaurant is decorated in warm yellow and white tones and has ceiling fans as well as the ubiquitous air-conditioning. Try the *sambal goreng udang* (fried shrimp with chili) for a spicy sensation, *sayur lodeh* (local vegetables cooked in coconut milk), or *kambing gan lembu* (mutton or beef in a mild curry sauce). Prices are very reasonable, but call ahead to make sure the restaurant won't be feeding a tour group at the time you'd like to dine here. ☒ *64 Lloyd Rd.,* ☏ *734–7117. AE, MC, V.*

$$ ✕ **Warung Wayan.** Indonesian cuisine reigns at this riverside restaurant. The charcoal-grilled items are particularly good. If you want to sample Balinese as opposed to Javanese or Indonesian-Chinese food, order the Balinese *satay* (pieces of beef, pork, and chicken on a wooden skewer and that are barbecued or roasted; but don't eat them with peanut sauce; they don't go together in Balinese cooking) and *ayam panggang Wayan* (barbecued chicken) with its wonderful tangy sauce. A Javanese speciality—*tahu telor* (meltingly soft bean curd deep-fried with a crunchy egg coating)—is a must. Prices for wine and beer are very reasonable by Singapore standards. ⊠ *50A Boat Quay,* ☎ *538–3889. AE, DC, MC, V.*

$–$$ ✕ **House of Sudanese Food.** Sudanese food, born of an isolated province
  ★   in western Java, is a cuisine unique from the rest of Indonesia. It combines raw, fresh vegetables with meat and fish in a piquant sweet-spicy mix. Order several small dishes and one seafood entrée and share them with your travel companions. You might start with *keredok,* a vegetable salad in a spicy peanut dressing; continue with *taupok goreng isi,* bean-curd-skin rolls stuffed with scallops, prawns, water chestnuts, and mushrooms; and *sedap ikan snapper bakar,* broiled red snapper basted in a sweet sauce. The prices at all three locations are very reasonable, making them hits with the lunchtime business crowd. ⊠ *55 Boat Quay,* ☎ *534–3775. AE, DC, MC, V.* ⊠ *Suntec City Mall, No. B1-063, Fountain Terrace, 3 Temasek Blvd.,* ☎ *334–1012. AE, DC, MC, V.* ⊠ *218 East Coast Rd.,* ☎ *345–5020. AE, DC, MC, V.*

Nonya

$$ ✕ **Blue Ginger.** Singapore's most popular Peranakan restaurant has two convenient locations—one in Chinatown, the other on Orchard Road. Furnishings are stylish and elegant, and colorful paintings by local artist Martin Loh abound. You might try such dishes as *udang goreng tauyu lada* (sautéed prawns with pepper in a sweet soya sauce), *ayam panggang Blue Ginger* (boneless chicken grilled and flavored with spiced coconut milk), and the mouthwatering *ngo heong* (homemade rolls of minced pork and prawns seasoned with five spices). If you're brave, sample the dessert made from the local infamous durian fruit (a large, thorny bit of produce that smells like old gym socks but has a caramel flavor). At the Tanjong Pagar location, request a second-floor table for an entertaining view of the street below. ⊠ *97 Tanjong Pagar Rd.,* ☎ *222–3928. AE, DC, MC, V.* ⊠ *The Heeren, No. 05-02C, 260 Orchard Rd.,* ☎ *835–3928. AE, DC, MC, V.*

$$ ✕ **Ivin's Restaurant.** Housed in the upscale suburb of Bukit Timah, just north of the city center (you'll need a cab to get here), this casual restaurant serves traditional Nonya food à la carte. Specialties include *ayam buah keluak* (chicken in a spicy-sour gravy with a black Indonesian nut that has a creamy texture and the smokiness of French truffles), *babi pongteh* (pork stewed in soy sauce and onions), *udang masak nanas* (prawns cooked with pineapple), and *pong tauhu* (a soup with bamboo shoots and minced chicken, prawn, and bean-curd dumplings). ⊠ *19/21 Binjai Park,* ☎ *468–3060. AE, DC, MC, V.*

Seafood

$$–$$$ ✕ **Palm Beach Seafood.** Forty years ago, this restaurant was on a beach, with tables set under coconut trees—hence the name. It's now in a shopping and leisure complex next to the National Stadium and covers three floors, with its downstairs restaurant seating around 550. What the place lacks in ambience, it more than makes up for in food quality, and the prices may well be the best in town for seafood. The most popular dishes include chili crabs served with French bread to mop up the sauce; prawns fried in black soy sauce or in butter and milk with curry leaves; and deep-fried crisp squid. Don't miss the *yu char kway,* deep-fried crullers stuffed with a mousse of squid and served with a tangy black sauce. ⊠ *Leisure Park, 5 Stadium Walk, Kallang Park,* ☎ *344–3088. Reservations not accepted. AE, MC, V.*

$$–$$$ ✕ **UDMC Seafood Centre.** You *must* visit this place at the East Coast Parkway, near the entrance to the lagoon, to get a true picture of the

way Singaporeans eat out, as well as real value (prices here are cheaper than in most other seafood restaurants). Walk around the eight open-fronted restaurants before you decide where to eat. Chili crabs, steamed prawns, steamed fish, pepper crabs, fried noodles, and deep-fried squid are the specialties. Restaurants include **Chin Wah Heng** (☎ 444–7967), **Gold Coast Seafood** (☎ 448–2020), **Golden Lagoon Seafood** (☎ 448–1894), **Jumbo Seafood** (☎ 442–3435), **Lucky View Seafood Restaurant** (☎ 241–1022), and **Red House Seafood Restaurant** (☎ 442–3112). ✉ *East Coast Pkwy. Reservations not accepted. AE, DC, MC, V. No lunch.*

Thai

$$–$$$
★
✕ **Thanying.** The owners and chefs at this restaurant in the Amara Hotel (☞ Chapter 4) are Thai, so it's no wonder that it has such exquisite, aristocratic, Thai decor and that the food (redolent of kaffir-lime leaves, basil, mint, ginger, and coriander) is cooked in the best palace tradition. Indeed, this restaurant has been so successful that the owners have opened a second one on Clarke Quay. Try the *gai kor bai toey* (marinated chicken in pandanus leaves and char-grilled to perfection), an exquisite Thai salad like *yam sam oh* (shredded pomelo tossed with chicken and prawns in a spicy lime sauce), *pla khao sam rod* (grouper, deep-fried until it's so crispy you can practically eat the bones), or one of the Thai curries. And of course, you won't want to miss the sour and hot *tom yam* soup. ✉ *Amara Hotel, Level 2, 165 Tanjong Pagar Rd.,* ☎ *222–4688. AE, DC, MC, V.* ✉ *Clarke Quay, Block D,* ☎ *336–1821. AE, DC, MC, V.*

$$
✕ **Yhingthai Palace.** The no-nonsense decor of this small, simple restaurant—just around the corner from the famous Raffles Hotel—makes it clear that food is the prime concern. Although the service can be slow, the well-prepared and moderately priced food is worth waiting for. The *yam ma muang* (sour mango salad) is an excellent and refreshing dish, while *hor mok talay,* seafood mousse served in charming terra-cotta molds, is light and flavorful. If you enjoy spicy dishes with plenty of herbs, try the *phad kra kai* (stir-fried minced chicken). The *kuay teow phad Thai* (fresh rice noodles fried with seafood) is delicious, and one of the lemony tom yam soups is almost obligatory. ✉ *13 Purvis St.,* ☎ *337–9429. AE, MC, V.*

4 Lodging

Singapore's hotels are a true delight, offering charm, efficiency, and every modern creature comfort—all at prices to suit a wide range of budgets.

OVER THE YEARS Singapore has been transformed from a popular tourist destination to a conventioneers' mecca teeming with tour groups and delegates. Singapore's lodging has visibly changed to accommodate this clientele: extensive refurbishment and growth with more automated service has been the trend. With that said, though, luxury still abounds, and there are places where exceptional personal service hasn't completely fallen by the wayside.

Singapore's hotels were once considered inexpensive compared to those in other world-class cities. Today, however, costs rival those in New York or London—a superior double room in a deluxe hotel can run more than S$400 a night; one with a private bath in a modest hotel, about S$150 a night. Further, during conventions and the peak months of August and December, hotel rooms can be scarce and prices can rise. Still, there are enough discounts and deals that no thrifty visitor should ever have to pay the published price (if you use a travel agent, make sure that he or she asks for a discount). There are also budget hotels (with shared bathroom facilities) with rates less than S$85 a night. And if all you're looking for is a bunk, walk along Bencoolen Street, where there are dormitory-style guest houses that charge no more than S$25 a night. (For more information on affordable lodgings, contact the Singapore Tourism Board or STB—see Visitor Information in the Gold Guide section—for its annually updated brochure, "Budget Hotels.")

Booking ahead—particularly for stays in August and December—will probably save you money and will definitely save you headaches. If, however, you gamble and arrive without reservations, the Singapore Hotel Association has two counters at Changi Airport that are staffed by people who can set you up with a room—often at a discount—with no booking fee.

Establishments in the $$$–$$$$ range offer such amenities as International Direct Dial (IDD) phones with bathroom extensions, TVs with international cable stations, room service, minibars, data ports for modems, no-smoking rooms or floors, in-room safes, and business and fitness centers loaded with the latest equipment. On the flip side, some smaller hotels—particularly those in converted shophouses—have a few rooms that lack windows, so be sure to ask for one that has them. For all of Singapore's high-tech advances—including traffic signals that chirp at you when it's safe to cross the street—there are some establishments that don't offer rooms equipped for people with mobility problems; those that do are indicated below. Unless otherwise noted, all rooms have air-conditioning and private baths.

Singapore

Singapore's hotels have developed in clusters. The best-known grouping is at the intersection of Orchard and Scotts roads. The luxurious Four Seasons is tucked behind the Hilton off Orchard Road, and the recently refurbished Grand Hyatt is on Scotts Road. Close by is the new Traders Hotel, which cuts out the frills and frippery found at luxury hotels, providing all the basic comforts at low rates.

In Raffles City, the megalithic Westins—the Plaza and the Stamford—stare down at the Raffles, the grande dame of Singapore's hotels, and the Inter-Continental's black-and-white marble gleams alongside turn-of-the-century shophouses. At the south end of the Shenton Way commercial district are a number of business-oriented hotels; to the south of the Singapore River, still another cluster has sprung up, one with boutique hotels as well as the Raffles-owned Merchant Court. Marina Square—a minicity created by a reclamation project that pushed back the seafront to make way for the Suntec City convention complex, more than 200 shops, and many restaurants—has a half dozen hotels, including the Pan Pacific and the Conrad International Centennial.

If you can't get enough of Sentosa Island's attractions, you'll find a couple of hotels there. If you like shopping and nightlife, then the Orchard and Scotts roads area is for you. If you're attending a convention or simply want an urban landscape with open spaces and river views, Marina Square is the logical choice. If you're doing business in the financial district, a hotel close to Shenton Way is ideal; if your business plans include a trip to the industrial city of Jurong, then a hotel on the Singapore River is best. Regardless of where you stay, it's easy to get around this compact city. Taxis and public transportation, especially the subway, make it possible to travel between areas swiftly, and no hotel is more than a 30-minute cab ride from Changi Airport.

$$$$ ☆ **Four Seasons.** Opened in 1995 by the owner of the adjacent Hilton, the Four Seasons is quieter and—dare we say it?—more refined, with luxuries intended to make it outshine the city's older hotels. (Drawn by the modern elegance, Britain's Spice Girls taped a music video here in 1998.) Guest rooms are spacious and gracious, with soft fabrics, peaceful Asian art, large bathrooms, two-line speakerphones with modem hookups, laser video, and CD players. Of the three restaurants, the Cantonese Jiang-Nam Chun (☞ Chapter 3) is the most memorable for its stunning art deco and art nouveau decor and its exotic fare. Some of the tennis courts are air-conditioned, and there's even a golf simulator. The hotel is linked to Orchard Road via an elevated passageway to the Hilton. ✉ *190 Orchard Blvd., 248646,* ☏ *734–1110,* 🖷 *733–0682. 237 rooms, 20 suites. 3 restaurants, bar, 2 pools, 4 tennis courts, health club, shops, business services, meeting rooms. AE, DC, MC, V.*

$$$$ ⊞ **Goodwood Park.** This venerable institution began in 1900 as a club for German expatriates and has since hosted the likes of the Duke of Windsor, Edward Heath, Noël Coward, and the great Anna Pavlova, who performed here. It has recently been renovated to bring its facilities up to world-class standing, though it still lacks many plush extras found in other luxury hotels. The Parklane Suites, each with a bedroom and a living-dining room, can be rented (for short- or long-term stays) for less than a double room in the main hotel; the drawback is the five-minute walk to all the hotel's facilities. Restaurants—which are popular with local diners—include the Gordon Grill, Min Jiang, and Chang Jiang (☞ Chapter 3). ✉ *22 Scotts Rd., 228221,* ☏ *737–7411 or 800/772–3890 (reservations in the U.S.),* 🖷 *732–8558. 171 rooms, 64 suites. 3 restaurants, coffee shop, 3 pools, beauty salon, exercise room, baby-sitting, business services, meeting rooms. AE, DC, MC, V.*

$$$$ ⊞ **Grand Hyatt Singapore.** Formerly the Hyatt Regency, this centrally located luxury hotel was extensively refurbished in 1998. Room rates here are among the highest in town, but promotional packages are frequently offered. The Grand Wing consists of one-, two-, and three-room apartments with two-line phones, extra bathrooms, work areas, and private mailboxes. Standard rooms are adequate but small. Dine at Pete's Place, for excellent pasta dishes; mezza9 for authentic Asian; and Scotts Lounge, for afternoon tea. Travelers with disabilities will find the amenities here to their liking. ✉ *10–12 Scotts Rd., 228211,* ☏ *738–1234,* 🖷 *732–1696. 266 rooms, 427 apartments. 3 restaurants, coffee shop, pool, beauty salon, massage, sauna, 2 tennis courts, badminton, exercise room, squash, business services. AE, DC, MC, V.*

$$$$ 🏨 **Hotel Inter-Continental Singapore.** This Bugis Junction hotel, built in 1995, appears to be just another modern, marbleized, posh hotel with all the latest amenities (including facilities for people with disabilities and "cyber-relations" officers, or computer consultants, on call). But in its 83 Shophouse Rooms—each one different from the next—the Peranakan style (the distinctive Malay-Chinese-European mix of design influences) reminds you of Singapore's multicultural heritage. There's a S$10 surcharge a night for a stay in these rooms, but a complimentary American breakfast is included. The remaining guest rooms have classical, clean, European lines. For a surcharge of S$50 a night you'll get more attentive service, a Continental breakfast, and evening cocktails. ✉ *80 Middle Rd., 188966,* ☎ *338–7600,* FAX *338–7366. 406 rooms. 3 restaurants, pool, health club, business services, meeting rooms. AE, DC, MC, V.*

$$$$ 🏨 **The Oriental.** Inside this pyramid-shape Marina Square hotel, the
★ level of service on everyone's part—from student trainees to seasoned doormen—is second to none. Subdued, modern elegance and personal attention are the hallmarks here. Rooms are understated, with soft hues of peach and green, handwoven carpets, and paintings of old Singapore. Of special note are the Italian-marble-tiled bathrooms with phones and radio and TV speakers. One-bedroom suites have lovely sitting rooms and separate washrooms. The Cherry Garden (☞ Chapter 3) prepares outstanding Hunanese food. Morton's, the Chicago-based steak house, has opened its first Asian branch here. More casual dining is available at Café des Artistes. Note that the hotel has facilities for people with disabilities. ✉ *5 Raffles Blvd., 039797,* ☎ *338–0066,* FAX *339–9537. 422 rooms, 100 suites. 5 restaurants, pool, massage, sauna, golf privileges, 2 tennis courts, health club, jogging, business services, meeting rooms, travel services. AE, DC, MC, V.*

$$$$ 🏨 **Raffles Hotel.** Opened by the Sarkies brothers in 1887 and visited
★ by such writers as Joseph Conrad, Rudyard Kipling, and Somerset Maugham, Raffles was the belle of the East during its heyday in the '20s and '30s but fell on hard times after World War II. True to form in this planned republic, millions of dollars have been spent to replace Singapore's noble old charm with a sanitized version of colonial ambience. The new Raffles is a glistening showpiece, especially from the outside; inside, antique furniture blends well with modern amenities (including facilities for people with disabilities). There are two lobbies: one for guests and the other for the constant flow of diners and curious tourists. Guest suites have teak floors, 14-ft ceilings, overhead fans, and '20s-style furnishings that tend to be stiff. Some suites are named after famous literary figures who once stayed here. ✉ *1 Beach Rd., 189673,* ☎ *337–1886,* FAX *339–7650. 104 suites. 2 restaurants, 2 bars, pool, exercise room, shops, business services. AE, DC, MC, V.*

$$$$ 🏨 **Ritz-Carlton.** The most dramatic of the luxury hotels in Marina Bay
★ is the Ritz-Carlton. It opened in 1996 with 32 floors of unobstructed water views as well as sculptures by Frank Stella and limited-edition prints by David Hockney and Henry Moore. All rooms are unusually large (travelers with disabilities will appreciate the facilities in some) and have bathrooms that seem better stocked than your local drugstore. Floors 30 to 32 are Club Floors where, for S$60 more a night, you can enjoy complimentary breakfast, noon snacks, afternoon tea, evening cocktails, after-dinner cordials, and personalized concierge services. For dining, there's Snappers for seafood, the Summer Pavilion for Cantonese cuisine, and the Asian- and European-accented Greenhouse. Check out the exclusive health club (local memberships cost S$25,000) and the live jazz in the lobby lounge every evening. ✉ *7 Raffles Ave., 039799,* ☎ *337–8888,* FAX *338–0001. 541 rooms, 59 suites. 3 restaurants, pool, spa, tennis court, health club, business services, meeting rooms. AE, DC, MC, V.*

76

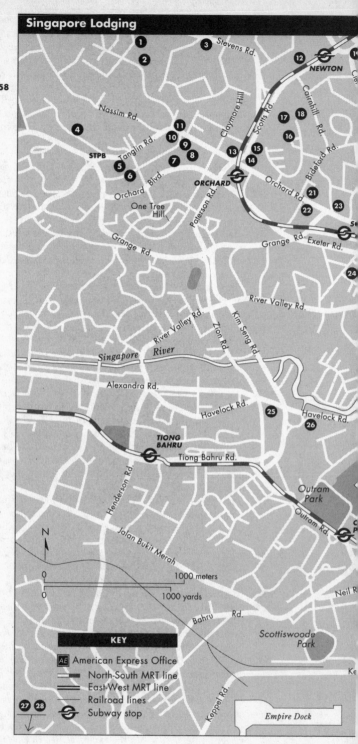

Singapore Lodging

KEY

AE American Express Office

North-South MRT line

East-West MRT line

Railroad lines

Subway stop

$$$$ ⊡ **Shangri-La.** This hotel has consistently been among Singapore's
★ top three since opening in 1971. To give the other two a run for their
money, approximately S$57 million has been earmarked for extensive
renovations of this hotel's Tower Wing, pool, lobby areas, and food
and beverage outlets in 1998–99. While refurbishments continue, the
Valley Wing (built at the start of the '90s) and its 137 rooms will be
the site of business-as-usual hotel activity. Prime Ministers and presi-
dents have stayed here, but all travelers are treated to the same excellent service. The Coffee Garden, designed after an English conservatory,
has light meals and a lunch buffet; you'll find haute Cantonese cuisine
in Shang Palace (☞ Chapter 3); and the Nadaman (☞ Chapter 3) serves
Japanese fare. (Travelers with disabilities take note: this hotel has
amenities for you.) ✉ *22 Orange Grove Rd., 258350, ☎ 737–3644;
0181/747–8485 (reservations in the U.K.); 800/942–5050 (reservations in Canada or the U.S.),* ℻ *737–3257. 823 rooms. 4 restaurants,
bar, putting green, 4 tennis courts, health club, squash, business services, meeting rooms. AE, DC, MC, V.*

$$$$ ⊡ **Sheraton Towers.** The pastel-decorated guest rooms here have all the
deluxe amenities, including small sitting areas with a sofa and easy chairs.
The Tower Rooms, at about S$60 more, include complimentary but-
ler service and breakfast. The best vantage point for the dramatic cas-
cading waterfall (the rocks are fiberglass) is from the Terrazza restaurant,
which has a superb high tea. Other restaurants are Domus for Italian
food and Li Bai (☞ Chapter 3) for refined Cantonese. The hawker stalls
at Newton Circus are close by. A large, comfortable lounge has live music
in the evening. ✉ *39 Scotts Rd., 228230, ☎ 737–6888,* ℻ *733–4366.
606 rooms. 2 restaurants, café, coffee shop, pool, massage, sauna,
dance club, business services, meeting rooms. AE, DC, MC, V.*

$$$ ⊡ **ANA Singapore.** Don't be deceived by the antique tapestries and
wood-paneled walls in the lobby of this glistening 14-story hotel near
the Botanic Gardens and the embassies. It has a full range of modern
facilities. Rooms are decorated in light colors and have writing desks,
bedside remote controls, and coffee- and tea makers. The Hubertus Grill
serves seafood, prime rib, and Continental cuisine; the Unkai special-
izes in Japanese food. ✉ *16 Nassim Hill, 238467, ☎ 732–1222,* ℻
*737–6684. 445 rooms, 17 suites. 2 restaurants, café, coffee shop,
pool, exercise room, dance club, business services. AE, DC, MC, V.*

$$$ ⊡ **The Beaufort.** This resort on Sentosa Island caters to leisure visitors,
but its remote location makes it seem more suited to business semi-
nars. Its best feature is the swimming pool, which overlooks the
Malacca Straits and is flanked by a romantic, open-air, seafood restaurant. The rooms—down concrete corridors, past pond-filled courtyards,
and in two symmetrical low-rise wings—don't share these fine views;
instead they look onto tropical parkland. Standard rooms (called
deluxe) aren't very large (though bathrooms are of a good size) and
have undistinctive pastel furniture. The Garden Rooms have larger bedrooms and work areas with better-quality furniture such as handmade
tortoiseshell desks, mosaic tables, and French banquette sofas. There
are also four luxurious two-bedroom villas, each with its own pool.
(This hotel has facilities for travelers with disabilities.) ✉ *2 Bukit
Manis Rd., Sentosa Island, 099891, ☎ 275–0331 or 800/637–7200
(reservations in the U.S.),* ℻ *275–0228. 175 rooms, 34 suites, 4 villas. 3 restaurants, pool, 2 tennis courts, exercise room, squash, business services, meeting rooms. AE, DC, MC, V.*

$$$ ⊡ **Boulevard Hotel.** A floor-to-ceiling sculpture dominates the airy atrium
lobby of this hotel, which caters to traveling executives. Guest rooms
have large desks and coffee- and tea makers. Rooms come in three sizes:
standard; deluxe, with a corner pantry; and executive, with a work desk
area. The hotel is at the top end of Orchard Road, away from the main

thoroughfare. ⊠ *200 Orchard Blvd., 248647,* ☎ *737–2911,* FAX *737–8449. 521 rooms. 3 restaurants, coffee shop, 2 pools, beauty salon, exercise room, dance club, business services, travel services. AE, DC, MC, V.*

$$$ 🏨 **Carlton Hotel.** This stark, pristine hotel near Raffles City has achieved a more relaxed ambience than when it first opened in 1988. Your footsteps will still echo through the lobby, but you'll find that the lounges to the side are quiet enclaves for sipping afternoon tea. All the hotel's amenities (including those for travelers with disabilities) are up-to-date. The upper five stories contain concierge floors, with express check-in, complimentary breakfast, and evening cocktails. Published prices have climbed recently; unless you can get a decent discount, they're steep for what the hotel offers. ⊠ *76 Bras Basah Rd., 189558,* ☎ *338–8333,* FAX *339–6866. 463 rooms, 14 suites. 2 restaurants, bar, café, coffee shop, lobby lounge, pool, exercise room, business services, meeting rooms. AE, DC, MC, V.*

$$$ 🏨 **Conrad International Centennial Singapore.** Though this impressive hotel is a high-rise—new in 1997—it's almost lost among the other towers of Marina Square. It's adjacent to the Singapore International Convention and Exhibition Centre (SUNTEC or Suntec City), so many of its rooms are often booked. The lobby is dominated by a grand marble staircase and a gold-leaf ceiling. The Asian art on permanent display was commissioned from the island's top artists and complements the Far Eastern decor and ambience. Rooms are similarly decorated, and have large bathrooms with the usual amenities. Travelers with disabilities will appreciate that the hotel has taken their needs into consideration; businesspeople will be grateful for the 24-hour business center and the well-equipped function rooms. The Golden Peony (☞ Chapter 3) serves one of the best dim sum lunches in the city. ⊠ *2 Temasek Blvd., 038982,* ☎ *338–8830,* FAX *338–8164. 484 rooms, 25 suites. 3 restaurants, 3 bars, pool, exercise room, business services, meeting rooms, travel services. AE, DC, MC, V.*

$$$ 🏨 **Crown Prince Hotel.** The large, sparse lobby greets you with Italian marble and glass chandeliers. For more drama, glass elevators run along the outside of the building so you can check out the traffic on Orchard Road. Though the pastel rooms are neat and trim, efficiency outweighs warmth here. The Cafe de Prince serves local and Western food, the Long Jiang (☞ Chapter 3) offers Szechuan food from a set menu, and the Sushi Nogawa is Japanese-owned. ⊠ *270 Orchard Rd., 238857,* ☎ *732–1111,* FAX *732–7018. 297 rooms, 6 suites. 3 restaurants, pool, business services, meeting rooms. AE, DC, MC, V.*

$$$ 🏨 **The Duxton.** Singapore's first boutique hotel consists of eight smartly
★ converted shophouses in Chinatown's Tanjong Pagar district. It remains a breath of fresh air: intimate and tasteful, with a whiff of Singapore's character before it sold out to steel girders and glass. The standard rooms, at the back of the building, are small and have colonial reproduction furniture. You may want to spend the extra S$120 a night for a small duplex suite. Breakfast is included, and afternoon tea is served in the lounge. The excellent French restaurant, L'Aigle d'Or (☞ Chapter 3), is off the lobby. ⊠ *83 Duxton Rd., 089540,* ☎ *227–7678 or 800/272–8188 (reservations in the U.S.),* FAX *227–1232. 38 rooms, 11 suites. Restaurant, business services. AE, DC, MC, V.*

$$$ 🏨 **Grand Plaza Parkroyal.** The builders of this two-year-old property integrated the century-old shophouses of the neighborhood with modern architecture, making an appealing statement at the junction of Coleman and Hill streets. The superb location has meant compromise, however, as the pool, fitness facilities, and regular rooms are smaller than those at similarly priced properties. The hotel has one large and prestigious tenant, though: the St. Gregory Marine Spa covers 7,000

square ft and has separate floors for men and women. There's also a medical clinic within the complex. ✉ *10 Coleman St., 179809,* ☎ *336–3456,* 𝔽𝔸𝕏 *339–9311. 338 rooms. 2 restaurants, bar, coffee shop, spa, exercise room, business services, meeting rooms. AE, DC, MC, V.*

$$$ ⊡ **Hilton International.** It may be short on glitter and dazzle, but the Hilton's rooms have all the amenities (including those for people with disabilities) of a modern deluxe property and at highly competitive rates. It's near shopping arcades that house some of Singapore's most exclusive boutiques. The rooms on the street side still have views, but those at the back have been blocked by the adjacent Four Seasons. The former Givenchy suites are now Executive Club floors with 72 rooms and suites and a clubroom all decked out in contemporary furniture with warm tones and black steel trim. Executive rooms, many with balconies, have two phone lines and a modem connection. Within the hotel are Checkers Brasserie; Tradewinds, a spot for rooftop and poolside dining; and the Harbour Grill, which has seafood and French cuisine. ✉ *581 Orchard Rd., 238883,* ☎ *737–2233,* 𝔽𝔸𝕏 *732–2917. 351 rooms, 72 suites. 3 restaurants, 2 bars, pool, health club, business services, meeting rooms. AE, DC, MC, V.*

$$$ ⊡ **Hotel New Otani.** Off by itself on the north bank of the Singapore River, this orange-brick-fronted hotel is striking against the greenery of Fort Canning Park. It attracts many Japanese travelers as part of the Liang Court complex, which houses more than 40 specialty shops, and the large Japanese department store Daimaru. Rooms come with coffee-, tea-, and soup makers. The hotel's location is best suited to business travelers who want to be close to Shenton Way. ✉ *177A River Valley Rd., 179031,* ☎ *338–3333,* 𝔽𝔸𝕏 *339–2854. 408 rooms. 2 restaurants, bar, pool, exercise room, business services, meeting rooms. AE, DC, MC, V.*

$$$ ⊡ **Hotel Phoenix.** During recent renovations, the Phoenix installed PCs with Internet access and exercise equipment in all its rooms, as well as a computerized massage chair in each of its executive rooms and suites. In the warmly decorated rooms, beds are dressed in down quilts and have electronic control panels beside them; the Business Executive Rooms can be converted into offices during the day. There's no on-site health club, so if the in-room gear isn't enough, take advantage of the free passes to the California Fitness Center two blocks away. The Phoenix Garden Café serves very good local and Western fare, but it can be noisy during dinner, perhaps owing to its basement location. The hotel is in the heart of the Orchard Road district and a five-minute drive to the convention center. ✉ *277 Orchard Rd., 238858,* ☎ *737–8666,* 𝔽𝔸𝕏 *732–2024. 290 rooms, 22 suites. Restaurant, bar, patisserie, nightclub, business services. AE, DC, MC, V.*

$$$ ⊡ **Mandarin Singapore.** The grand main lobby has translucent white-and-black Italian marble and a huge mural, *87 Taoist Immortals,* based on an 8th-century Chinese scroll. Guest rooms on the upper floors command fabulous views of the harbor, the city, and Malaysia beyond. The best rooms have VCRs and bedside remote controls; some have amenities for travelers with disabilities. Rooms in the South Tower have black-lacquer furniture with colorful silk cushions. Overall, however, the Mandarin is a little disappointing; tour groups are its mainstay. Dining options include the Pine Court (☞ Chapter 3); the Top of the M, a revolving restaurant; Chikuyotei, with Japanese fare; the 24-hour Chatterbox coffeehouse; and hawker-stand Chinese food. ✉ *333 Orchard Rd., 238867,* ☎ *737–4411,* 𝔽𝔸𝕏 *732–2361. 1,200 rooms. 3 restaurants, coffee shop, pub, pool, beauty salon, massage, sauna, tennis court, exercise room, squash, dance club, business services, meeting rooms. AE, DC, MC, V.*

$$$ 🏨 **Marina Mandarin.** Here, the John Portman–designed atrium narrows as it ascends 21 floors to a tinted skylight, and the lobby is relatively peaceful. Pastel guest rooms are modern and smart and have coffee- and tea makers; for the best view, ask for a room overlooking the harbor. Rooms on the concierge floor—the Marina Club—cost about 25% more and have such extras as terry-cloth robes, butler service, and free breakfast and cocktails. Also available are accommodations for businesspeople who don't need all the extras of the concierge floor but who do need efficient hotel services. The on-site Peach Blossoms restaurant serves Chinese cuisine for lunch and dinner and the Ristorante Bologna (☞ Chapter 3) has northern Italian fare; the Cricketeer pub is a pleasant place for an evening drink. ⊠ *6 Raffles Blvd., 039594,* ☎ *338–3388,* ℻ *339–4977. 575 rooms. 3 restaurants, pub, pool, massage, sauna, 2 tennis courts, exercise room, squash, dance club, business services. AE, DC, MC, V.*

$$$ 🏨 **Merchant Court Hotel.** The trend toward developing "no frills" hotels for business travelers led the Raffles Group to open Merchant Court in 1997. It's across from Clarke Quay and is a free shuttle ride away from the Raffles City Shopping Centre. Standard rooms, albeit small, are comfortable; larger executive rooms have a few more amenities. A stay in a Merchant Club room gets you free use of laptop computers and fax machines as well as complimentary breakfast and cocktails. All rooms have refrigerators for you to stock, and there's a coin-op laundry with video games on the second floor. In addition, the hotel can comfortably accommodate travelers with disabilities. The Ellenborough Market Café offers a nightly Asian/Western buffet. The fitness facilities are top-notch, though the locker rooms are cramped and ill-equipped. ⊠ *20 Merchant Rd., 058281,* ☎ *337–2288,* ℻ *334–0606. 470 rooms, 6 suites. Restaurant, 2 bars, refrigerators, pool, exercise room, business services, meeting rooms. AE, DC, MC, V.*

$$$ 🏨 **Meridien Singapore Orchard.** Slightly away from much of the hustle and bustle on Orchard Road, this hotel—its large atrium lobby reminiscent of a train station—is part of what seems to be an abandoned shopping complex. Rooms are done in pastels and have such Asian touches as silk-screen murals; some rooms have balconies loaded with potted plants. Quarters on Le Club Président concierge level have extra amenities. In addition to the hotel's dining room, you'll find rotisserie buffets, local specialties, and Western fare in the relaxed Café Georges. ⊠ *100 Orchard Rd., 238840,* ☎ *733–8855,* ℻ *732–7886. 407 rooms. 2 restaurants, bar, pool, exercise room, business services. AE, DC, MC, V.*

$$$ 🏨 **Orchard Hotel.** Its location close to the activity on Orchard Road, several embassies, and the Botanic Gardens has no doubt contributed to this hotel's popularity. The pastel guest rooms are comfortable and functional, and there are facilities for people with disabilities. Rooms in the 17-story Orchard Wing are larger and more expensive than standard rooms. Rooms on the top four floors are part of the Premier and Harvesters' clubs; amenities here include separate check-in, in-room fax services, and complimentary breakfast and evening cocktails. The formal Hua Ting restaurant offers Cantonese and Shanghainese dishes, and the Orchard and Sidewalk cafés serve light fare till 1 AM. ⊠ *442 Orchard Rd., 238879,* ☎ *734–7766,* ℻ *733–5482. 680 rooms. Restaurant, bar, 2 cafés, tea shop, pool, exercise room, business services, meeting rooms, travel services. AE, DC, MC, V.*

$$$ 🏨 **Orchard Parade Hotel.** Previously known as the Ming Court Hotel, this 30-year-old property at the corner of Tanglin and Orchard roads underwent a S$40-million transformation that was completed in mid-1998. Mediterranean in style (there's a Spanish feel throughout the place), the rooms are spacious, especially the Junior Suites. Several of these are set aside for families with young children and have one or two extra single beds and a dining area. The hotel's location makes it a favorite with leisure travelers, and all the on-site restaurants are leased to well-known eateries. Club Chinois (☞ Chapter 3) adds a touch of elegance to this "new" kid on the block. ✉ *1 Tanglin Rd., 247905,* ☎ *737–1133,* FAX *733-0242. 368 rooms, 19 suites. 4 restaurants, bar, coffee shop, dance club, nightclub, meeting rooms, travel services. AE, DC, MC, V.*

\$\$\$ ▥ **Pan Pacific.** Of the five Marina Square hotels, this one is the largest (which can make it seem impersonal) and the least expensive (which may enable you to overlook its impersonal air). It caters to tour groups and conventioneers, with amenities (such as PCs in all the rooms) to please the budgets and needs of business travelers—from junior executives to senior management. Upper-floor guest rooms have better views and more amenities; those on the Pacific Floor have butler service and complimentary breakfast and cocktails. Your eatery options include the rooftop Chinese restaurant and the Japanese and Italian dining rooms. ✉ *7 Raffles Blvd., 039595,* ☎ *336–8111,* FAX *339–1861. 747 rooms, 37 suites. 4 restaurants, café, coffee shop, pool, 2 tennis courts, exercise room, playground, business services, meeting rooms. AE, DC, MC, V.*

\$\$\$ ▥ **The Regent.** A good 10-minute walk from Orchard and Scotts roads, the Regent appeals to those who want a quiet haven. Relaxed, comfortable public rooms are done in soft tones and decked out with Asian carpets and wood paneling. The clubby second-floor cocktail lounge, The Bar, is a peaceful refuge within this refuge. Rooms have pastel color schemes, big beds, writing desks, and marble bathrooms; some have balconies. The Tea Lounge serves, of course, high tea daily. Capers offers an alfresco setting for its international cuisine, the Summer Palace serves Cantonese cuisine prepared by Hong Kong chefs; and Maxim's de Paris has a belle epoque decor and French cuisine. (Travelers with disabilities take note: this hotel has amenities for you.) ✉ *1 Cuscaden Rd., 249715,* ☎ *733–8888,* FAX *732–8838. 393 rooms, 48 suites. 4 restaurants, bar, lobby lounge, pool, spa, business services. AE, DC, MC, V.*

\$\$\$ ▥ **Royal Crowne Plaza Singapore.** The lobby here makes a statement with Italian marble floors, two grand staircases, Burmese teak paneling, stained-glass skylights, and handwoven tapestries. Rooms were recently upgraded to the tune of S\$20 million, and there are facilities for travelers with disabilities. The Executive Club floor has a private lounge for complimentary breakfast and evening cocktails. Paolo & Ping's (☞ Chapter 3) is a fun, informal restaurant off the lobby. ✉ *25 Scotts Rd., 228220,* ☎ *737–7966,* FAX *737–6646. 495 rooms. 2 restaurants, bar, pool, exercise room, business services, travel services. AE, DC, MC, V.*

\$\$\$ ▥ **Singapore Marriott.** Formerly the Dynasty, this striking 33-story, pagoda-inspired property dominates Singapore's "million-dollar corner"—the Orchard and Scotts roads intersection. Before Marriott took over, the three-story lobby was done in rich, deep red—the Chinese color for good fortune—with 24 remarkable carved-teak wall panels. Such decoration has been replaced by light-color walls and fake palm trees. Rooms are Western in style, with light-gray carpets, pink vinyl wallpaper, pink-gray upholstery, and ample wood; there are amenities for people with disabilities. The hotel's location—rather than its character—is now its selling point, though it may be the only lodging in the country with an outdoor basketball court. The Crossroads Café is a great spot for people-watching. ✉ *320 Orchard Rd., 238865,* ☎ *735–5800,* FAX *735–9800. 364 rooms, 19 suites. 2 restaurants, café, coffee shop, pool, basketball, exercise room, nightclub, business services, meeting rooms. AE, DC, MC, V.*

$$$ ⊞ Westin Plaza and Westin Stamford. Catering to business executives, the Plaza is the smaller and higher-priced of these Raffles City twins; the 70-story Stamford, one of the tallest hotels in the world, attracts tours and conventions. These hotels are a hub of their own, with a dozen restaurants—of which the Compass Rose (☞ Chapter 3) is the highlight—more than 100 shops, and convention facilities (including the largest column-free meeting rooms in the world). All rooms have balconies, and the hotel can fulfill the needs of those with disabilities. The 29 Stamford Crest Suites are extremely well appointed with such amenities as a complimentary breakfast and minibar and a separate exercise room. ⊠ *2 Stamford Rd., 178882,* ☎ *339–6633,* FAX *336–5117. Stamford 1,263 rooms; Plaza 764 rooms, 29 suites. 12 restaurants, 2 pools, 6 tennis courts, health club, squash, dance club, business services, convention center, meeting rooms, travel services. AE, DC, MC, V.*

$$ ★ ⊞ Albert Court Hotel. Rare in Singapore are small hotels that have gone to the expense and effort of restoring existing structures (and installing facilities for people with disabilities). The Albert Court, which is only a few minutes' walk to Little India, is one. Furnishings are simple, but wood paneling creates a warm, comfortable atmosphere. The staff is enthusiastic, and this attitude infects the mostly European guests. You can relax and grab a bite at the small coffee shop, open from 7 AM to 11 PM. ⊠ *180 Albert St., 189971,* ☎ *339–3939,* FAX *339–3252. 135 rooms, 1 suite. Bar, coffee shop. AE, MC, V.*

$$ ⊞ Allson. This hotel's published rates are lower than those at similar hotels, such as the nearby Carlton. All rooms have rosewood furniture and little extras such as coffee- and tea makers and IDD phones. Rooms on the Excellence Floor are more expensive but more spacious. This hotel has a great location: it's near Raffles City Tower, Marina Square, the historic colonial district, Little India, Bugis Street, and the Arab District, and it's only a 10-minute subway or bus ride to Orchard Road. ⊠ *101 Victoria St., 188018,* ☎ *336–0811,* FAX *339–7019. 450 rooms. 3 restaurants, café, coffee shop, pool, business services. AE, DC, MC, V.*

$$ ⊞ Amara Hotel. At the south end of the business district, this 18-story hotel is convenient to the train station and the commercial and port facilities and is one of Singapore's better deals if you get a discount (usually available). Although the hotel itself lacks character, it's part of a vibrant shopping and entertainment complex and close to Chinatown's Tanjong Pagar. Rooms are warm, with pastel colors, large sofas, one king-size or two queen-size beds, and bedside remote-control panels. The Royal Club concierge floor has butler service. Don't miss the nightly S$22 poolside steamboat and barbecue buffet with more than 40 items. (Travelers with disabilities should consider a stay at this hotel.) ⊠ *165 Tanjong Pagar Rd., 088539,* ☎ *224–4488,* FAX *224–3910. 337 rooms. 2 restaurants, coffee shop, pool, 2 tennis courts, jogging, squash, nightclub, business services. AE, DC, MC, V.*

$$ ⊞ Apollo Singapore. Another business-traveler haven, this semicircular, 19-story hotel has relatively inexpensive, clean, and bright rooms. There are on-site Chinese, Indonesian, and Japanese restaurants; a coffee shop; and evening entertainment. The hotel is south of the Singapore River and west of Chinatown and the business district. A daytime shuttle bus runs hourly to Orchard Road. ⊠ *405 Havelock Rd., 169633,* ☎ *733–2081,* FAX *733–1588. 345 rooms. 3 restaurants, coffee shop, exercise room, dance club. AE, DC, MC, V.*

$$ ⊞ The Concorde. Once appropriately called the Glass Hotel, the Concorde has a glass canopy that curves down from the ninth story over the entrance, which faces southeast for good fortune. Decorated in autumn hues, rooms are modern and have standard amenities. A stay in one on the three executive floors gets you complimentary breakfast and cocktails. For dining and entertainment, head for the fourth floor, where there are French, Japanese, and Chinese restaurants; the Chinese restaurant frequently has floor shows. The hotel lies just south of the Singapore River and west of the business district. ⊠ *317 Outram Rd., 169075,* ☎ *733–0188,* FAX *733–0989. 515 rooms. 3 restaurants, pool, massage, sauna, steam room, exercise room, tennis court, business services, meeting rooms. AE, DC, MC, V.*

$$ 🏨 **Elizabeth Hotel.** Once the truly budget Queen's Hotel, this establishment in a quiet area off Orchard Road was expanded in 1997 and was given a new name and higher rates. Standard rooms are modest; those in the four-story deluxe wing have refrigerators. Travelers with disabilities will be comfortable here. ⊠ *24 Mt. Elizabeth, 228518,* ☎ *738–1188,* FAX *732–3866. 247 rooms. Restaurant, bar, coffee shop, pool, exercise room, business services, meeting rooms. AE, DC, MC, V.*

$$ 🏨 **Excelsior Hotel.** This central-city hotel is across the street from nearly 1,000 shops; close to its older sister, the Peninsula hotel; and a block from Raffles City. Guest rooms are reasonably large and well maintained and have IDD phones. Its popular Annalakshmi restaurant (☞ Chapter 3) serves vegetarian Indian fare, and there's a 24-hour café. ⊠ *5 Coleman St., 179805,* ☎ *338–7733,* FAX *339–3847. 266 rooms, 5 suites. 3 restaurants, bar, pool, travel services. AE, DC, MC, V.*

$$ 🏨 **Furama Hotel.** This modern curvilinear building, on the doorstep of Chinatown and a 10-minute walk from the commercial district, stands out amid the surrounding shophouses. Tour groups and Japanese businessmen call this place home. The helpful staff will direct you to interesting sights, and there are daily guided walking tours through Chinatown. After hoofing it around, you can rest in the popular poolside café. ⊠ *10 Eu Tong Sen St., 059804,* ☎ *533–3888,* FAX *534–1489. 356 rooms. 2 restaurants, bar, café, pool, beauty salon, sauna, steam room, business services, meeting rooms. AE, DC, MC, V.*

$$ 🏨 **Harbour View Dai Ichi.** If you want to be away from all the hurly-burly but still still near the business district, this 29-story hotel will be perfect for you. Rooms are small, neat, and functional; two are in Japanese tatami style (most of the clientele is from Japan), and the hotel's main restaurant is the Kuramaya. There's also a Continental restaurant. ⊠ *81 Anson Rd., 079908,* ☎ *224–1133,* FAX *222–0749. 416 rooms. 2 restaurants, coffee shop, pool, massage, sauna, exercise room, business services. AE, DC, MC, V.*

$$ 🏨 **Le Meridien Changi.** Aside from its location 10 minutes from the airport, this hotel has no particular merits, except for golfers. Some rooms are designed for the physically challenged. ⊠ *1 Netheravon Rd., 508502,* ☎ *542–7700,* FAX *542–5295. 280 rooms. Restaurant, coffee shop, pool, golf privileges, exercise room, bicycles, baby-sitting, business services. AE, DC, MC, V.*

$$ 🏨 **Peninsula Hotel.** Near the Padang and between the fashionable Orchard Road and commercial district areas, this hotel offers the basic creature comforts. The lobby is small and nondescript. The fairly spacious guest rooms are clean, and those on the 17th floor and up have good views. There's no on-site restaurant, but a coffee shop serves the basics, and there are several reasonably priced restaurants nearby. ⊠ *3 Coleman St., 179804,* ☎ *337–2200,* FAX *339–3847. 299 rooms, 8 suites. Coffee shop, in-room safes, minibars, room service, pool, exercise room, nightclub. AE, DC, MC, V.*

$$ 🏨 **Plaza Hotel.** The rooms in this Little Araby hotel include IDD phones, coffee- and tea makers, and sensor-touch bedside control panels. Service is friendly, though a bit laid-back. The three on-site restaurants offer Cantonese and Thai cuisine, Western and regional fare, and spicy Oriental-style steaks. With a full house, the hotel can be quite lively. There's entertainment in the evenings; if you want to be the evening's entertainment, check out the 18-room Singsation karaoke club. ⊠ *7500A Beach Rd., 199591,* ☎ *298–0011,* ℻ *296–3600. 350 rooms. 2 restaurants, 2 bars, refrigerators, pool, steam room, exercise room, business services. AE, DC, MC, V.*

$$ 🏨 **Rasa Sentosa.** A vast, arc-shape building facing the sea, this Sentosa Island resort getaway is popular with both conventions and Singaporean families escaping to the beach for the weekend (room rates are lower during the week). The motel-like rooms are small though all have balconies; ask for a room facing the water, otherwise your view will merely be of a grassy knoll. The main restaurant serves Cantonese fare, and the café dishes up Western and Asian food. Children love this place for its pool with water slides, its playground, its nursery, and its video-games room. Adults appreciate the many recreational activities, including rock-wall climbing, golf, and windsurfing. Travelers with disabilities will find that the hotel caters to their needs as well. You can get to the island on a free shuttle bus from the Shangri-La hotel, which owns this resort. ⊠ *101 Siloso Rd., Sentosa Island 098970,* ☎ *275– 0100; 0181/747–8485 (reservations in the U.K.); 800/942–5050 (reservations in Canada and the U.S.),* ℻ *275–0355. 459 rooms. 3 restaurants, bar, lobby lounge, pool, massage, health club, Ping-Pong, windsurfing, boating, recreation room, video games, nursery, playground. AE, DC, MC, V.*

$$ 🏨 **Seaview Hotel.** Off the East Coast Parkway, midway between Changi Airport and Singapore city, this high-rise hotel is more convenient for travelers in transit than for those here to see the sights. Guest rooms offer the basic amenities, and there are restaurants and shops on the premises and in the area. The nearby East Coast Park offers many outdoor activities, including water-sports facilities. ⊠ *26 Amber Close, 439984,* ☎ *345–2222,* ℻ *345–1741. 435 rooms. 2 restaurants, bar, coffee shop, room service, pool, nightclub. AE, DC, MC, V.*

$$ 🏨 **Traders Hotel.** For value (try to take advantage of the frequent pro-
★ motional rates) and service, this hotel is hard to beat. It has all the necessary comforts—including those for travelers with disabilities—but no frills. There's only one coffee shop for dining and no fancy room service, but scores of restaurants and a supermarket are just steps away; the Orchard Road area is also nearby. Rooms are comfortable, with writing desks and plenty of light from the bay windows. There are spacious gardens and a pool. ⊠ *1A Cuscaden Rd., 249716,* ☎ *738–2222; 0181/ 747–8485 (reservations in the U.K.); 800/942–5050 (reservations in Canada; the U.S.),* ℻ *831–4314. 543 rooms. Coffee shop, pool, exercise room, business services, meeting rooms. AE, DC, MC, V.*

$$ 🏨 **York Hotel.** Near busy Orchard Road, this classic European hotel is a quiet oasis. The tower has only suites, and the poolside wing has split-level cabanas and rooms surrounding a garden. All guest quarters have two queen-size beds. The White Rose Cafe serves Asian and Western fare. ⊠ *21 Mt. Elizabeth, 228516,* ☎ *737–0511,* ℻ *732– 1217. 335 rooms, 69 suites. 2 restaurants, bar, pool, beauty salon, sauna, exercise room. AE, DC, MC, V.*

$ 🏨 **Hotel Royal.** This modest hotel has the standard amenities and in-room IDD phones. On the premises is an international forwarding service that can be useful for anyone—especially shoppers—who wishes to send excess baggage back home. The hotel is near Newton Circus and a 20-minute walk from Orchard Road. ⊠ *36 Newton Rd., 307964,* ☎ *253–4411,* ℻ *253–8668. 331 rooms. 3 restaurants, coffee shop, minibars, refrigerators, pool, meeting rooms, travel services. AE, DC, MC, V.*

$ 🏨 **Inn at Temple Street.** One of the latest additions to Chinatown's unique
★ boutique hotel scene, the Inn at Temple Street opened in early 1998 and occupies five beautifully restored shophouses. The attractive Per-

anakan decor—a fusion of 19th-century European, Chinese, and Malay furnishings and color schemes—reminds you of the neighborhood's rich cultural traditions. Ask for a room with a view of the street below, which is slated to become a pedestrian mall. ⊠ *36 Temple St., 058581,* ☎ *221–5333,* FAX *225–5391. 42 rooms. Coffee shop, bar, in-room safes, refrigerators. AE, DC, MC, V.*

$ 🛏 **Metropole Hotel.** This very modest, very basic hotel near Raffles City has simply furnished rooms. Rare in budget lodgings, you'll find both a helpful staff and room service. ⊠ *41 Seah St., 188396,* ☎ *336–3611,* FAX *339–3610. 54 rooms. Restaurant, coffee shop, room service. AE, DC, MC, V.*

$ 🛏 **Metropolitan YMCA, Tanglin Centre.** A 10-minute walk to Orchard Road, this YMCA (which admits women) has rooms with air-conditioning and private baths. There are even a few suites. The budget restaurant offers wholesome English breakfasts, as well as Chinese, Malay, Nonya, and Western meals. ⊠ *Tanglin Centre, 60 Stevens Rd., 257854,* ☎ *737–7755,* FAX *235–5528. 93 rooms. Coffee shop, pool, exercise room, meeting rooms. AE, DC, MC, V.*

$ 🛏 **Regalis Court.** This charming, 43-room, boutique hotel—which
★ opened in mid-1997—once housed the Singapore Ballet Academy of British colonial days. The rooms have a Peranakan-inspired decor (earth tones, reds, and browns) with classical European touches and such novel items as reproductions of clunky black telephones and old alarm clocks. You can open your windows (be sure to ask for a room that has them) to the quiet residential neighborhood, and a Continental breakfast is included in the room rate. Only a few minutes' walk to Orchard Road, the hotel is not well known and attracts savvy independent travelers from around the globe. Check out the Indonesian Rajah Inn (☞ Chapter 3) restaurant for inexpensive, tasty dishes. ⊠ *64 Lloyd Rd., 239113,* ☎ *734–7117,* FAX *736–1651. 43 rooms. Restaurant, breakfast room, in-room safes, no-smoking rooms. AE, DC, MC, V.*

$ 🛏 **RELC International Hotel.** This is less a hotel than an international
★ conference center often used by Singapore's university for seminars. However, the upper floors contain bargain guest rooms that are large and basically comfortable and have plenty of light. The building is in a residential neighborhood, up a hill beyond the Shangri-La hotel, a 10-minute walk to the Orchard and Scotts roads intersection. Because of its good value, it's often booked, so reservations well in advance are strongly advised. Breakfast is included, and there are coffeemakers in the rooms. ⊠ *30 Orange Grove Rd., 258352,* ☎ *737–9044,* FAX *733–9976. 128 rooms. Coffee shop, coin laundry. AE, DC, MC, V.*

$ 🛏 **Royal Peacock.** Living up to its name, this brightly painted shop-house boutique hotel opened in 1997 on the once notorious Keong Saik Road (it was known for its red lanterns and ladies of the night, who are still here but are in state-controlled brothels). The standard rooms don't have windows, so ask for a deal on a superior or deluxe room (listed at S$180). Breakfast and coffee and tea fixings are included in all prices. The hotel is within the central business district in Chinatown, and it has facilities for travelers with disabilities. ⊠ *55 Keong Saik Rd., 089518,* ☎ *223–3522,* FAX *221–1770. 76 rooms. Bar, café, minibars, business services. AE, DC, MC, V.*

$ 🛏 **Transit Hotel.** At last: a lodging truly geared to bleary-eyed travelers en route to still another destination. This new hotel is *inside* Changi

Airport on Level 3 of the departure lounge in Terminal 1. (Note: if you stay here, you don't go through immigration control.) Rooms are clean, fresh, and basic. Rates are for six-hour periods—a double is S$56—and include use of the swimming pool, sauna, and fitness center. Nonguests may also use the pool (S$10), the sauna and showers (S$10), or just the shower (S$5). ⊠ *Terminal 1, Changi Airport,* ☎ *543–0911; 0800/96–3562 (reservations in the U.K.); 800/690–6785 (reservations in the U.S.),* ☏ *545–8365. Pool, sauna, health club, nursery. AE, DC, MC, V.*

$ ☷ **YMCA International House.** This well-run YMCA at the bottom of Orchard Road offers hotel-like accommodations for men and women—with double (S$105) and single (S$90) rooms—as well as dormitory-style quarters (S$25); S$5 will buy you temporary YMCA membership. All rooms have private baths, color TVs, and IDD phones. In addition to an impressive gym, you'll find a rooftop pool and squash and badminton courts. There's also a McDonald's at the entrance. ⊠ *1 Orchard Rd., 238824,* ☎ *336–6000,* ☏ *337–3140. 111 rooms. Pool, exercise room, squash. AE, DC, MC, V.*

Bintan Island, Indonesia

Bintan's resorts dot wide sandy beaches on the northern coast. Each hotel has a wide range of restaurants, bars, and other facilities. Since there are really only six establishments (the hotels in Tanjung Pinang, the island's main city, are substandard), book as far in advance as possible. On weekends Singaporeans and expats take full advantage of the island's clean waters, just 45 minutes from one of the world's busiest ports.

The resorts accept Singapore dollars for rooms and for meals (price categories assigned below are based on Singapore dollars), though credit card purchases for other items may be charged in Indonesian rupiahs at, no doubt, a better rate of exchange. The newest resorts, such as Club Med and Sol Elite Bintan, have been offering promotional specials, so always ask about discounts when booking. All resorts have their marketing offices in Singapore, and it's best to make reservations before arriving on Bintan; for more information contact **Bintan Resort Management** (☎ 543–0039). If, for some reason, you need to dial an establishment directly, the country code for Indonesia is 62, and the area code for Bintan is 771.

At press time, plans for shuttle bus service between the resorts were afoot. If, however, you have to rely on a taxi to get around, you must book it in advance from a car rental agency at the ferry terminal. Ask the front desk staff of your hotel to help with the arrangements. Although most people come here to relax or frolic in a beach resort environment, consider taking a guided day trip outside of your resort; it will definitely enhance your Indonesian experience (☞ Tour Operators *in* the Gold Guide section).

$$$$ ☷ **Banyan Tree Bintan.** You'll find romance, luxury, and top-notch ser-
★ vice during a stay here. Accommodations are in private, Balinese-style villas that stand on stilts and overlook a horseshoe-shape bay. Fifty-five villas have a whirlpool tub on a deck that faces the South China Sea. The more luxurious Pool Villas also have either a private swimming pool or plunge pool, two bedrooms with king-size beds, a bathroom with a sunken bath, a spacious dressing room, and a kitchen

(though you can make your own meals, most people just ask for a staff chef to drop by and whip up a special meal or two; there's no grocery store nearby). Rooms have green and brown color schemes, Indonesian pottery, elevated beds that are draped with mosquito netting, and sea views—truly idyllic. ⊠ *Site A4, Lagoi, Tanjong Said,* ☎ *462–4800 (in Singapore) or 771/26918 (in Bintan),* FAX *462–2800 (in Singapore) or 771/81348 (in Bintan). 74 villas. 2 restaurants, 2 pools, outdoor hot tub, spa, 18-hole golf course, 2 tennis courts, beach, dive shop, dock, snorkeling, windsurfing, fishing, meeting rooms. AE, MC, V.*

$$$ 🏨 **Club Med Ria Bintan.** This resort opened in late 1997 with all the amenities of a luxury Club Med, including many, many water and land activities—there's even a circus school for children, complete with a trapeze that gives parents heart palpitations. The resort is popular with Europeans, Japanese families, and Club Med junkies from around the world, so its staff members are multilingual. You might feel as if you're on the French Riviera: there are numerous chaises longues around the pools and on the private beach; the TV in your room has French satellite television; and wines served at meals are distinctly French. Among the facilities are an excellent children's activity center and a well-equipped exercise room and spa. The general feeling here is that you never need to leave the resort for anything; everything is terribly well organized (great if you want to be involved, not so great if you're seeking solitude). The comfortable rooms have balconies (the sunset views are terrific) and well-equipped baths. ⊠ *North coast,* ☎ *738–4222 (in Singapore),* FAX *738–0770 (in Singapore). 307 rooms. 4 restaurants, bar, 2 pools, spa, 2 tennis courts, aerobics, archery, health club, beach, water slide, cabaret, dance club, baby-sitting, children's programs, nursery, playground, coin laundry, meeting rooms. AE, MC, V. FAP.*

$$–$$$ 🏨 **Hotel Sedona.** Japanese visitors and locals alike are drawn to this enormous villa complex. Amenities include two pools—one of them *very* large—water-sports facilities, a spa, a mah-jongg hall, tennis, golf, karaoke, and a children's center. Although right next to the beach, this hotel isn't as aesthetically appealing or relaxed as some of the other resorts. Still, it *is* a golfer's paradise with two 18-hole courses—one designed by Jack Nicklaus, the other by Ian Baker-Finch—that have driving ranges and putting greens. The stunning view of the Nicklaus course from the golf club's alfresco café is itself inspiring. The rest of the grounds are equally well landscaped; you can rent a bicycle for an hour or two and take a tour of them. Rooms and suites are clean and well kept, if a bit stark in their furnishings; the Sedona Club Suites have huge balconies and sunken tubs. You won't lack for a place to eat: there are seven on-site restaurants that offer a variety of cuisines. ⊠ *Pasir Panjang Beach, north coast,* ☎ *223–3223 (in Singapore) or 771/91388 (in Bintan),* FAX *421–7878 (in Singapore) or 771/91399 (in Bintan). 401 rooms, 15 suites. 7 restaurants, 2 pools, massage, spa, 2 driving ranges, 2 18-hole golf courses, 2 putting greens, 4 tennis courts, health club, Ping-Pong, volleyball, beach, snorkeling, water slide, windsurfing, jet skiing, fishing, bicycles, billiards, dance club, video games, baby-sitting, children's programs, playground, laundry service, business services, meeting rooms, travel services. AE, DC, MC, V.*

$$ 🏨 **Sol Elite Bintan.** Another new addition to Bintan's north coast is the sprawling Sol Elite, one of the Spanish-run Sol Melia properties. Rooms are bright, clean, and relatively spacious; those facing the sea have balconies. For about S$100 more a night, you can stay in one of the two- to four-bedroom villas. The public areas are well maintained and cheery; the buildings are painted in dazzling primary colors. To get away from it all, head for the beach; most guests opt for the pool area so it's often deserted. Organized activities include staff-led lawn games and instruction on how to properly open a coconut. Buffet breakfast in El Patio coffee shop is included in the rates, and the lively Cantores Karaoke Lounge is one of Bintan's few nightspots. ⊠ *Nirwana Gardens,* ☎ *334– 3332 (in Singapore) or 771/311–798 (in Bintan),* FAX *334–2065 (in Singapore). 245 rooms, 14 villas. 2 restaurants, 2 bars, pool, croquet, volleyball, beach, snorkeling, nightclub, video games, playground, business services, meeting rooms, travel services. AE, DC, MC, V. BP.*

$–$$ 🏨 **Mayang Sari.** Set on a bay with an exquisite palm-lined beach, the relaxed, friendly Mayang Sari is a quiet retreat—the perfect place to read a novel or go beachcombing. The chalet-style cabins have high ceilings, Indonesian teak furnishings, large beds, and private verandas. This, Bintan's first resort property, is reminiscent of what Bali might have been like in the 1960s: tall palm trees lining the beach, friendly service, decent prices, gentle breezes. The on-site Mayang Terrace restaurant serves delicious Indonesian dishes at affordable prices. The gift shop seems to have sporadic opening hours, but again, the price of the goods makes it worth checking out. ⊠ *Northwest coast at Tanjong Tondang,* ☎ *732–8515 (in Singapore) or 771/92580 (in Bintan),* FAX *732–3959 (in Singapore) or 771/92576 (in Bintan). 56 beach and garden cabins. Restaurant, 2 bars, beach, recreation room, baby-sitting, laundry service, meeting room. AE, MC, V.*

$ 🏨 **Mana Mana.** College students and other young Europeans and Australians flock to this resort because of its affordable rates; water-sports enthusiasts of all ages are drawn by the facilities at its beach club. Accommodations are in small, no-smoking huts with TVs and baths (shower only). Most of the cabins are in a garden setting; only the lobby and alfresco restaurant-bar front the beach. The on-site gift shop stocks souvenirs, clothing, knapsacks, and jewelry, but the prices are on the high side. ⊠ *North coast,* ☎ *346–1984 (in Singapore),* FAX *440– 3132 (in Singapore). 50 rooms in 25 huts. Restaurant, bar, beach, snorkeling, windsurfing, boating. AE, MC, V.*

5 Nightlife and the Arts

Risqué nightlife is a thing of the past in Singapore. Now it's good, clean fun in new areas for managed frivolity. Jazz bars, state-of-the-art discos, and nightclubs abound, along with a symphony orchestra and dance and theater troupes. Whatever your tastes, you'll find plenty of choices.

EATING OUT ONCE CONSUMED so much of Singapore-ans' time and money that there were few other forms of entertainment. Now, entering a new century and relatively unfazed by the Southeast Asian economic crisis of the late '90s, the city just keeps adding activities to keep its mostly under-30 population entertained. The Singapore Tourism Board (☞ Visitor Information *in* the Gold Guide section) has monthly listings of events. You can also find schedules for major performances in the local English-language newspaper, the *Straits Times,* or in the free weeklies *I.S.* and *This Week Singapore,* available at most hotel reception desks.

Tickets to events are available at box offices or through **SISTIC,** a ticketing service that operates Monday–Saturday 10–10 and Sunday and holidays noon–10. There are offices at Scotts Shopping Centre, Raffles City, Specialists Centre, Suntec City Mall, Parco Bugis Junction, and Takashimaya (☞ Chapter 7). You can also call the company's hot line (☎ 348–5555) and reserve tickets for a S$3 service charge.

NIGHTLIFE

Several areas of town come alive at night. Bugis Street, once a bawdy area, has been sanitized with boutique shopping, cafés, bars, and the only air-conditioned outdoor mall in Asia. More authentic is Chinatown's Tanjong Pagar, where shophouses have been turned into hotels, stores, restaurants, teahouses, and bars. On the Singapore River, you'll find similar offerings in former godowns and shophouses at Clarke Quay and Robertson Quay. Wet your whistle with a beer or a glass of wine on a tongkang before taking a walk along Boat Quay, which was developed with less stringent government supervision. Here you can enjoy the natural flavor of Singapore with an interesting mix of reasonably priced restaurants and bars. Though not very lively, Chinatown's Duxton Hill does have two or three jazz bars.

Trendy, glitzy music and dance clubs that have everything from jazz to disco are popular with the young and the restless. The distinction between a disco and a place with live music and a dance floor has become blurred; one thing both places share is a decibel level that allows for only snatches of conversation. You'll also usually find a cover charge or a "first-drink" charge (cover plus one free drink) of about S$15 weeknights and S$25 weekends. Certain places allow women in for free or at a reduced rate.

Older Singaporeans often prefer nightclubs with floor shows and hostesses, also called "public relations officers" or PROs. Depending on the establishment, "booking the hostess" requires either a flat hourly fee or a gratuity at the end of the evening. (Be forewarned that some hostesses may be prostitutes with their *mamasans,* or madams, urging them to go after your wallet.) It's also common practice to buy a bottle of brandy (for as much as S$300), which some consider a high-status drink (whereas whiskey is "bad smelling and shows poor taste"). You are under no obligation to select a hostess or buy a bottle of brandy, however.

The truly risqué disappeared long ago from Singapore. Prostitution is legal only in certain areas, such as parts of Geylang, which has red-light districts. Brothels are numbered with large, backlit signs, and some hotels rent rooms in two-hour time slots. With typical Singaporean efficiency, prostitutes are registered and are subject to regular medical checks.

Bars and Pubs

Brewerkz. Beer lovers need look no farther than this large pub on Riverside Point, across from the restaurants and shops of Clarke Quay. Brewmaster Scott Robinson offers seven ales and bitters (the most popular is the India Pale Ale) and chef James Chew serves an eclectic selection of Eastern and Western favorites (the kitchen is open from noon to midnight). The best buy is the set lunch menu (about S$15); unbelievably for Singapore, the price includes two glasses of beer and coffee or tea. Check out the Cigar Divan Room, and the large interior room, which rebroadcasts NFL and NBA games. ⊠ *No. 01-05/06 Riverside Point, 30 Merchant Rd.,* ☎ *438–7438.* ⊘ *Sun.–Thurs. noon–1 AM; Fri.–Sat. noon–3 AM.*

Father Flanagan's. This Irish pub in the Chijmes complex gets its fair share of homesick Dubliners, but the good pub grub and variety of brews make it popular with the local business crowd, too. ⊠ *Chijmes complex (lower level), 30 Victoria St.,* ☎ *333–1418.* ⊘ *Sun.–Tues. noon to midnight; Wed.–Thurs. noon–1 AM; Fri.–Sat. noon–2 AM.*

Hard Rock Cafe. Hamburgers and light fare are served at this pub-café, and a live band plays in the evenings. It's much like other establishments in the chain, with a casual, festive, atmosphere; plenty of rock memorabilia; a bar; booth tables; pool tables; and souvenir shops so you can get your Hard Rock Singapore T-shirt. ⊠ *No. 02–01 HPL House, 50 Cuscaden Rd.,* ☎ *235–5232.* ☒ *On evenings with live bands: 1st drink S$12.* ⊘ *Weekdays 11 AM–2 AM, weekends 11 AM–3 AM.*

Ice Cold Beer. Expats tend to gather at this lively pub on a small pedestrian street off Orchard Road. Beers from around the world dominate, ranging from S$5 specials to S$14 a pop, and good hot dogs are available for S$5. There's never a cover charge; the music tends to be rock from the '70s and '80s. Happy hour is from 5 to 9 Monday through Saturday; it turns into "happy day" on Sunday. ⊠ *5 Emerald Hill Rd.,* ☎ *735–9929.* ⊘ *Daily 5 PM–2 AM.*

Moods. This pub attracts a local university crowd, even though it's in the heart of the Orchard and Scotts roads' shopping area, behind the Royal Crowne Plaza Hotel. It's a good place to stop when you're tired of seeing all those other tourists and expats. ⊠ *No. 01-02 Scotts Walk, 25 Scotts Rd.,* ☎ *734–8098.* ⊘ *Nightly 5 PM–1 AM.*

Muddy Murphy's. A longtime favorite, due to its wine and cheese promotions, weekly Sunday brunches, and excellent Irish bands, "Muddy's" is in the heart of the shopping belt. Here's a place to wind down when your feet won't take you any farther. ⊠ *No. B1-01/06 Orchard Hotel Shopping Arcade, 442 Orchard Rd.,* ☎ *735–0400.* ⊘ *Mon.–Sat. 8 PM–1 AM; Sun. 3 PM–1 AM.*

Pop Cat. A pub with a difference: this is 1950s kitsch, Chinatown style. Wacky theme bashes, such as "Squirt" (a water pistol shootout), are regular events. The music is eclectic—anything from Japanese pop to jazz to cutting edge. Creative and entertainment types tend to hang out here. ⊠ *42/42A Pagoda St.,* ☎ *226–6229.* ⊘ *Weekdays 11 AM–midnight; Sat. 11 AM–1 AM.*

Que Pasa. For wine lovers, this friendly pub is a sure bet. Small and intimate, it has a mix of local and expat twenty- to thirtysomething customers. ⊠ *7 Emerald Hill Rd.,* ☎ *235–6626.* ⊘ *Nightly 5 PM–2 AM.*

Riverbank Restaurant & Pub. This riverside terrace is a great place to start your evening. Wander in here, watch others as they wander around Boat Quay, and then wander on out for some casual barhopping. ⊠ *Boat Quay,* ☎ *538–1135.* ⊘ *Nightly 6 PM–2 AM.*

Wild West Tavern. One of Clarke Quay's plethora of restaurants and bars, this is less pricey than most and quite appealing for a beer and a chat. As the name may imply, expect an authentic Hollywood-style saloon—but without the cowboys. ✉ *12 Clarke Quay,* ☎ *334–4180.* ⊙ *Nightly 4 PM–midnight.*

Comedy Club

Boom Boom Room. Two years ago, you wouldn't find the delightful unsavoriness of old Bugis Street here, but this comedy house has gotten a bit more daring in its twice-nightly shows. A basic knowledge of the local "Singlish" would certainly help in understanding many of the jokes. Be prepared for cross-dressing and jibes aimed at individuals in the audience. A DJ spins disks between shows. ✉ *Bugis Village,* ☎ *339–8187.* ✏ *S$15 and up.* ⊙ *Tues.–Sun. 8 PM–2 AM.*

Discos and Dance Clubs

Caesars. The decor and the waitresses clad in lissome togas give this disco an air of decadent splendor. DJ-spun music plus imported live bands make it a hot venue for entertainment. ✉ *No. 02–04 Orchard Towers (front block), 400 Orchard Rd.,* ☎ *235–2840.* ✏ *1st drink Sun.–Thurs. S$15, Fri.–Sat. S$24.* ⊙ *Sun.–Thurs. 8 PM–2 AM; Fri.–Sat. 8 PM–3 AM.*

Europa Music Bar. It's easy to have fun at this busy club where young Singaporeans let down their hair. There are stage shows as well as contests and prizes for the serious drinking crowd. ✉ *No. B1–00 International Building, 360 Orchard Rd.,* ☎ *235–3301.* ✏ *Cover charges vary.* ⊙ *Weeknights 6 PM–1 AM, weekends 6 PM–2 AM.*

Fire. One of Singapore's steady favorites, Fire has live music danced to by a lively (very young and local) crowd. Drinks are paid for by coupons, so work out the cost before making the purchase. Upstairs, would-be artists sing their lungs out in 12 computerized karaoke rooms. ✉ *No. 04-19 Orchard Plaza, 150 Orchard Rd.,* ☎ *235–0155.* ⊙ *Nightly 9 PM–2 AM.*

Heaven. Opened in 1998, Heaven should be around for a while, owing to the good reputation of its sister club in Kuala Lumpur. Although not as mammoth as Zouk or Venom (☞ *below*), Heaven's clever interiors, VIP Lounge, and varied mix of tourists and locals almost ensure its success. Women (who must be 21 to enter) don't pay a cover charge, and they receive two free drinks after 10:30 PM on Tuesday and Thursday; men have to pay a first-drink charge and must be at least 23 to get in. The music ranges from soul to "garage" to "happy house." ✉ *No. 01-01A Orchard Parade Hotel, 1 Tanglin Rd.,* ☎ *732–7808.* ✏ *1st drink S$18, S$25 on weekends.* ⊙ *Nightly 8 PM–3 AM.*

The Jump. By day, it's a Tex-Mex American style restaurant; at night, it turns into a busy disco featuring retro tunes for the over-25 set. (Your ID may be checked to make sure you fall into this age bracket.) The long lines and ubiquitous cover charges don't deter the yuppies who frequent this spot. ✉ *Chijmes complex (interior courtyard), 30 Victoria St.,* ☎ *338–9388.* ✏ *Fri.–Sat. S$20 men, S$15 women.* ⊙ *Sun.–Wed. noon–1 AM; Thurs.–Sat. noon–3 AM.*

Neo Pharoahs. Housed in a quaint, three-story shophouse, this dance club is more personal than the larger, warehouse-style discos. The third-floor main dance hall has British house music; the ground and second floors have a combination of acid jazz, R&B, and '70s and '80s funk. The place attracts a mix of expats and locals, mostly in their mid-20s to mid-40s. ✉ *56 Cairnhill Rd.,* ☎ *736–3098.* ✏ *Cover charges vary.* ⊙ *Weeknights 8 PM–1 AM, weekends 8 PM–2 AM.*

Pleasure Dome. Upscale and expensive with decent live bands, private rooms, and a Members' Lounge, this club is always busy with the young and well-to-do. The adjoining wine and cigar bar, **Le Château,** is great place to chill when the crowd gets too noisy. The cover charge varies, but expect to pay at least S$20, and don't bother going if you're under 25. ⊠ *No. B1-02 Specialists Shopping Centre, 277 Orchard Rd.,* ☎ *834–1221.* ⊘ *Weeknights 6 PM–1 AM, weekends 6 PM–2 AM.*

Sparks. An offshoot of the popular Fire disco, this club has karaoke rooms, live music, and laser shows. It's on the seventh floor of the upscale Takashimaya where, so it would seem, the revelers have just made purchases. Foreign dance bands often stop here for one-night shows. ⊠ *Ngee Ann City, Tower B, Level 7,* ☎ *735–6133.* ☎ *Cover charges vary, but start at S$12 weeknights and S$20 weekends.* ⊘ *Mon.– Sat. 8 PM–2 AM.*

Venom. This lavish, 10,000-square-ft penthouse disco used to be Studebaker's, and it reopened in 1998 to rave reviews after a S$1.4-million renovation. All the praise must have gone to the staff's collective head, as attitude reigns supreme here. Security guards, cell phones in hand, try to give the impression celebrities are always in the house. Don't bother coming unless you're decked out in the latest Italian designer fashions. ⊠ *Pacific Plaza Penthouse, 12th floor, 9 Scotts Rd.,* ☎ *734– 7677.* ☎ *S$20 weeknights, S$25 Fri.–Sat. and eve of public holidays.* ⊘ *Tues.–Sun. 6 PM–2 AM.*

Zouk, Velvet Underground, and Phuture. You'll need a taxi to get here and back, but every cabbie knows where it is. A huge dance emporium that's remained open for more than two years, Zouk is an institution of sorts. Sprawling and mammoth, it's really three clubs in one: a younger set flocks to Zouk itself; a more sophisticated crowd fills Velvet, the place for true disco divas; and experimental music lovers head for Phuture. Visiting DJs from around the world serve as hosts, and the club consistently gets rave reviews from pop culture critics in the United Kingdom. When the lights come up at 3 AM, the crowd swiftly disappears into the dozens of waiting taxis outside. ⊠ *17 Jiak Kim St.,* ☎ *738–2988.* ☎ *Men S$28–S$35, women S$20–S$25; cover includes 2 drinks.* ⊘ *Wed.–Sun. 6 PM–3 AM.*

Music Clubs

Jazz

Bar & Billiard Room. Light acoustic jazz is offered from Monday through Saturday in Singapore's best known hotel. There's no cover charge. ⊠ *Raffles Hotel, 1 Beach Rd.,* ☎ *331–1746.* ⊘ *Daily 11:30 AM–12:30 AM; live music begins at 8:30 PM.*

The Bar at the Regent. Jazz duos and trios often perform at this Four Seasons Hotel sister property. Your only cost will be your bar tab. ⊠ *The Regent Singapore, 1 Cuscaden Rd.,* ☎ *733–8888.* ⊘ *Daily 4 PM–1 AM.*

Harry's Quayside. This is a comfortable place to hang out and listen to a mix of jazz, blues, and old-time rock. Occasionally the live band, which starts performing at around 9:30 PM, gets carried away and turns the show into a good old-fashioned jam session. Food is served upstairs, and there are fine waterfront views. ⊠ *28 Boat Quay,* ☎ *538– 3029.* ⊘ *Sun.–Thurs. 11 AM–midnight; Fri.–Sat. 11 AM–2 AM.*

Saxophone. At this club, which has both jazz and popular rock, the volume is loud and the space is compact (read: standing room only). However, there's a terrace outside where you can sit and still hear the music. Saxophone was a pioneer of the Singapore jazz scene, and the customers keep coming, so the sound must be right. ⊠ *23 Cuppage Terr.,* ☎ *235–8385.* ⊘ *Tues.–Sun. 6–1.*

Somerset Bar. The jazz and contemporary music played here has attracted a loyal following. With a larger space than the Saxophone, it offers room to sit and relax, making it popular with an older crowd. There's a happy hour from 5 PM to 7 PM nightly. ⊠ *Westin Plaza (3rd* *floor), 4 Stamford Rd., ☎ 338–8585. ۞ Nightly 5 PM–2 AM; music starts around 9 PM.*

Rock

Anywhere. Crowds gather, especially on weekends, in this smoke-filled room to hear decent live music. If you're in your forties and divorced, you'll feel at home. ⊠ *No. 04–08 Tanglin Shopping Centre, 19 Tanglin Rd., ☎ 734–8233. ☜ 1st drink: Sun.–Thurs. S$12, Fri.–Sat. S$18. ۞ Sun.–Thurs. 8 PM–2 AM; Fri.–Sat. 8 PM–3 AM.*

Crazy Elephant. Billed as Singapore's "only rock-and-roll blues bar," jam sessions are held every here Sunday, and a live band appears every night except Monday. Cover charges vary. ⊠ *No. 01-07 Clarke Quay, ☎ 337–1990. ۞ Weeknights 5 PM–1 AM, weekends 5 PM–2 AM.*

Roomful of Blues. Blues lovers and local musicians flock to this club—really a combination café and high-tech studio—in a neighborhood northeast of the city. The music is eclectic ('70s funk, rock, R&B, punk, heavy metal), and local bands play on Saturday nights. Dress is very casual. ⊠ *Macpherson Rd., ☎ 289–6718. ۞ Daily 10 AM–midnight.*

World Music

Fabrice's World Music Bar. Hopping, busy, crowded—this bar is true to its name, with live Latin, African, European, and American music. It opens in the evening with "early sessions"; the wilder music and raucous crowds fill the room later in the night. Cover charges vary. ⊠ *Marriott Hotel (basement level), 320 Orchard Rd., ☎ 738–8887. ۞ Nightly 8 PM–2 AM.*

Nightclubs

Apollo Theatre Restaurant and Nightclub. This club is very popular with Chinese businessmen, who come here to be entertained by a steady stream of Chinese singers and hostesses and to enjoy the Hunanese cuisine. ⊠ *Apollo Singapore Hotel, 405 Havelock Rd., 17th floor, ☎ 235–7977. ☜ Brandy S$270; hourly hostess fee S$25. ۞ Nightly 8 PM–2 AM.*

Lido Palace Niteclub. Promoting itself as the "palace of many pleasures," this lavish establishment offers Chinese cabaret, a band, a DJ-spun disco, hostesses, karaoke, and—for those who wish to dine—Cantonese cuisine. ⊠ *Concorde Hotel, 317 Outram Rd., 5th floor, ☎ 732–8855. ☜ 1st drink S$30. ۞ Nightly 9 PM–3 AM; shows at 9:30 and 12:30.*

Neptune. At this sumptuous two-story club, designed as an Oriental pavilion, you can dine on Cantonese food or take a seat in the gallery for nondiners. Local, Taiwanese, and Filipino singers entertain in English and Chinese; occasionally a European dance troupe is added to the lineup. For the most fun, go with a group. The club is operated by the Mandarin Hotel, so call ahead to be sure it's not already booked for private functions. (It's also the only nightclub in Singapore that has a license allowing it to feature the occasional topless cabaret show.) ⊠ *Overseas Union House, 7th floor, Collyer Quay, ☎ 224–3922 or 737–4411. ☜ Drink minimum S$8; with dinner, drink minimum S$15. ۞ Nightly 8 PM–2 AM.*

THE ARTS

Each year sees more arts events—particularly orchestral and dramatic performances—added to Singapore's cultural calendar. The many sporadic Chinese, Indian, and Malay happenings and festivals add further color. Springtime is especially busy with such well-attended events as an international film festival; a comedy festival; WOMAD (World of Music, Arts, and Dance); the Festival of Arts; and performances by Theatreworks, the Singapore Dance Theatre, and the Singapore Symphony Orchestra.

Some of the best performances take place at the **Victoria Theatre and Memorial Hall** (✉ 11 Empress Pl., ☎ 339–6120 for information; 338–8283 for bookings), two adjoining buildings at the Padang. These Victorian structures are home to the 85-member Singapore Symphony Orchestra, which is renowned for its large repertoire of well-known classics and works by Asian composers. Other performances here include those by music and dance groups from all over Southeast Asia and by Singapore's various theatrical and operatic societies. You'll also find Chinese opera and Indian classical dance presentations.

Singapore hopes that **The Esplanade—Theatres on the Bay** (✉ The Esplanade Co. Ltd., 60 Raffles Ave., ☎ 337–3711), which was under construction at press time and was due to open in 2001, will become as famous a landmark as Sydney's Opera House. In 1999, impressive construction works for this complex were well underway alongside Marina Bay and next to both the central business district and the colonial district. The Esplanade is slated to contain the 2,000 seat **Lyric Theatre** and the 1,800 seat **Concert Hall,** which will have a 39-ft-high pipe organ with 4,489 pipes and the necessary acoustics to match. Also planned are three smaller studios and numerous outdoor performance spaces. In keeping with Singapore's two obsessions—shopping and eating—expect to see a retail complex and food and beverage outlets.

Indian music, drama, and dance performances are staged during major festivals at the more important temples, including the **Sri Mariamman Temple** (✉ 244 South Bridge Rd., ☎ 223–4064) and the **Chettiar Temple** (✉ 14 Tank Rd., ☎ 737–9393). Themes are from the ancient epics—tales of gods, demons, and heroes. For more information, contact the **Hindu Endowment Board** (☎ 373–4590).

At **The Substation** (✉ 45 Armenian St., ☎ 337–7535 for information; 337–7800 for tickets) you'll find all of the arts combined. Actors, artists, and musicians do what they do best at this theater-gallery-restaurant and often gather for alfresco cover drinks (daily from noon to 8:30 PM).

Dance

Periodic performances by companies such as the **Singapore Dance Theatre** (✉ Fort Canning Centre, 2nd floor, Cox Terr., ☎ 338–0611) are given in Fort Canning Park. Take along a picnic to enjoy before the show, which will start at about 7 PM or so.

The **Kala Mandhir Temple of Fine Arts** (☎ 339–0492) and the **Nrityalaya Aesthetics Society** (☎ 336–6537) are Indian dance schools that perform regularly throughout the year at different venues. **Sriwana** (✉ No. 02-494 Block 125, 11 Tampines St., ☎ 783–2434) is recognized for its innovative presentations of traditional Malay dances.

Music

Orchestras

The **Singapore Symphony Orchestra** gives concerts on Friday and Saturday evenings twice a month at the Victoria Concert Hall. Tickets cost S$8–S$80 and are available at the box office (Monday–Saturday 10–6 and up to 8:30 on the night of a concert) or through SISTIC (☞ *above*). You should also check local listings for performances by the following noteworthy groups: **Singapore Chinese Orchestra** (✉ People's Association, Room 5, Block B, 9 Stadium Link, ☎ 344–8777); the

Singapore Youth Orchestra (✉ ECA Branch, No. 02-03, Block 2, 51 Grange Rd., ☎ 831–9606); and the **Singapore Lyric Theatre** (✉ No. 03-06 Stamford Arts Centre, 155 Waterloo St., ☎ 336–1929), which specializes in opera.

Chinese Opera

The dramatic *wayangs* (Chinese operas) reenact Chinese legend through powerful movement, lavish costumes, outrageous masks, and heavy makeup. Performances are held on temporary stages set up near temples, in market areas, or outside apartment complexes. They're staged all year, but most frequently in August and September, during the Festival of the Hungry Ghosts. Street performances—such as those at Clarke Quay held on Wednesday and Friday at 7:45 PM—are free. You'll need to buy tickets to shows by the **Chinese Theatrical Circle** (☎ 235–2911) and other groups that perform at different venues, including the Victoria Theatre and Memorial Hall, throughout the city.

The wayangs are full of action. Gongs and drums beat, devils leap, maidens weep, and heroes reap the praise of an enraptured audience. The characters are fancifully weird—take a look behind the stage and watch the actors apply their makeup—and gorgeously costumed. With Chinese TV programming mostly in Mandarin, street wayangs—spoken in dialect, though totally different from the conversational dialect—have become popular with the older generation, who rarely have a chance to be entertained in their own language. Do try to seek out a wayang. It's an experience you won't soon forget. And don't be bashful about asking a fellow spectator who the characters portrayed are.

Theater

The Necessary Stage (☎ 738–6355) performs highly experimental works and is an established and respected company. In 1998, the bilingual (Mandarin and English) **Practice Theatre Ensemble** (☎ 337–2529) was very involved with an Asian version of *King Lear* that was staged in Japan.

The **Singapore Repertory Theatre** (SRT; ✉ Telok Ayer Performing Arts Centre, 182 Cecil St., ☎ 221–5585), is the country's most popular troupe, staging local and international plays and musicals. (*The Golden Child*, by local playwright David Hwang, for example, went from here to Broadway.)

6 Outdoor Activities and Sports

From biking and hiking to golf and tennis to waterskiing and windsurfing, the Garden Isle offers land and water sports in scenic settings.

DESPITE THE HEAT, Singapore is one of the best cities in Asia for outdoor activities, for it's one of few that are not polluted. The government has taken care to set aside a significant portion of the island for recreation, so you can go waterskiing or scuba diving, take a jungle hike, or play beach volleyball. Virtually all Singapore hotels have swimming pools, and there are 19 public swimming complexes, some of which are superb. Be sure to drink lots of water, and try to schedule the most strenuous activities for early morning or late afternoon.

BEACHES AND PARKS

Bintan Island, Indonesia. Whether you're in Singapore for business or pleasure, you may be able to slip in a quick side trip to Indonesia— it's that close. Bintan Island, which is just 45 minutes by ferry away from Singapore's east coast, has recently become a resort haven. You can frolic on its beaches, golf its courses, and experience Indonesian cuisine and culture.

East Coast Park. This park stretches for 8 km (5 mi) on reclaimed land between the road to the airport and the seashore. Here you'll find well-planned recreational facilities, including an excellent beach and a water-sports lagoon where you can rent sailboards, canoes, and sailboats. If you prefer swimming in a pool, the **Aquatic Centre** has four—including a wave pool—as well as a giant water slide called the Big Splash. "Holiday chalets" set among the palm trees beside the beach can be rented by the day. Restaurants and changing facilities are available.

Nearby Islands. The islands of **Kusu** and **St. John's** (☞ *also* Chapter 2) have reasonable small beaches and swimming facilities. On weekends, they're crowded with locals.

Sentosa Island. Billed as Singapore's leisure resort, Sentosa offers a range of recreational facilities in addition to its museums, waxworks, fountains, and other attractions (☞ *also* Chapter 2). There's a reasonable beach and a swimming lagoon, with changing and refreshment facilities, as well as rowboats, sailboards, and canoes for rent. You can camp here, play golf or tennis, bike, roller skate (the rink is said to be the largest in Southeast Asia and skate rentals are only S$2 per hour), or join the beach volleyball games. The island gets very crowded on weekends.

PARTICIPANT SPORTS

Archery

The **Archery Association of Singapore** (✉ 5 Binchang Walk, ☎ 258-1140), founded in 1967, has 18 affiliated clubs, most of which welcome enthusiasts. The range at 131 Portsdown Road is open daily and offers day and night (floodlit) shooting. The fee is S$25 for visitors.

Bicycling

Look for signs that point to one of the many **bicycle kiosks** dotting designated bike paths. You can rent bikes for about S$3–S$8 an hour, with a deposit of S$20–S$50. There are many such kiosks in East Coast Park, Sentosa Island, Pasir Ris, Bishan, and Pulau Ubin (an island on Singapore's northeast coast). Cycling through the beaches and parks along the highway to the airport is a very pleasant way to sightsee.

Bowling

There are a number of bowling centers in Singapore; the cost per string is about S$2.80 on weekdays before 6 PM, S$3.90 on weekends and after 7 PM weekdays. For general information contact the **Singapore Tenpin Bowling Congress** (☎ 440–7388). **Leisure Bowl** (⊠ Leisure-Dome, 5 Stadium Walk, Kallang Park, ☎ 345–0545) has 30 lanes. Other alleys include **Jackie's Bowl** (⊠ 452B East Coast Rd., no phone) and **Plaza Bowl** (⊠ Textile Centre, 8th floor, Jalan Sultan, ☎ 292–4821).

Fitness Facilities

Hotels

If you absolutely *have* to work out in a gym, consider a stay at one of these hotels with fabulous fitness facilities. Because most hotel clubs offer annual memberships to Singaporeans, you'll find the facilities busy early in the morning, at midday, and early in the evening.

Four Seasons (⊠ 190 Orchard Blvd., ☎ 734–1110). Tennis lessons are offered by Peter Burwash International pros on indoor, air-conditioned courts. You'll also find two pools (one for adults only), a fully equipped fitness center, massage, a golf simulator, saunas, and steam rooms. Continental breakfast is served free to members; hotel guests must pay S$18 plus tax.

Marina Mandarin (⊠ 6 Raffles Blvd., ☎ 338–3388). If you're a guest here, you can play a couple games of squash or tennis and then take a dip in the outdoor pool. Or you can head for the gym—which has Nautilus-type equipment, a Universal gym, free weights, and treadmills—before relaxing in the steam room or sauna. If you need still more relaxation, massage therapy is an option, too.

Oriental (⊠ 5 Raffles Blvd., ☎ 338–0066). Here you'll find a jogging track, tennis and squash courts, and a splendid outdoor pool with an underwater sound system and a view of the harbor. The fifth-floor health club includes a hot tub, massage, steam and sauna rooms for men and for women, free weights, a Universal gym, stationary bikes, and treadmills. Runners should try the waterfront path across the street from the hotel; maps are provided in your room.

Ritz-Carlton (⊠ 7 Raffles Ave., ☎ 337–8888). The health and fitness club here is so exclusive that it has the highest-priced membership for locals in Singapore: S$25,000 plus annual fees. If you're a hotel guest, take advantage of being able to use the state-of-the-art gymnasium, the pool and outdoor Jacuzzi, the sauna, and the steam facilities for free.

Shangri-La (⊠ 22 Orange Grove Rd., ☎ 737–3644). Here the amenities include a good-size outdoor pool and a smaller indoor one; a modern health club with a Universal gym, stationary bikes, treadmills, and other equipment; tennis and squash courts; and a three-hole golf course, where you can jog in the early morning. The site also has spacious, separate, "wet" areas—which include saunas, steam rooms, and Jacuzzis—for men and women.

YMCAs/YWCAs

The following YMCA/YWCA complexes have fitness facilities and offer temporary memberships: **Metropolitan YMCA** (⊠ 60 Stevens Rd., ☎ 737–755), **Metropolitan YMCA International Centre** (⊠ 70 Palmer Rd., ☎ 222–4666), **YWCA Fort Canning** (⊠ 6 Fort Canning Rd., ☎ 338–4222), and the **YMCA International House** (⊠ 1 Orchard Rd., ☎ 336–6000).

Flying

The **Republic of Singapore Flying Club** (⊠ East Camp Building, 140B Seletar Airbase, ☎ 481–0502 or 481–0200) offers visiting membership to qualified pilots and has aircraft available for hire (approximately S$270 per hour plus S$65 per hour for a temporary one-month membership). You can't fly solo unless you have a Singapore license. A piloted ride for up to three people can be arranged for about S$270 an hour.

Golf

Some of the top hotels will make arrangements for their guests to golf at local courses. This can include making all the necessary bookings, including equipment reservations, at the club of your choice and arranging for a limousine to take you there. You might check before leaving home to see whether your club has any reciprocal arrangements with a Singapore club. Several excellent Singapore courses accept nonmembers, though some limit this to weekdays. Most clubs are open daily 7–7; some offer night golfing until 11. Driving ranges offer you the chance to practice your drives for as little as S$2 for 50 balls.

Changi Golf Club. This hilly nine-hole course on 50 acres is open to nonmembers on weekdays. ⊠ *345 Netheravon Rd.,* ☎ *545–5133.* 🖾 *Greens fee: S$49. Caddy fee: S$15.*

Jurong Country Club. Here you'll find an 18-hole, par-71 course on 120 acres, as well as a driving range. Half the holes are on flat terrain; the other nine are on small hills. ⊠ *9 Science Centre Rd.,* ☎ *560–5655.* 🖾 *Greens fee: S$123.60 weekdays, S$185.40 weekends and holidays. Caddy fee: S$25.75.*

Keppel Club. This 18-hole course close to the city also has a driving range. ⊠ *Bukit Chermin,* ☎ *273–5522.* 🖾 *Greens fee: S$123.60 Tues.–Fri., S$185.40 weekends and holidays. Caddy fee: S$40. Closed Mon.*

Seletar Country Club. Laid out in 1932 by the Royal Air Force, this is considered the best nine-hole course on the island. ⊠ *Seletar Airbase,* ☎ *481–4745.* 🖾 *Greens fee: S$45 Tues.–Fri., S$60 weekends and holidays. No caddies; trolley fee: S$4. Closed Mon.*

Sembawang Country Club. Because of its hilly terrain, this 18-hole, par-70 course is known as the "commando course." There are also squash courts available. ⊠ *Km 17, Sembawang Rd.,* ☎ *257–0642.* 🖾 *Greens fee (includes cart): S$113.30 weekdays, S$139.05 weekends and holidays. No caddies.*

Sentosa Golf Club. Here you can play on the 18-hole **Tanjong course** on the southeastern tip of the island or the 18-hole **Serapong course.** At both courses visitors can only play weekdays. ⊠ *Sentosa Island,* ☎ *275–0022.* 🖾 *Greens fees (includes cart): Tanjong S$164.80; Serapong S$123.60–S$144.20. No caddies.*

Running

Singapore is a great place for runners: there are numerous parks, and a number of leading hotels offer jogging maps. Serious runners can tackle the 10-km (6.2-mi) **East Coast Parkway track,** then cool off with a swim at the park's sandy beach. One of the most delightful places to run is the **Botanic Gardens** (off Holland Road and not far from Orchard Road), where you can jog on the paths or on the grass until 11 at night. The best time to run in Singapore is in the morning or evening; avoid the midday sun. It's safe for women to run alone. Remember to look right when crossing the road—in the British manner, driving is on the left. Several full or half-marathons are organized in Singapore during the year.

Sailing

Folks at the **Changi Sailing Club** (⊠ Netheravon Rd., ☎ 545–2876) can provide general information about sailing. You can rent Sunfish and sailboards at the **Europa Sailing Club** (⊠ 1210 East Coast Pkwy.,

☎ 449–5118). Sailboat rentals are also available on **Sentosa Island** (☞ Beaches and Parks, *above*).

Scuba Diving

The most interesting (and cleanest) diving is found off the coasts of nearby islands, though the currents are treacherous. The cost can run anywhere from S$380 to S$600, including scuba equipment. For information on local opportunities, contact **Marsden Bros.** (☎ 778–8287) or **Pro Diving Services** (☎ 291–2261). **Scuba Corner** (✉ No. 02-47 Millennia Walk, 9 Raffles Blvd., ☎ 338–6563) is a dive shop that runs trips to the outer islands.

Tennis, Squash, and Racquetball

Several hotels have their own tennis and squash courts (☞ Fitness Facilities, *above*), and there are a few public squash and racquetball courts as well. One public court complex is **Kallang Squash and Tennis Centre** (✉ National Stadium, ☎ 440–6839), where courts cost around S$10 an hour, depending on the time of day. At the **Singapore Tennis Centre** (✉ 1020 East Coast Pkwy., ☎ 442–5966) court costs range from S$7 to S$12 an hour. The **Tanglin Tennis Courts** (✉ Minden Rd., ☎ 473–7236) charges S$3.50 an hour during the day and S$9.50 in the evenings.

Waterskiing

The center of activity is Ponggol, a village in northeastern Singapore. **Ponggol Water Ski Centre** (✉ 17th Ave., ☎ 386–3891) is open daily 9–5:30 and charges S$60 an hour weekdays, S$70 an hour on weekends for a boat with ski equipment. Some of the local boats are for hire at considerably lower rates—about S$40 an hour. Negotiate directly, and make sure the proper safety equipment is available. Another popular place to water-ski is along the Kallang River, where world championships have been held. For rentals, try **Bernatt Boating and Skiing** (✉ 53 Jalan Mempurong, ☎ 257–5859). Rentals are usually S$70 an hour on weekdays, S$75 on weekends.

Windsurfing

At the **Europa Sailing Club** (☞ Sailing, *above*) sailboards rent for S$20 for two hours, S$10 per hour thereafter. Half-day lessons are available weekdays 2–6 for S$90, with a minimum of three people per class, and subject to the availability of instructors. Windsurfing is available on **Sentosa Island** (☞ Beaches and Parks, *above*) from 9:30 to 6:30.

SPECTATOR SPORTS

In addition to the sports listed below, golf, tennis, cycling, auto racing, swimming, badminton, and squash competitions are held from time to time. Some of these attract top professionals from abroad, and it may be easier to see these top athletes here than in countries where competitions are more heavily attended. A number of unique happenings—such as dragon-boat races and a kite-flying festival—are also organized annually. Most events are detailed in the newspapers. You can also get information from the **National Sports Council** (☎ 345–7111 ext. 663).

Cricket

From March through September, matches take place on the Padang grounds in front of the old **Cricket Club** (☎ 338–9271) every Saturday at 1:30 PM and every Sunday at 11 AM. Entrance to the club during matches is restricted to members, but you can watch from the sides of the playing field.

Horse Racing

You'll find on-site racing as well as live telecasts of Malaysian races at the **Singapore Turf Club.** There's a strict dress code: shorts, sleeveless T-shirts, and sandals aren't allowed in the public stands; smart casual is the way to go in the air-conditioned members enclosures (which foreigners need a passport to enter). ✉ *Head Office: Bukit Timah Race Course,* ☎ *460–3400.* 💷 *Public stands S$5.15 and S$10.30; members enclosures, S$20.60.* ☉ *Weekends 1:30 PM–6 PM.*

Polo

The **Singapore Polo Club** (✉ Thomson Rd., ☎ 256–4530) has both local and international matches. Spectators are welcome to watch Tuesday, Thursday, Saturday, and Sunday matches, which are played in the late afternoon.

Rugby

Rugby is played on the **Padang** grounds in front of the Singapore Cricket Club. Kickoff is usually at 5:30 PM on Saturday from September through March.

Soccer

Soccer is the major sport of Singapore; important matches take place in the **National Stadium** at Kallang. Details are published in the daily papers, and ticket reservations can be made through the National Sports Council (☞ *above*). The main season is September through March.

Track and Field

In recent years, most Asian countries have become keen on track-and-field events. Singapore has the **National Stadium** at Kallang for major events as well as nine athletic centers with tracks. International meets are usually detailed in the daily press and arouse considerable nationalistic feeling. For information and details on how to book seats for major meets, call the National Sports Council (☞ *above*).

7 Shopping

You can get just about anything you want in Singapore—for a price. Sleek shopping malls exist cheek by jowl with two-story shophouses and indoor/outdoor markets. Shopping here is a sport to be savored. With persistence and luck, you may find some of Singapore's surprising bargains.

WITH AN INCREDIBLE RANGE of goods—brought in from all over the world and sold in an equally incredible number (and variety) of shops—Singapore is truly a shopping fantasyland. Unfortunately, the bargains for which the city was once famous no longer exist. Though you can still find deals on handcrafted rosewood furniture, Chinese objets d'art, and carpets, prices for most items are the same as or higher than those in the United States. You should know the costs of goods you intend to buy—especially photographic and electronic items—at home. Though prices don't vary much from shop to shop, compare a few shops to feel secure about your price.

If you have (or wish you had) the money to spend on haute couture, head over to the Orchard and Scotts roads area to browse in the boutiques of the Hilton International arcade—which leads to the Four Seasons Hotel arcade—where every designer imaginable has a store. A 10-minute walk farther up Orchard Road takes you to the Tanglin Shopping Centre with its distinctive gift shops. For truly singular gifts check out the shops around Temple Street and Sago Street in Chinatown, where you'll find such things as Chinese herbal medicines, paper funerary items, and religious sculptures.

Stop into at least one of the Watson's drugstores scattered throughout the city. You'll find bags of prawn chips from Indonesia, tapioca chips from Malaysia, and bar snacks or lobster balls from Singapore; cookies from Australia; mints from England; and candied jellies from Japan. All make great gifts (if they're not eaten before you get them home).

For small, inexpensive souvenirs, take the MRT to the Bugis stop. On one side of Victoria Street is the Parco Bugis Junction—an air-conditioned, semioutdoor, multilevel shopping center. On the other side are an array of market stalls that sell everything from fake designer watches at S$18 each to silk boxer shorts and scarves (three for S$10). "Dollar" stores abound here, and they're full of such inexpensive and indispensable consumer goods as cans of "prickly heat" talcum powder (three for S$1) or packages of one-use, throwaway underwear (S$3 for five pairs).

For real deals, savvy locals flock to the weekly garage sales—usually held by expats leaving the country—advertised in the Saturday classifieds of the *The Straits Times*. At these, furniture and goods are sold at bargain-basement prices by people who literally can't take it with them.

Shopping Essentials

Bargaining

Although department stores, chain stores, and some independent stores do not offer discounts—their items are tagged with fixed prices—bargaining is common in Singapore. Shops that are reluctant to offer discounts usually have a FIXED-PRICE STORE sign in their windows (price tags may have the same message). If you don't like to bargain, stick to the department stores, which usually have the lowest initial ("first") price. If you don't mind bargaining, visit a department store first to get an idea of established prices, and then shop around.

Price tags in places that allow bargaining may say "recommended price." Local shops in upscale complexes or malls tend to give a 10%–15% discount on clothes. However, at jewelry stores, the discount can be as high as 40%–50%; carpet dealers also give hefty reductions. At less-upscale complexes, the discounts tend to be greater. Stalls and shops around visitor attractions have the highest initial asking prices, so bargaining here yields deep discounts

Everyone has his or her own method of bargaining, but in general, when a vendor tells you a price, ask for the discounted price, then offer even less. The person will probably reject your offer but come down a few dollars. With patience, this can continue and earn you a few more dollars off the price. If you don't like haggling, walk away after hearing the discounted price. If the vendor hasn't hit bottom price, you'll be called back.

Complaints

To avoid even having to worry about problems with goods or services, look for shops that have the Singapore Tourism Board's gold circular logo in their windows. This indicates that the retailer has been distinguished for excellent service and fair pricing among other things. Members need to be approved by the **Consumers Association of Singapore** (⊠ No. 04–3625, 164 Bukit Merah Central, 150164, ☏ 270–4611) and the tourist board (☞ Visitor Information *in* the Gold Guide section). If you do end up with complaints about either a serious disagreement with a shopkeeper or defective merchandise, lodge them with the tourist board; rest assured that staff members will follow up on them. The consumers association can also help. If you encounter retailer malpractice, you can get full redress through the Small Claims Tribunals—something retailers dread, because the tourist board publishes the names and addresses of miscreants ordered to make redress to visitors.

Electrical Goods

Singapore's current is 220–240 volts at 50 cycles, like that in Australia and Great Britain. Canada and the United States use 110–120 volts at 60 cycles, so before you buy appliances, verify that you can get special adapters, if required, and that these will not affect the equipment's performance. These days, most electrical goods sold are 110–220 volts compatible. Check the sticker on the apparatus you are about to buy.

Guarantees and Receipts

Make sure you get international guarantees and warranty cards with your purchases. Check the serial number of each item against its card, and don't forget to mail the card in. Sometimes guarantees are limited to the country of purchase. If the dealer cannot give you a guarantee, he's probably selling an item intended for the domestic market in its country of manufacture; if so, he has bypassed the authorized agent and should be able to give you a lower price. Though your purchase of such an item isn't illegal, you have no guarantee. If you decide to buy it anyway, be sure to check that the item is in working order before you leave the shop.

Be sure to ask for receipts, both for your own protection and for customs. Though shopkeepers are often amenable to stating false values on receipts, customs officials are wary and knowledgeable.

How to Pay

All department stores and most shops accept credit cards—American Express, Diners Club, MasterCard, and Visa—and travelers checks. Many tourist shops also accept foreign currency; just be sure to check the exchange rates before agreeing to any price—some store owners try to skim extra profit by giving an unfair rate of exchange. Retailers work at a low profit margin and depend on high turnover; they assume you will pay in cash. Except at the department stores, paying with a credit card will mean that your "discounted price" will reflect the commission the retailer will have to pay the credit card company.

Imitations

Copyright laws passed in early 1987 impose stern penalties on the selling of pirated music recordings and computer software. However, Singapore still has a reputation for pirated goods. If you're buying a computer, for example, some stores are quite amenable to loading it with all the software you want. Pirated CDs and video laser discs can be found at certain market stalls, as can incredibly authentic-looking wristwatches from every designer on the globe. The greatest of the fakes is the "solid gold" Rolex, which comes complete with serial number for less than S$100. It looks so good you could have a problem at customs—though you're more likely to have a customs problem (either in Singapore or at home) if it's discovered that you've purchased a counterfeit item.

Shipping

All stores that deal with valuable, fragile, or bulky merchandise know how to pack well. Ask for a quote on shipping charges, which you can then double-check with a local forwarder. Check whether the shop has insurance covering both loss and damage in transit. You might find you need additional coverage. If you're sending your purchases home by mail, check with **Singapore Post** (☎ 800/222–5777), the national postal service, about regulations.

Touts

Touting—soliciting business by approaching people on the street with offers of free shopping tours and special discounts—is illegal (maximum fines are S$5,000, and prison sentences of up to six months are possible). Nevertheless, it continues inside one or two shopping centers, especially Lucky Plaza. Each center has its band of men looking for people to interest in their special stash of fake designer watches. The touts at the top of Tanglin Road can be particularly bothersome. Some taxi drivers tout as well. Avoid all touts and the shops they recommend; a reputable shop doesn't need them. The prices will end up being higher—reflecting the tout's commission—and the quality of the goods possibly inferior.

Shopping Districts

Throughout the city are complexes full of shopping areas and centers. Many stores will have branches that carry much the same merchandise in several of these areas.

Orchard Road

The heart of Singapore's preeminent shopping district, Orchard Road is bordered on both sides by tree-shaded, tiled sidewalks lined with modern shopping complexes and deluxe hotels that house exclusive boutiques. Also considered part of this area are the shops on Scotts Road, which crosses Orchard, and two shopping centers—**Supreme House** on Penang Road and **Singapore Shopping Centre** (which was under renovation at press time).

Orchard Road is known for fashion and interior design shops, but you can find anything from Mickey Mouse watches to Chinese paper kites and antique Korean chests. The interior-design shops have unusual Asian bric-a-brac and such original items as a lamp stand made from old Chinese tea canisters or a pair of bookends in the shape of Balinese frogs. Virtually every Orchard Road complex, with the exception of the Promenade, has a clutch of department stores selling electronic goods, cigarette lighters, pens, jewelry, cameras, and so on. Most also have money changers, a few inexpensive cafés, and snack bars.

Though there's reference to an "Orchard Road price," which takes into account the astronomical rents some shop tenants have to pay, the department stores have the same fixed prices here as at all their branches. Small shops away from the center may have slightly cheaper prices.

Chinatown

Once Singapore's liveliest and most colorful shopping area, Chinatown lost a great deal of its vitality when the street stalls were moved into the **Kreta Ayer Complex** off Neil Road, **Chinatown Point** off Trengganu Street, and the **People's Park Complex** on Eu Tong Sen Street. Still, this neighborhood is fun to explore. The focus is on the Smith, Temple, and Pagoda street blocks, but nearby streets—Eu Tong Sen Street, Wayang Street, and Merchant Road on one side and Ann Siang Hill and Club Street on another—can yield some interesting finds.

Chinese kitchenware can be fascinating, and Temple Street has an abundance of unusual plates, plant pots, teapots, lacquered chopsticks, and so on. Paraphernalia for Chinese funerals is particularly prevalent around Sago Street. Nearby Sago Lane was lined, not so long ago, with "death houses," where elderly people went to await death. This may sound gruesome, but funerary items are among the most creative examples of folk art in the world. They include paper replicas of life's necessities, to serve the dead in their afterlife. There are some famous craftsmen on Ann Siang Hill. Just around the corner, on Club Street, are several wood-carvers who specialize in creating idols of Chinese gods. On Merchant Road, a vendor of costumes for Chinese operas welcomes customers. And on Chin Hin Street, you can buy fragrant Chinese tea direct from a merchant.

South Bridge Road in Chinatown is the street of goldsmiths. Dozens of jewelers here specialize in 22K and even 24K ornaments in the characteristic orange color of Chinese gold. Each assistant, often shielded by a metal grill, uses an abacus and a balance to calculate the value of the piece you wish to buy. You must bargain here. South Bridge Road is also home to many art galleries.

Little India

Serangoon Road is affectionately known as Little India. For shopping purposes, it begins at the **Zhujiao Market,** better known as the KK Market, on the corner of Serangoon and Buffalo roads. Some of the junk dealers and inexpensive-clothing stalls form a bazaar known as Mustafa Centre. This is a fun place to poke about and look for bargains.

All the handicrafts of India can be found on Serangoon Road: intricately carved wood tables, shining brass trays, hand-loomed table linens, fabric inlaid with tiny mirrors, brightly colored pictures of Hindu deities, and garlands of jasmine for the gods. And the sari shops! At dozens of shops here you can get the 6½ yards of voile, cotton, Kashmiri silk, or richly embroidered Benares silk required to make a sari. For the variety, quality, and beauty of the silk, the prices are very low. Other Indian costumes, such as long or short *kurtas* (men's collarless shirts) and Punjabi trouser sets, are unusual and attractive buys. Should you overspend and find yourself with excess baggage, there are several luggage shops on Serangoon Road where you can buy an old-fashioned tin trunk big enough to hide a body in.

Arab Street

The Arab Street shopping area really begins at Beach Road, opposite the Plaza Hotel. This old-fashioned street is full of noteworthy buys. A group of basket and rattan shops first catches your eye. There are quite a few jewelers here, and even more shops selling loose gems and necklaces of garnet and amethyst beads. The main business is batiks (textiles bearing hand-printed designs) and lace.

Brassware, prayer rugs, carpets, and leather slippers are sold in abundance on Arab Street and its side streets, which have appealing names such as Muscat Street and Baghdad Street. Two noteworthy complexes in the vicinity are Beach Road's **Golden Mile Food Centre,** which is devoted to good food on the lower floors and junk and antiques on the top floors, and Jalan Sultan's **Textile Centre,** which offers a wide variety of batiks.

Katong

The quiet east-coast suburb of Katong, just 15 minutes from town via the Pan Island Expressway, has old-fashioned shophouses along its main street, some selling inexpensive children's clothes and one dealing in antiques. Off the main road is the even more old-fashioned Joo Chiat Road, which gets more and more interesting as it approaches Gelang Road. Its shops sell Chinese kitchenware, antiques, baby clothes, and lots of offbeat items.

Holland Village

Holland Village, 10 minutes west of town by taxi, is a bit of a yuppie haunt, but it's the most rewarding place to browse for unusual and inexpensive Asian items, large and small. Many shops here specialize in Korean chests. Behind the main street is Lorong Mambong, a street of shophouses jammed with baskets, earthenware, porcelain, and all sorts of things from China and Thailand. One complex to look for in this area is the **Holland Village Shopping Centre** on Holland Avenue. A 10-minute walk along Holland Avenue from Holland Village is **Cold Storage Jelita,** which also has several shops.

Centers and Complexes

Shops in multilevel buildings and shopping complexes are often listed with a numerical designation such as "No. 00-00." The first part of this number indicates what floor the shop is on. The second part indicates its location on the floor. When the phone number of an individual shop is not given in this section, you'll find it listed with the shop under a specific merchandise category, below.

Centrepoint (⊠ 176 Orchard Rd.). This spacious and impressive center has the **Robinsons** department store as its anchor tenant. One of the liveliest complexes, Centrepoint also has jewelry, silverware, and fashion shops; furniture stores that sell Philippine bamboo and Korean chests; and a large basement supermarket.

Delfi Orchard (⊠ 402 Orchard Rd.). Delfi is full of wedding boutiques, art galleries, and jewelry shops. **Waterford Wedgwood** and **Royal Selangor Pewter** are also here, along with a well-stocked golf shop.

Far East Plaza (⊠ 14 Scotts Rd.). This center is where the young and trendy gather to see and be seen. The shops are geared to them, and there's a bargain-basement atmosphere about the place. A forecourt offers fast-food restaurants (including a McDonald's and Canadian Pizza—the best in the city), outdoor tables, and entertaining people-watching.

Forum Galleria (⊠ 583 Orchard Rd.). Here you'll find a huge **Toys 'R' Us,** as well as an assortment of boutiques, including **Guess! Kids.**

Funan Centre (⊠ 109 North Bridge Rd.). Next to the Peninsula Hotel on North Bridge Road and High Street, this shopping center will thrill computer and information-technology lovers.

The Heeren Shops (⊠ 260 Orchard Rd.). This new complex at Orchard and Grange roads houses a huge **HMV** music store; **True Colours,** a futuristic makeup boutique; **Electric City,** an electronics superstore; and a branch of the popular Nonya restaurant, **The Blue Ginger.**

Hilton Shopping Gallery (⊠ 581 Orchard Rd.). Most of Singapore's upscale hotels have a boutique or two in their lobbies, but the Hilton

Singapore Shopping Complexes and Markets

NEWTON

Nassim Rd.

Claymore Hill

Scotts Rd.

Cairnhill Rd.

Clemenceau Ave.

Cavenagh Rd.

Tanglin Rd.

Bideford Rd.

ORCHARD

Orchard Blvd.

Orchard Rd.

Paterson Rd.

One Tree
Hill

ORCHARD
ROAD

Grange Rd.

Grange Rd.

Exeter Rd.

SOMERSET

Singapore River

River Valley Rd.

River Valley Rd.

Zion Rd.

Kim Seng Rd.

Alexandra Rd.

Havelock Rd.

Havelock Rd.

TIONG
BAHRU

Tiong Bahru Rd.

Henderson Rd.

Outram
Park

Outram Rd.

N

Jalan Bukit Merah

OUTRAM
PARK

Neil Rd.

Cantonment Rd.

1000 meters

1000 yards

Bahru Rd.

Spottiswoode
Park

Keppel Rd.

KEY

Keppel Rd.

Empire Dock

AE American Express Office

North-South MRT line

East-West MRT line

Railroad lines

Subway stop

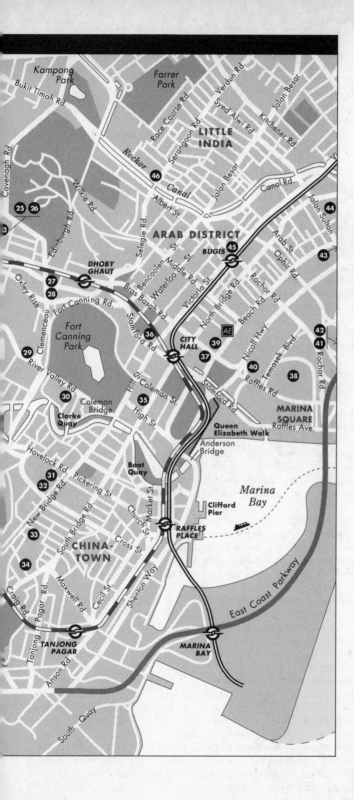

has an extensive shopping arcade full of them. It is home to several top names—**Giorgio Armani, Matsuda, Valentino**—and, through a boutique called **Singora,** many other Italian and French fashion houses. Among its other top-flight tenants are **Gucci, Davidoff, Dunhill, L'Ultimo,** and **Louis Vuitton.** This gallery leads to a similar arcade with still more expensive boutiques that's attached to the Four Seasons.

Liang Court Complex (✉ 177 River Valley Rd.). Liang Court is off the beaten track but only five minutes by cab from Orchard Road and worth the drive. The department store **Daimaru** is here; half of its floor space has been transformed into selected designer boutiques, such as **Dunhill,** and areas that sell books, silk, pearls, and other specialty items.

Lucky Plaza (✉ 304 Orchard Rd.). This plaza has gone downhill as its shops have moved to trendier, newer buildings. What stores remain are geared toward tourists. Plan to bargain furiously, particularly with the many jewelers who are, it seems, involved in a perpetual price-cutting war.

Marina Square. Part of an elegant complex that begins east of the Nicholl Highway downtown (a five-minute walk from the Raffles City MRT station), it includes Millennia Walk (look up to admire the architecture) and houses **Metro,** a large department store that has great sales; **DFS,** a massive duty-free shop; two cineplexes for film buffs; and about 200 small shops, including the English store **Mothercare.**

Ngee Ann City (✉ 391 Orchard Rd). Although the Japanese store **Takashimaya** takes up most of this complex, you'll find a number of small boutiques as well.

Orchard Point and Orchard Plaza (✉ No. 220 and No. 150 Orchard Rd.). These side-by-side centers don't have the popular appeal of some other complexes but will reward dedicated shoppers with good finds. Reptile bags can be found in the basement shops of Orchard Point. (Note that Orchard Plaza houses several brothels; you might want to avoid it at night.)

Palais Renaissance (✉ 390 Orchard Rd.). Across the road from the Hilton hotel is this new high-fashion center. Targeted at those who seek status labels at high prices, the Palais Renaissance is chic, opulent, and overpriced. It's a delight to wander through regardless of whether you're well heeled or not. Here **Prada, DKNY, Gianni Versace,** and **Krizia** compete as much in the design of their stores as in the design of their merchandise. Perfumes, jewelry, and travel accessories are also expensively represented in this extravagant marbled emporium.

The Paragon (✉ 290 Orchard Rd.). The glossy Paragon has more than 15 men's fashion boutiques and counts **Gucci** and **Sonia Rykiel** among its more popular tenants. It also has the **Metro** department store.

Parco Bugis Junction (✉ 230 Victoria St.). Linking the Hotel Inter-Continental and the Bugis MRT station, this shopping center has the Japanese department store **Seiyu** as its major tenant. It also houses a host of boutiques, restaurants, cafés, a cineplex, and the **Amusement Wonder Park Namco.** Bargain hunters might want to stop by the *pasar malam* (night market) at Bugis Village.

Parkway Parade (✉ 80 Marine Parade Rd.). This excellent and very attractive center is 15 to 20 minutes east of town by expressway. On weekdays you can shop here in peace and quiet; on weekends, it's uncomfortably crowded. The focus is on up-to-date and affordable fashions. Things get started around noon.

People's Park Complex and Centre (✉ Eu Tong Sen St.). Though not new and glossy, this Chinatown center has an international reputation and is always entertaining. Everything is sold here: herbs, Chinese medicines, cameras, stereo equipment, clothes, luggage. Shopkeepers are much more aggressive here than in town, and if you haven't done your homework, you can get taken.

The Promenade (⊠ 300 Orchard Rd.). The elegant architecture (there's a spiral walkway with a gentle slope instead of escalators) here is matched by the elegance of the tenants. Its fashion stores carry some of the hottest names, including **Charles Jourdan, Dolce&Gabbana,** and **Issey Miyake.** Home-decor shops sell superb Asian odds and ends.

Raffles City and Raffles Hotel Arcade. Bordered by Stamford, North Bridge, and Bras Basah roads, this complex has a confusing interior. If you get lost, you're sure to come across many shopping finds, some of them in the Japanese department and grocery store **Sogo.** You'll also find several fashion boutiques, the **Times** bookshop, and a post office branch. Across the road is the Raffles Hotel Arcade, whose 60 boutiques sell high fashion and art. There's also a tourist board office here.

Scotts Shopping Centre (⊠ 6–8 Scotts Rd.). One of the best places in Singapore for affordable fashion that stops just short of haute couture, Scotts also has a basement food court with local and delicatessen food, plus activities and demonstrations to keep shoppers entertained.

Shaw House (⊠ 350 Orchard Rd.). **Isetan,** a large Japanese department store, is the major anchor in this complex. The **Kinokuniya** bookstore is excellent for volumes on Japan. **Etienne Aigner** is a good place for leather items.

Specialists Centre (⊠ 277 Orchard Rd.). This center is the home of the **John Little** department store, better known as JL, and assorted boutiques.

Stamford Court and Stamford House. This corner of North Bridge and Stamford roads has more speciality shopping centers than any other section of downtown Orchard Road. Check out the fine array of furniture and home decor stores here, as well as antiques, sculpture, fine art, and gift shops.

Suntec City Mall. At the corner of the Nicholl Highway and Raffles Boulevard in the Marina Bay area, this large complex is divided into four zones: the Tropics (lifestyle products and services), the Entertainment Centre (housing the French superstore **Carrefour**), the Fountain Terrace (an array of restaurants, pubs, and a food court), and the Galleria (high-end boutiques). You could shop and dine here and not even bother seeing the rest of Singapore.

Tanglin Shopping Centre. This center, where Orchard Road meets Tanglin Road, has a good selection of antiques shops, especially in a small, self-contained section at ground level. **Moongate** is one of Singapore's oldest dealers in fine antique porcelain. **Antiques of the Orient** is the only shop in town that specializes in antique maps. The contemporary interior-design shops, as well as the food court in the basement, are excellent, too.

Wisma Atria (⊠ 435 Orchard Rd.). Come here if only to see the aquarium that wraps around the elevator. If you want to shop as well, this center has such grand names in fashion as **Dior** and **Fendi.** You'll also find the **Isetan** department store.

Department Stores

Singapore has one homegrown chain—**Metro**—that offers a wide range of affordable fashions and household products. When shopping for locally designed and manufactured fashion as well as brands such as Esprit, Metro is the best bet. The designs are up-to-the-minute, and the prices are good by local standards and unbelievably good by international standards. Look for Metros in Far East Plaza, Marina Square, and the Paragon.

Locally owned **Tang's** (⊠ 320 Orchard Rd., ☎ 737–5500), also known as Tang's Superstore or C. K. Tang's, is next to the Marriott Hotel. It looks upscale, but it has some of the best buys in town. Its fashions are, at best, improving, but its accessories are excellent—especially the costume jewelry—and its household products are unsurpassed.

Two Chinese department stores under different ownership, but with the same name, **Overseas Emporium,** are in the **People's Park Complex** (☎ 535–0555) and the **People's Park Centre** (☎ 535–1948). Both offer basically the same goods: Chinese silk fabric, silk blouses, brocade jackets, crafts, children's clothes, and china.

Singaporeans enjoy Japanese department stores. **Isetan**—in **Wisma Atria** (☎ 733–7777), **Shaw House** (☎ 733–1111), and **Parkway Parade** (☎ 345–5555)—always has good specials, and the fashion departments for men and women are well stocked. **Daimaru** (☎ 339–1111), in Liang Court, has some very unusual goods. **Sogo** (☎ 339–1100) opened in Raffles City as did **Seiyu** in the Parco Bugis Junction Complex (✉ 230 Victoria St., Bugis MRT, ☎ 223–2222).

The English **Robinsons** (☎ 733–0888), in Centrepoint, is Singapore's oldest department store. It recently shed its fuddy-duddy image and rethought its pricing and is once again one of the best. **John Little** (☎ 737–2222), at the Specialists Centre, has a full range of offerings but is now targeting the young and trendy. There are still good sales here, however. The **Marks & Spencer** in the basement of Lane Crawford at the corner of Scotts and Orchard is the biggest of several outlets in town.

Markets

Stalls crowding upon stalls in covered, open spaces of the city's **food markets** make for a hectic, colorful scene. The range of foodstuffs is staggering, and some of the items may turn your stomach. The live animals eyed by shoppers will tug at your heartstrings. Usually a food market is divided into two sections: the dry market and the wet market, which has squirming fish, crawling turtles, strutting chickens, and cute rabbits that are sold for the pot (the floors are continually sluiced to maintain hygiene). The wet market at the **Chinatown Point** is the most fascinating; the dry market at **Cuppage Centre** (on Cuppage Rd., off Orchard Rd.), where the flower stalls are particularly appealing, is a better choice for the squeamish.

The old-style street bazaars are all gone now, but in the **Sungei Road** area, site of the once-notorious Thieves Market, a few street vendors creep back each weekend. The stalls sell mainly inexpensive shirts, T-shirts, children's clothes, and underwear, as well as odds and ends such as inexpensive watches, costume jewelry, and sunglasses. A few sell plastic household items.

The **Kreta Ayer** complex in Chinatown may be modern, but it has all the atmosphere of a bazaar. All the street vendors from Chinatown were relocated here. The shops sell cassette tapes, clothing from China, toys, and a lot of gaudy merchandise.

Some of Chinatown's elderly junk peddlers refuse to leave the streets. In the afternoon, they line up along **Temple Street** and lay out a strange variety of goods—old bottles, stamps, bits of porcelain or brass, old postcards, and the like—on cloths.

Shops and stalls also cluster at the **Bugis Street** mall and at **Telok Ayer,** but some merchandise tends to be overpriced. Since 1996, several "dollar stores" have opened at Bugis, where items—from Indonesia, Malaysia, Korea, Thailand, and other parts of Asia—that you never thought you'd ever need are for sale. They are great shops for those on a budget who have to pick up several souvenirs for the folks back home.

Specialty Shops

Antiques and Curios

Most antiques stores have a variety of small items—porcelain, brass-ware, idols, and so on—as well as Chinese furniture, which may be of blackwood inlaid with mother of pearl, or namwood stained red with elaborate carvings picked out in gold. Falling halfway between souvenir shops and antiques stores, curio shops sell a fascinating variety of goods, mainly from China. Reverse-glass paintings, porcelain vases, cloisonné, wood carvings, jewelry (agate, jade, lapis lazuli, malachite), ivory carvings, embroidery, and idols represent just a fraction of their treasures. Note that some curio dealers style themselves as antiques shops, as do some vendors who sell rosewood items or reproduction furniture. (Strictly speaking, antiques in Singapore are defined as items that are more than 80 years old.)

If you don't have time to step outside of the Orchard Road shopping mecca, good places to see genuine antiques are the Tanglin Shopping Centre's **Antiques of the Orient** (☎ 734–9351), which specializes in maps, ceramics, and furniture; **Moongate** (☎ 737–6771), which sells porcelain; and **Tatiana** (☎ 235–3560), which carries primitive art and antique Indonesian batik and ikat (a woven fabric of tie-dyed yarns).

Off Orchard Road on Cuppage Road is a row of restored shophouses. Here, **Babazar** (⊠ 31A–35A Cuppage Terr., ☎ 235–7866) is full of wonderful jewelry, furniture, clothes, art, knickknacks, and antiques. **Keng of Tong Mern Sern** (⊠ 226 River Valley Rd., ☎ 734–0761), near the Chettiar Temple, is a rabbit warren full of antiques. The store's sign says, WE BUY JUNK, WE SELL ANTIQUES.

For curios, try **Lim's Art & Crafts** (⊠ Top floor, ☎ 735–2966) in the Scotts Shopping Centre. For museum-quality Asian antiques, visit the **Paul Art Gallery** in Holland Park (⊠ 68 Greenleaf Rd., ☎ 468–4697). In the east end, about a 20-minute walk on Sims Avenue from the Kallang MRT, is **Poh Antiques and Junks** (⊠ 139 Sims Ave., no phone), which has Buddhist and Hindu sculptures as well as assorted kitsch from this century. It opens when the owner feels like opening—but even if it's closed when you get there, Sims Avenue around Geylang and Lorong 9 is an interesting neighborhood in which to stroll.

Art

Singapore has more than its share of fine artists. Established names—Chen Wen Hsi for Chinese brush painting, Thomas Yeo for abstract landscapes, and Anthony Poon for contemporary graphics—fetch high prices. Among the artists who are gaining recognition are Wan Soon Kam, Ng Eng Teng (a sculptor who re-creates the human figure in cement, stoneware, and bronze), James Tan (known for his traditional and abstract Chinese brush paintings), and Teng Juay Lee (who specializes in orchids). Nostalgic scenes of the Singapore of yesteryear are captured in watercolors and oils by artists such as Gog Sing Hoi, Ang Ah Tee, and Ong Kim Seng, known for his scenes of the Singapore River and Chinatown. Some delightful paintings can be had for as little as S$300.

For a range of art, try **Art Forum** (⊠ 56 Monk's Hill Terr., ☎ 737–3448), but call before visiting. There are also many galleries on South Bridge Road in Chinatown. If you wish to see Chinese calligraphy in the works, Yong Cheong Thye practices his art at the **Yong Gallery** (⊠ 17 Erskin Rd., ☎ 226–1718) in Chinatown.

Other galleries include: **Cicada Gallery of Fine Arts** (⊠ 31 Ann Siang Rd., ☎ 225–6787), **Opera Gallery** (⊠ No. 02-12H, 391 Orchard Rd.,

☎ 735–2618), **Plum Blossoms Gallery** (✉ Raffles Hotel, 1 Beach Rd., ☎ 334–1198), and **Shenn's Gallery** (✉ 37 Blair Rd., ☎ 223–1233).

Batik

A traditional craft item of Singapore, Malaysia, and Indonesia, batik is now also important in contemporary fashion and interior design. **Blue ~~Ginger~~ Design Centre** (✉ 1 Beach Rd., ☎ 334–1171) and **Design Batik** (✉ 1 Beach Rd., ☎ 776–4337), both at the Raffles Hotel, sell clothes and fabrics in modern designs. Blue Ginger is especially innovative, and has opened a branch at the **Merchant Court Hotel** (✉ 20 Merchant Rd., ☎ 536–4986). **Tang's** department stores (☞ *above*) sell inexpensive batik products, including a good range of men's shirts. Traditional batik sarong lengths can be bought in the shops on Arab Street and in the **Textile Centre** on Jalan Sultan.

Cameras

Photographic equipment may not be the bargain it once was, but the range of cameras and accessories available can be matched only in Hong Kong. It's especially important that you establish the price at home before buying here. Film and film processing remain excellent buys. All department stores carry cameras, and there are so many in Lucky Plaza that you can do all your comparison shopping in one spot.

For personalized service try **Cathay Photo** (☎ 339–6188) on the second floor of Marina Square. For camera repairs, **Goh Gin Camera Service Centre** (✉ 150 Orchard Rd., Orchard Plaza, ☎ 732–6155) may be able to help.

Carpets

Carpets are very attractively priced in Singapore. Afghan, Pakistani, Persian, Turkish, and Chinese carpets—both antique and new—are carried by reputable dealers. Carpet auctions, announced in the newspapers, are good places to buy if you know your stuff. In shops, it's acceptable to bargain—in fact, it's integral to the rather lengthy proceedings.

Good shops include: **Amir & Sons** (✉ No. 03–01, ☎ 734–9112) in Lucky Plaza, **Hassan's** (✉ No. 03–01, ☎ 737–5626) in the Tanglin Shopping Centre, and **Qureshi's** (✉ No. 05–12, ☎ 235–1523) in Centrepoint.

Clothing

CASUAL OUTFITS

In department stores and small boutiques all over the island—but especially on Orchard Road—locally made women's fashions and Japanese imports sell for a song. Brands such as Chocolate and Ananas offer colorful, reasonably made, very fashionable garments. Two of the better-known chain stores are the **East India Company** (✉ 11 Stamford Rd., ☎ 336–0448) and the **British India Company** (✉ 11 Stamford Rd., ☎ 334–6806), both of which are in the Capitol Building. **Trend** (☎ 235–9446) is a popular Centrepoint boutique.

Shoes are good buys, too, especially in the Metro and Tang's department stores (☞ Department Stores, *above*), but sizes here are smaller than in the West, and some women may have a problem getting the right fit.

HIGH FASHION

Singapore has its own designers, including London-based Benny Ong, who sells through Tang's and China Silk House (☞ Silk, *below*) and Song & Kelly, a Singaporean/British couple who are winning raves internationally. You should also look for the designs of Jut Ling, Thomas Wee, and Celia Loe in the more upscale department stores and boutiques. For European couture, check the arcades of the Hilton International and the Mandarin, as well as the more fashionable shopping centers, especially the Palais Renaissance.

Boutiques that carry a number of designers include **Club 21** (☎ 738–8778), which has men's and women's fashions and is in the Four Seasons arcade; **Glamourette** (☎ 737–5939) in the Promenade; and **Link** (☎ 736–0645) in the Palais Renaissance.

Men's fashions are represented by **Hermès** (✉ 541 Orchard Rd., ☎ 734–1353) in Liat Towers, **Mario Valentino** (☎ 338–4457) in Marina Square, and **Ralph Lauren** (☎ 738–0298) in Takashimaya.

Jewelry

Singapore is a reliable place to buy jewelry, and there are so many jewelers that prices are competitive. Never accept the first price offered, no matter how posh the store. (All jewelers give enormous discounts, usually 40% or more, but some, especially in hotels, don't mention this until pressed.) The Singapore Assay Office hallmarks jewelry, though the procedure is time-consuming and not many jewelers submit to it unless required for export.

In Chinatown, particularly along South Bridge Road and in People's Park, there are dozens of jewelers who sell 22K gold. Many of these are old family firms, and prices are calculated by abacus based on the weight of the ornament and the prevailing price of gold. The bargaining procedure can take quite some time. On Orchard Road, the jewelry shops are often branches of Hong Kong firms or are local firms modeled along the same lines. They sell 18K set jewelry, often in Italian designs, as well as loose investment stones.

Cartier has shops in **Takashimaya** (☎ 734–2427) and in **Millennia Walk** in Marina Square (☎ 339–3294). One of the many small jewelers in Takashimaya is the **Hour Glass** (☎ 734–2420), which carries a large selection of designer watches. **Je T'Aime** (☎ 734–2275) in Wisma Atria is a reputable firm. **Larry's** (☎ 732–3222), with branches in Raffles City and other malls, is a popular store. You'll find the antique silver and gold jewelry of the Straits Chinese at **Petnic's** (✉ 41A Cuppage Rd., ☎ 235–6564). **Tiffany & Co.** recently opened a two-story store at Ngee Ann City (☎ 735–8823).

Luggage and Accessories

Luggage is a bargain in Singapore, and every complex contains several stores that carry designer names including Charles Jourdan, Dunhill, Etienne Aigner, and Louis Vuitton. Department stores also carry such brands as Samsonite and Delsey. The **Escada** boutique (☎ 336–8283) at the Promenade and the Millennia Walk has a range of accessories and custom-made luggage.

Pewter and Dinnerware

Malaysia is the world's largest tin producer, and pewter is an important craft item in the region. Modern pewter items are heavily influenced by Scandinavian design. Items range from jewelry and tiny figurines to coffee and tea sets. Sake sets, bowls, vases, ornamental plates, clocks, and traditional beer tankards are also available. Some items are specifically aimed at the tourist trade, such as Raffles plates and Chinese zodiac plaques.

For dinnerware, **Christofle** (☎ 733–7257) has a boutique in the Hilton. **Royal Selangor Pewter** (✉ Main office: 32 Pandan Rd., ☎ 268–9600), the largest pewter concern in Singapore, has a great product range displayed at the showrooms in the Paragon, Delfi Orchard, Clarke Quay, Raffles Hotel, Marina Square, and Raffles City. Also try the **Waterford Wedgwood Shop** (✉ No. 01–01 Delfi Orchard, ☎ 734–8375).

Silk

Chinese silk is easy to find in Singapore. All the emporiums have special departments that sell the fabric or clothes (tailored and ready-to-wear) made from it. **China Silk House,** which has outlets in the **Tanglin Shopping Centre** (☎ 235–5020) and in **Centrepoint** (☎ 733–0555), has a wide range of fabrics in different weights and types. You'll also find silk clothing, including a line designed for the shop by Benny Ong.

For Indian silk in sari lengths check out the many shops in the Serangoon Road area. You pay only a fraction of what it would cost elsewhere to buy the 6.5 yards of silk—which could be the thin Kashmiri type or the heavier, embroidered Benares type—required to make a sari. The major store for Indian textiles is **P. Govindasamy Pillai** (PGP; ✉ Campbell La., ☎ 297–5311). To enter it, you must first walk into Kuna's Handicraft Shop, which will lead you to the PGP Supermarket and the sari shop upstairs.

Thai silk, in different weights for different purposes, comes in stunning colors. Specialty shops sell it by the meter or made up into gowns, blouses, and dresses. The **Siam Silk Company** (✉ 87 Tanjong Pagar Rd., ☎ 323–4800) is a good place to look.

Tailoring

There are tailors and tailors—what you end up with depends on how well you choose. Tailors who offer 24-hour service rarely deliver, and their quality is often suspect. Another indication of danger is not seeing a tailor on the premises. Anyone can set up shop as a tailor by filling a store with fabrics and then subcontracting the work; the results from such places are seldom felicitous. Allow four to five days for a good job. **Justmen** (☎ 737–4800) in the Tanglin Shopping Centre is one of a number of excellent men's tailors. For women, shops such as the Tanglin branch of **China Silk House** (☞ Silks, *above*) offer good tailoring.

8 Portraits of Singapore

*From Lion City to Asian Tiger:
A Brief History*

The Peoples of Singapore

A Nation of Contradictions

The Flavors of Asia

FROM LION CITY TO ASIAN TIGER: A BRIEF HISTORY

MODERN SINGAPORE dates its history from the early morning of January 29, 1819, when a representative of the British East India Company, Thomas Stamford Raffles, stepped ashore at the mouth of the Singapore River, beginning the process that would quickly turn a sleepy backwater into one of Asia's main commercial and financial centers. But let us go a bit farther back.

The Early Days

Though little is known of Singapore's early history, it is clear that by the 7th century AD Malays had a settlement here known as Temasek—"sea town." According to legend, a 13th-century prince of Palembang (Sumatra) landed on the island while seeking shelter from a storm and sighted a strange animal, which he believed to be a lion but was more likely a tiger. The prince subsequently fought and defeated the ruler of the settlement and proclaimed himself king, then renamed the island Singa Pura, Sanskrit for "lion city." (More appropriately, Singapore is today referred to as one of the Asian Tigers, in recognition of its economic success.)

The first recorded history of Singapore, from a Chinese chronicler who visited in 1330, describes a thriving Malay settlement. By the 14th century, Singa Pura had become an active trading city important and wealthy enough to build a walled fortress—and to make others covet the island. Drawn into a battle between the Java-based Majapahit empire and the Siamese kingdom for control of the Malay Peninsula, Singa Pura was destroyed and the settlement abandoned to the jungle.

In 1390 or so, Iskandar Shah (or Parameswara, as the Portuguese called him), another Palembang prince, broke from the Majapahit empire and was granted asylum on the island. After killing the local chieftain, he installed himself as ruler but was driven out before long by the Javanese and fled north into the peninsula. Singa Pura became a Thai vassal state until it was claimed by the Malacca Sultanate, which Iskandar Shah had established and brought to great prominence a few years after fleeing the island.

When, in 1511, the Portuguese seized Malacca, the Malay admiral fled to Singa Pura and established a new capital at Johor Lama. Obscurity engulfed Singa Pura in 1613, when the Portuguese reported laying waste to a small Malay settlement at the mouth of the river.

Enter Raffles

With the development of shipping routes to the West around the Cape of Good Hope and the opening of China to trade, the Malay Peninsula became strategically and commercially important to the West. To protect its shipping interests, the British secured Penang in 1786 and threw the Dutch out of Malacca in 1795. (The Dutch had thrown the Portuguese out earlier.) In 1818, to prevent any further northward expansion by the Dutch, who controlled the East Indies (now Indonesia), Lord Hastings, governor-general of India, gave tacit approval to Thomas Stamford Raffles, an employee of the British East India Company, to secure a British trading settlement and harbor on the southern part of the Malay Peninsula.

On January 29, 1819, Raffles made an exploratory visit to Singa Pura, which had come under the dominion of the Sultan of Johore. When Raffles arrived, the two sons of the previous sultan, who had died six years earlier, were in dispute over who would inherit the throne. Raffles backed the claim of the elder brother, Tunku Hussein Mohamed Shah, and proclaimed him sultan.

Offering to support the new sultanate with British military strength, Raffles persuaded the sultan to grant the British a lease allowing them to establish a trading post on the island in return for an annual rent; within a week the negotiations were concluded. (A later treaty ceded the island outright to the British in return for increased pensions and cash payments for the sultan and his island representative.)

Thus began the continual rapid changing and adapting that characterizes Singapore to this day: within three years, the small fishing village, surrounded by swamps and jungle and populated by only tigers and 200 or so Malays, had become a boomtown of 10,000 immigrants, administered by 74 British employees of the East India Company. In 1826 Singapore joined Penang and Malacca in Malaya to form the British India–controlled Straits Settlements (named for the Strait of Malacca, also called the Straits—the channel between Sumatra and the Malay Peninsula that connects the Indian Ocean with the South China Sea). In 1867 the Straits Settlements became a crown colony.

As colonial administrators and businessmen, the British led a segregated life, maintaining the British lifestyle and shielding themselves from the local population and the climate. In the humid tropical heat, they would promenade along the Padang (cricket green), men in high-collared, buttoned-up white linen suits and women in grand ensembles complete with corsets, petticoats, and long kid gloves. In part, they believed that maintaining a distance and the appearance of invulnerability would help them win the respect and fear of the locals. Indeed, the heavily outnumbered colonials needed all the respect they could muster. But holding on to familiar ways also gave the colonials a sense of security in this foreign land where danger was never far away—in the mid-1850s, for example, five people a week were carried off by tigers.

As Singapore grew, the British erected splendid public buildings, churches (including St. Andrew's Cathedral, built to resemble Netley Abbey in Hampshire, England), and hotels, often using Indian convicts for labor. The Muslim, Hindu, Taoist, and Buddhist communities—swelling rapidly from the influx of fortune-seeking settlers from Malaya, India, and South China—built mosques, temples, and shrines. Magnificent houses for wealthy merchants sprang up, and the harbor became lined with *godowns* (warehouses) to hold all the goods passing through the port.

It was certainly an exotic trade that poured through Singapore. Chinese junks came loaded with tea, porcelain, silks, and artworks; Bugis (Indonesian) schooners carried in cargoes of precious spices, rare tropical hardwoods, camphor, and produce from all parts of Indonesia. These goods, and more like them from Siam (now Thailand), the Philippines, and elsewhere in the region, were traded in Singapore for manufactured textiles, coal, iron, cement, weapons, machinery, and other fruits of Europe's industrial revolution. Another major product traded here by the British was opium, grown in India and sold to the Chinese.

Meanwhile, much of the island was still covered by thick jungle. As late as the 1850s, there were dozens of tigers still to be found here. Early experiments with agriculture (spices, cotton, coffee, and the like) were soon abandoned, as almost nothing except coconuts would grow successfully in the sandy and marshy soil. (Singapore does, however, have the distinction of having introduced the rubber plant to Malaya: in 1877 the first seedlings were successfully grown here by botanist H. N. Ridley, then director of Singapore's Botanic Gardens, from plants brought out of Brazil.)

With the advent of steamships (which found Singapore's deep-water harbor ideal) and the opening of the Suez Canal in 1869, the port thrived as the "Gateway to the East." Its position at the southern end of the Straits made it a vital link in the chain of ports and coaling stations for steamers. Shipyards were established to repair the oceangoing cargo carriers and to build the ever-increasing number of barges and lighters bringing cargo ashore to the godowns. With the development of the rubber industry in Malaya starting in the 1870s, Singapore became the world's top exporter of the commodity.

The 20th Century

By the turn of the century, Singapore had become the entrepôt of the East, a mixture of adventurers and "respectable middle classes." World War I hardly touched the island, although its defenses were strengthened to support the needs of the British navy, for which Singapore was an important base. Until 1921 the Japanese and the British were allies and no need was felt to maintain a large naval presence in the region, but then the United States, anxious about Japan's growing military strength, prevailed on Britain to cancel its treaty with the Japanese, and defense of Singapore became a priority. A massive military expansion took place: barracks were created for up to 100,000 troops, and Sentosa Island was heavily fortified with huge naval guns.

As the likelihood of war in the Pacific grew, Singapore's garrison was further strengthened, and naval shipyards and airfields were constructed. The British were complacent about the impregnability of Singapore, expecting that any attack would come from the sea and assuming that they were well prepared to meet such an attack. But the Japanese landed to the north, in Malaya. The two British battleships that had been posted to Singapore were sunk, and the Japanese land forces raced down the peninsula on bicycles.

When the Japanese made their first bombing runs on Singapore, all the city's lights were on. The key to turn off the switch was in the governor's pocket, and he was at the movies. The big guns on Sentosa Island sat idle, trained vainly on the quiet sea; they were not designed to fire on land forces. In February 1942 the Japanese captured Singapore.

Huge numbers of Allied civilians and military were sent to Changi Prison; others were marched off to prison camps in Malaya or to work on the notorious "Death Railway" in Thailand. The 3½ years of occupation was a time of privation and fear for the civilian population; up to 100,000 deaths are estimated during this period. The Japanese surrendered on August 21, 1945, and the Allied military forces returned to Singapore. However, the security of the British Empire was never again to be felt, and independence for British Southeast Asia was only a matter of time.

Military control of Singapore ended in 1946. The former Straits Settlements crown colony was dissolved, and the island became a separate crown colony, with a partially elected legislative council representing various elements of the community. The first election was held in 1948. In the 1950s, the degree of autonomy allowed Singapore increased and various political parties were formed. One of these was the People's Action Party (PAP), established in 1954 under the leadership of a young Chinese lawyer, Lee Kuan Yew, who had recently graduated from Oxford.

In 1957 the British government agreed to the establishment of an elected 51-member legislative assembly. General elections in 1959 gave an overwhelming majority—43 of 51 seats—to the PAP, and Lee Kuan Yew became Singapore's first prime minister. In 1963 Singapore became part of the Federation of Malaysia, along with the newly independent state of Malaysia.

Mainly due to the Malays' anxiety over a possible takeover by the ethnic Chinese, the federation did not work. When it broke up two years later, Singapore became an independent sovereign state (its independence day—August 9, called National Day—is celebrated each year in grand style). In 1967 Singapore issued its own currency for the first time, and in the general election of 1968 the PAP won all 58 seats in Parliament.

In 1971 the last of the British military forces left the island. The economic future of the nation seemed unsure: how could it survive without the massive British military expenditure? But Singapore did more than survive—it boomed. The government engaged in programs for rapid modernization of the nation's infrastructure to attract foreign investment and to help its businesses compete in world markets.

The electorate stayed faithful to Lee Kuan Yew and the PAP, returning the party almost unchallenged in one election after another. It was something of a surprise when, at a by-election in 1981, a single opposition member, Indian lawyer J. B. Jeyaretnam, was elected to Parliament, followed by a second non-PAP member in the general election of 1984. Today the PAP's popular majority is the lowest it has ever been. Nevertheless, the party is still sufficiently entrenched to hold all but a few of the parliamentary seats. Lee has stepped down from the all-powerful post of prime minister, but as elder statesman ("senior minister") he still acts as the guiding hand behind the PAP and, hence, the government. In recent years he has encouraged freer expression (to some extent, at least), and consequently more and more citizens have begun voicing their criticism of the government's sometimes heavy-handed dictates.

THE PEOPLES OF SINGAPORE

MODERN SINGAPOREANS are proud of their nation's multiracial heritage. In 1911 the census found 48 races speaking 54 languages, though some of these races have dwindled since then. Once 5,000 strong, the Armenian community, which built the Armenian Apostolic Church of St. Gregory in 1835, numbers fewer than 50 today. The Sephardic Jews, mostly from India and Iran, have moved out of Singapore to Israel, Australia, and elsewhere; just two synagogues, one on Waterloo Street and one on Oxley Rise, survive. The fortunes amassed by Bugis from the Celebes (now Sulawesi) in Indonesia—pirates before Raffles arrived, later turned real-estate investors—have passed into the hands of the few Bugis families who remain.

Still, numerous ethnic communities exist: Filipinos, Japanese, and Thais, Germans, Swiss, and Italians. There are also about 20,000 Eurasians—half British, Dutch, or Portuguese; half Filipino, Chinese, Malay, Indian, Thai, Sri Lankan, or Indonesian. An overwhelming 97% of the population, however, come from among just three ethnic groups: Chinese, Malay, and Indian. It had been Lee's wish to make Singapore multiracial, but increasingly in his later years Lee has spoken of Singapore as a Sinic society and sought immigrants from Hong Kong.

The Chinese

Raffles had one ambition for Singapore— to make it a thriving trading port that would secure British interests in the Orient and undermine the Dutch. To achieve these goals, he made the island a free port. Traders flocked to Singapore, and soon so did thousands of Chinese in search of work. Every year during the northeast monsoon, junks crammed to the gunnels with half-starved Chinese would ride the winds to Singapore. Many arrived intent only on saving money and then returning to their families on mainland China. However, most did not make the return journey.

These immigrants were from many different ethnic groups with different languages, different foods, different clothes, and often different religions. Each group carved out its own section of Chinatown, the part of Singapore that Raffles's master plan (drawn up with the intention of avoiding racial tensions) had allotted the Chinese, and there they lived basically separate lives.

The largest group of immigrants was the **Hokkien,** traders and merchants from southern Fukien Province, who now make up 43% of the Chinese population and still work predominantly as merchants. The early arrivals settled in Amoy Street. One of Singapore's oldest temples, the Temple of Heavenly Happiness, was built in 1841 by Hokkien immigrants in honor of the goddess of the sea, and here they made offerings in thanks for their safe voyage.

On Philip Street in Chinatown is the Wak Hai Cheng Bio Temple, also dedicated to a goddess of the sea. It was built by the **Teochews,** the second-largest immigrant group (constituting 22% of Singapore's Chinese), who came from the Swatow region in Guangdong Province. The temple suggests one of their chosen professions— they dominate the port and maritime labor force—but they also make a strong showing as cooks.

The **Cantonese** are the third-largest group, making up 16.5% of the Chinese population. They are often artisans and craftsmen. Their Fuk Tak Chi Temple on Telok Ayer Street is dedicated to Tua Pek Kong, who can bring prosperity and safety to a voyage. Southern neighbors of the Teochews on the mainland, the Cantonese dedicate enormous amounts of time and energy to eating. Three-fourths of all the Chinese restaurants in Singapore serve Cantonese food.

The **Hakka**—who had lived a nomadic existence in Fukien, Guangdong, and Szechuan provinces—remember old times at the Ying He Hui Guan (Hakka Clan Association Hall), just off Telok Ayer Street, which served as a sort of foster home for immigrants stepping off the junks a century ago. The **Hainanese,** many of whom work in hotel or domestic service, were employed as cooks by the colonials (you'll often see "breaded pork cutlet" on the menus at Hainanese restaurants).

By the 1920s, the number of **Straits Chinese**—those born in Singapore or in Malaya—exceeded the number of mainland-born Chinese in Singapore. Though some continued to consider themselves "overseas Chinese," an increasing number began to recognize Singapore as their home. The Straits Chinese British Association (formed at the turn of the century) served as a forum for exchanging views on Singapore's future and, unofficially, worked alongside the colonial administration in the island's development. Chinese families that had made fortunes in the 19th century began sending their children to British universities. These graduates became businessmen, politicians, and statesmen. Today Chinese constitute 76% of Singapore's total population.

One of Singapore's most interesting aspects is the more than two dozen festivals celebrated so colorfully each year, and more than half of these are Chinese, based on traditions brought over from the mainland. Even the keenest Chinese businessman does not discount *joss*—fortune—and festivals are considered important in ensuring good joss, by appeasing ancestral spirits during the Festival of the Hungry Ghosts, celebrating the birthday of the mischievous Monkey God, or ushering in the Chinese New Year.

The Malays

When Raffles landed on the island in 1819, there were perhaps 100 Malay houses in a small fishing village on the banks of the Singapore River. Aside from the Malays, there were about 30 *orang laut* (sea gypsies) living farther upriver in houseboats. (The orang laut, aborigines from Johore, were later decimated by an epidemic of smallpox, but there were still families living in waterborne settlements until after the Second World War. Since then they have come ashore, intermarried with Malays, and become mainstream Singaporean.)

To help develop Singapore as a free port, the East India Company encouraged Malays to migrate from the peninsula. By 1824 their numbers had grown to more than 5,000, and today Malays account for 15% of Singapore's ethnic mix.

Malays, in contrast to the Chinese, did not adapt to the freewheeling entrepreneurial spirit that engulfed Singapore. Overwhelmingly Muslim, they sought fulfillment in serving the community and winning its respect rather than in profit making. Their lives traditionally centered on the *kampong,* or village, where the family houses are built around a central compound and food is grown for communal use. Kampongs have mostly disappeared from Singapore, but one does remain on the island of Pulau Sakeng. If you visit this island, you will immediately feel the pervasive community spirit and the warmth extended to visitors. With luck, you may even get to witness the traditional Malay sport called *sepak tatraw*—similar to badminton, except that the feet, arms, and body are used instead of rackets.

The early Malays chose to be fishermen, woodcutters, or carpenters rather than capitalists, and today they continue to concentrate on the community and their relationship with Allah. (No visitor to Singapore can fail to hear the plaintive call to prayer five times a day from the Sultan Mosque, whose gold-painted domes and minarets tower above the shophouses.) Hence, wealth and power have, for the most part, eluded the Malay community.

Still, the culture has infiltrated all aspects of Singapore life. Though there are four "official" languages—Malay, Mandarin, Tamil, and English—Malay is the national language, used, for example, in the national anthem, "Majulah Singapura" (May Singapore Prosper). Singaporeans have incorporated Malay food into their cooking as well. Nonya (Malay for "woman" or "wife"), or Peranakan, cuisine is one aspect of the blending of Chinese and Malay cultures, featuring Chinese ingredients prepared with local spices.

The Indians

At least seven centuries before Christ, Indian merchants were crossing the Bay of Bengal to trade in Malaya. Some settled in, and their success in trade made them respected members of the community. Hindu words were absorbed into the Malay language; Singapore's name, in fact, derives from the Sanskrit *singa pura* ("lion city").

With success stories floating back to the Indian subcontinent, little encouragement was needed to entice other Indians to seek their fortunes in the new Singapore. Some, however, had no choice. Seeing a way of both ridding Calcutta of its miscreants and building an infrastructure in Singapore, the East India Company sent Indian convicts to the island in chains and put them to work draining marshes and erecting bridges, churches, and other public buildings. For themselves, the Indians built Sri Mariamman, Singapore's oldest and most important Hindu temple, in 1862 (it has since been expanded and repainted).

In fact, serving time in Singapore during the mid-19th century was not so bad. The convicts were encouraged to learn a trade, and often, after their term was served, they opted to stay. Many Tamils from South India went as indentured laborers to work Malaya's rubber plantations and, when their time was up, moved to Singapore.

The majority of Indians in Singapore are, in fact, Hindu Tamils from South India. There are also Muslims from South India and, in smaller numbers, Bengalis, Biharis, Gujaratis, Marathis, Kashmiris, and Punjabis, from the north, west, and east of India. From Sri Lanka come other Hindu Tamils, as well as the Sinhalese (often mistaken for Indians), who are neither Hindu nor Muslim but follow the gentle teachings of Hinayana Buddhism. The Sinhalese traditionally work in jewelry and precious gems; incidentally, they are among Singapore's finest cricket players—witness their domination of the teams playing at the prestigious Singapore Cricket Club.

During the colonial period, the Indians in Singapore regarded India, and more particularly their region, as their true home. They would send money back to their families and dream of returning. Of all the immigrant groups, they were the least committed to the future of Singapore. When the Japanese occupied the island in World War II, some 20,000 Singaporean Indians volunteered for the Japanese Indian National Army, led by Subhas Chandra Bose, which took advantage of local sentiment and Japanese expansionist goals in an attempt to evict the British from India. This collaboration left Singapore's Chinese and Malay communities—both of which had suffered greatly at the hands of the Japanese—distrustful of the Indians. However, India, after independence, actively discouraged expatriates from returning.

Today, Indians, who account for 7% of Singapore's population, increasingly see themselves as Singaporean. Their respect for education has taken them into the influential professions of law, medicine, and government. Nevertheless, the Tamil-language newspaper gives more space to events in South India than to local events, and Indians remain deeply tied to their community and traditional customs. Hinduism remains a powerful force—Singapore has more than 20 major temples devoted to Hindu gods—and some of the Tamil Hindu festivals (such as Thaipusam) are expressed with more feverish ritualism than in India. Indian food, too, remains true to its roots; it has been said that one can eat better curries in Singapore than in India.

A NATION OF CONTRADICTIONS

FROM ECONOMICS TO FOOD, Singapore is a nation of contradictions. Except for Japan, it has the best-educated, most knowledgeable, and most worldly-wise society in Asia, but the government still tries in many ways to regulate its citizens' lives. Although Singapore has no enemies—Communism no longer poses a threat, and the island's relations with its immediate neighbors, Malaysia and Indonesia, are vastly improved—it continues to maintain one of the largest armies in the world proportionate to population and has a ruthlessly efficient and intrusive intelligence agency, the Internal Security Department, or ISD, which is tireless in its pursuit of dissent. Despite the fact that Singapore is a bastion of capitalism, the government owns many of the largest local companies and frequently interferes with economic decisions. The government is so prudish that it bans *Cosmopolitan* as well as *Playboy,* yet the national airline promotes itself with slogans on the order of "Singapore Girl you're a great way to fly." And although Singapore has many "hawker centers," each with an ethnic mélange of food stalls, which offer some of the best street food in the world, young Singaporeans flock to American fast-food restaurants. . . .

For any Westerner accustomed to Asian cities choked by pollution, traffic jams, and snarled communications, Singapore is an oasis. The airport is so efficient, the taxis are so numerous, and the roads are so good that a visitor arriving at Changi Airport, on the eastern tip of the island, 12 miles from downtown, can reach his hotel room there 30 minutes after stepping off the plane. That visitor can drink water from the tap; get business cards, eyeglasses, or a tailor-made suit the day after placing an order; and ride a modern subway system whose underground stations as well as its trains are air-conditioned. An international phone call can be direct-dialed as quickly in Singapore as in the United States. Business can be conducted in English, because it is the language that all the schools use. (Only one out of five Singaporeans speaks English at home, though.) While the dreary high-rise buildings convey no atmosphere, Singapore has retained enough greenery to make it a pleasant city for walking. Every block has trees and flowers; the island's entire east coast, facing the South China Sea, is a string of parks and beaches, and only half an hour from downtown are a nature preserve and some semirural areas with farms. No litter mars a walk through Singapore's streets, because a litterbug must pay a fine of up to US$700 and undergo counseling. (Cigarette butts count as litter, and many of Singapore's litter baskets—there are 45,000 of them—are equipped with ashtrays.) Everything in Singapore is clean; everything in Singapore works.

In a nation known for efficiency, the government is most efficient of all. In other parts of Asia, government services can take an eternity to arrive and then come bound in red tape, the instrument for cutting the tape being a bribe. But in Singapore, when someone calls to report a pothole, the Public Works Department fills it within 48 hours. The Telecommunication Authority will install a new phone the day after the order is received. Secretaries are so conscientious that a journalist gets unsolicited wake-up calls to make sure he'll be on time for early-morning interviews with their bosses. A bribe, whether a little tip to an employee or a large payoff to a high-ranking minister, represents a ticket to jail. A postman was once arrested for accepting a gift of one Singapore dollar—equal [at the time] to 62 American cents. A civil servant who receives a present in the mail must send it to a government agency, which puts a price tag on it and then offers to sell it back to the recipient. If the employee doesn't want to buy it, the gift is sold at an auction. Such is the shame attached to corruption that in 1986, when the minister of national development was accused of accepting a bribe to save private land from government acquisition, he committed suicide.

The government of Singapore, ever fearful of snakes in its capitalist Garden of Eden, loves to make rules. The walls of buildings are plastered with rules, telling people what they can't do and how much they have to pay if they dare to try it. The fines represent considerably more than a slap on the wrist, and they're enforced often enough to make most potential miscreants think twice. . . . Few proscribed activities are left to the imagination, as opposed to being posted; for example, in the Botanic Gardens, where PROHIBITED signs threaten to outnumber plant-identification markers, a pictograph warns against shooting at birds with slingshots. Nor do violations always depend for discovery on a passing policeman. Trucks and commercial vans are required to install a yellow roof light that flashes when the vehicle exceeds the speed limit. When a taxi exceeds the maximum speed on freeways of 48 miles an hour, loud chimes go off inside; the chimes are so annoying that the driver is likely to slow down. At some intersections, cameras photograph the license plates of cars that pass through as the light is changing to red; the drivers receive bills for that offense in the mail.

TODAY, SINGAPORE is a city with almost no poverty. Hong Kong may have grown as rapidly, but in Hong Kong the gap between rich and poor is visible everywhere. By contrast, I never saw anyone in Singapore shabbily dressed, and everyone appeared to have at least a passable place to live. Food is cheap and plentiful. Even low-income Singaporeans have access to high-quality medical care; doctors at public hospitals in the United States might look enviously at the public wards of Singapore General Hospital.

But Singapore was not always so prosperous or so tidy. When Lee Kuan Yew [who was prime minister from 1959 until he stepped behind the scenes in 1990] took power, he found himself governing a mosquito-infested swamp dotted with pig and chicken farms, fishing villages, and squatter colonies of tin-roofed shacks. The streets of the central city were lined with shophouses—mostly two-story buildings with ornate façades. A family would operate a business on the ground floor and live on the second floor. Often without plumbing and electricity, and housing as many as 10 people to a room, the shophouses may have presented a picturesque sight for tourists, but they were far less agreeable for their occupants. "The Chinese, who constitute the main current of the city, live in utter filth and poverty," *Asia Scene,* a travel magazine, reported in 1960. "Their poverty is phenomenal. One must see with his own eyes to believe it." Compounding the problem of poverty were racial and political tensions, coming both from the Malay minority and from young Chinese infused with the ideals of the Maoist revolution; these tensions frequently spilled out into the streets.

In not much more than a decade, Singaporeans were passing from poverty to affluence, and the nation's economy from a basket case to the powerhouse of southern Asia. The explanation for this transformation, as for nearly everything else that happens in Singapore, rests with Lee Kuan Yew. Lee has put his stamp on Singapore to an extent that few political leaders anywhere in the world have ever matched. Tough and authoritarian although operating under a pretense of democracy, uninterested in personal wealth among a people who devote their lives to financial gain, often rude and contemptuous in a country that runs annual campaigns promoting the virtues of courtesy, Lee embodies as many contradictions as does Singapore itself.

— Stan Sesser

Stan Sesser has written extensively about Southeast Asia. While researching the article from which this essay is excerpted, he interviewed Lee Kuan Yew twice. The article, which originally appeared in *The New Yorker,* is reprinted in Sesser's *The Lands of Charm and Cruelty: Travels in Southeast Asia.*

THE FLAVORS OF ASIA

SINGAPORE'S DINING SCENE reflects the three main cultures that have settled here—Chinese, Indian, and Malay—as well as the many other influences that contribute to the island's diverse mix. Singapore's history as a port through which the products of the famed Spice Islands were traded has left its people in love with spicy food. But it's not necessarily the kind of spiciness that burns the roof of your mouth; often, spicy here means well flavored, seasoned to perfection.

Spice Traditions

Basically, there are two schools of spicy cooking, both well represented in Singaporean cuisine. The first is the Indian tradition, which uses dried spices such as cardamom, cloves, cumin, fennel, fenugreek, white and black pepper, chili peppers, powdered turmeric root, and mustard and poppy seeds. These spices are sometimes used whole but are more often ground into a powder (broadly referred to as curry powder) or made into a paste used as a base for gravies. (In Asia, gravies are thickened not with flour or cream but usually with these pastes.)

The second school is Southeast Asian, and it relies mainly on fresh roots and aromatic leaves. Typically, lemongrass, turmeric root, galangal, ginger, garlic, onions, shallots, and other roots are pounded into smooth pastes, with candlenuts and shrimp paste, to again form a base for gravies and soups. Leaves—such as turmeric, lime, coriander, several varieties of basil—add a distinctive bouquet.

The Cuisines of Many Cultures

Chinese

Chinese make up about 76% of Singapore's population, and this predominance is reflected in the wide assortment of restaurants representing their ethnic groups. The following is a sampling of the many Chinese cuisines represented in Singapore.

The best-known regional Chinese cuisine is **Cantonese,** with its fresh, delicate flavors. Vegetable oil, instead of lard, is used in the cooking, and crisp vegetables are preferred. Characteristic dishes are stir-fried beef in oyster sauce; steamed fish with slivers of ginger; and deep-fried duckling with mashed taro.

Dim sum is a particularly Cantonese style of eating, featuring a selection of bite-size steamed, baked, or deep-fried dumplings, buns, pastries, and pancakes, with a variety of savory or sweet flavorings. Popular items are the *cha shao bao* (a steamed bread bun filled with diced, sweetened, barbecued pork) and *shao mai* (a steamed mixture of minced prawns, pork, and sometimes water chestnuts). The selection, which might comprise as many as 50 offerings, may also include such dishes as soups, steamed pork ribs, and stuffed green peppers. Traditionally, dim sum are served three on a plate in bamboo steamer baskets on trolleys that are pushed around the restaurant. You simply wait for the trolleys to come around, then point to whichever item you would like. The more elegant style now is to order dim sum à la carte so that they will be prepared freshly for you.

If you walk around Ellenborough Market, you'll notice the importance of dried ingredients in Chinese cooking. The people here are **Teochew** (or Chao Zhou), mainly fisherfolk from Swatow in the eastern part of Guangdong Province. Though their cooking has been greatly influenced by the Cantonese, it is quite distinctive. Teochew chefs cook with clarity and freshness, often steaming or braising, with an emphasis on fish and vegetables. Oyster sauce and sesame oil—staples of Cantonese cooking—do not play a large role in Teochew cooking; Teochew chefs pride themselves on enhancing the natural flavors of the foods.

Characteristic Teochew dishes are *lo arp* and *lo goh* (braised duck and goose), served with a vinegary chili-and-garlic sauce; crispy liver or prawn rolls; stewed, preserved vegetables; black mushrooms with fish roe; and a unique porridge called *congee,* which is eaten with small dishes of salted vegetables, fried whitebait, black olives, and preserved-carrot omelets.

Szechuan food is very popular in Singapore, as the spicy-hot taste suits the local palate. This style of cooking is distinguished by the use of bean paste, chilies, and garlic, as well as nuts and poultry. The result is dishes with pungent flavors of all sorts, harmoniously blended. Simmering and smoking are common forms of preparation, and noodles and steamed bread are preferred accompaniments. Characteristic dishes to order are hot-and-sour soup, sautéed chicken or prawns with dried chilies, camphor- and tea-smoked duck, and spicy fried string beans.

Pekingese cooking originated in the imperial courts. It makes liberal use of strong-flavored roots and vegetables, such as peppers, garlic, ginger, leeks, and coriander. Dishes are usually served with noodles or dumplings and baked, steamed, or fried bread. The most famous dish is Peking duck: the skin is lacquered with aromatic honey and baked until it looks like dark mahogany and is crackly crisp. Other choices are clear winter melon soup, emperor's purses (stir-fried shredded beef with shredded red chili, served with crispy sesame bread), deep-fried minced shrimp on toast, and baked fish on a hot plate.

The greatest contribution to Singaporean cuisine made by the many arrivals from China's **Hainan** island, off the north coast of Vietnam, is "chicken rice": whole chickens are lightly poached in a broth flavored with ginger and spring onions; then rice is boiled in the liquid to fluffy perfection and eaten with chopped-up pieces of chicken, which are dipped into a sour and hot chili sauce and dark soy sauce.

Also popular here are Fukienese and Hunanese restaurants. **Fukien** (also known as Hokkien) cuisine emphasizes soups and stews with rich, meaty stocks. Garlic and dark soy sauce are often used, and seafood is prominent. Dishes to order are braised pork belly served with buns, fried oyster, and turtle soup.

Hunanese cooking is dominated by sugar and spices and tends to be more rustic. One of the most famous dishes is beggar's chicken: a whole bird is wrapped in lotus leaves and baked in a sealed covering of clay; when it's done, a mallet is used to break away the hardened clay, revealing a chicken so tender and aromatic that it is more than worthy of an emperor. Other favorites are pigeon soup in bamboo cups, fried layers of bean-curd skin, and honey ham served with bread.

Hakka food is very provincial in character and uses ingredients not normally found in other Chinese cuisines. Red-wine lees are used to great effect in dishes of fried prawns or steamed chicken, producing gravies that are delicious when eaten with rice. Stuffed bean curds and beef balls are other Hakka delicacies.

Indian

Most Indian immigrants to Singapore came from the south, from Madras (now known as Tamil Nadu) and Kerala, so **South Indian** cultural traditions tend to predominate here. In Little India, many small and humble restaurants can be found. Race Course Road is a street of curries: at least 10 Indian restaurants, most representing this fiery-hot cooking tradition, offer snacks or meals served on banana leaves. The really adventurous should sample the Singapore Indian specialty fish-head curry. Like all the food served here, this dish, with its hot, rich, sour gravy, is best appreciated when eaten without utensils—somehow, eating with the fingers enhances the flavor!

South Indian cuisine, generally more chili-hot than northern food, relies on strong spices like mustard seed and uses coconut milk liberally. Meals are very cheap, and eating is informal: just survey the cooked food displayed, point to whatever you fancy, then take a seat at a table. A piece of banana leaf will be placed before you, plain rice will be spooned out, and the rest of your food will be arranged around the rice and covered with curry sauce.

Vegetarian cuisine is raised to a high art by South Indian cooks. Other tempting South Indian dishes include fish *pudichi* (fish in coconut, spices, and yogurt), fried prawns and crabs, mutton or chicken *biryani* (a meat-and-rice dish), *brinjal curry* (spiced eggplant), *keema* (spicy minced meat), *vindaloo* (hot spiced meat), *dosai* (savory pancakes), *appam* (rice-flour pancakes), sour lime pickle, and *papadam* (deep-fried lentil wafers). Try a glass of *rasam* (pepper water) to aid digestion and a glass of *lassi* (yogurt drink) or beer to cool things down.

Since the 1960s, **North Indian** food has made a mark in Singapore. Generally found in the more posh restaurants, this cuisine blends aromatic spices with a subtle Persian influence. The main differences between northern and southern Indian cuisine are that northern food is less hot and more subtly spiced than southern and that cow's milk is used as a base instead of coconut milk. North Indian cuisine also uses yogurt extensively to tame the pungency of the spices and depends more on puréed tomatoes and nuts to thicken gravies.

The signature North Indian dish is Tandoori chicken (marinated in yogurt and spices and cooked in a clay urn, or *tandoor*) and fresh mint chutney, eaten with *naan, chapati,* and *paratha* (Indian breads). Another typical dish is *rogan josh,* lamb braised gently with yogurt until the spices blend into a delicate mix of aromas and flavors. *Ghee,* a nutty clarified butter, is used—often in lavish quantities—to cook and season rice or rice-and-meat dishes (*pulaos* and *biryanis*).

In general, North Indian food is served more elegantly than is South Indian food. The prices are also considerably higher. (Beware of ordering prawns in South Indian restaurants, though—they often cost as much as S$8 apiece.)

The **Indian Muslim** tradition is represented in the Arab Street area. Opposite the Sultan Mosque, on North Bridge Road, are small, open-fronted restaurants serving *roti prata* (a sort of crispy, many-layered pancake eaten with curries), *murtabak* (prata filled with spiced, minced mutton and diced onions), *nasi biryani* (saffron-flavored rice with chicken or mutton), and various curries. These places are for the stouthearted only; they are cramped and not really spic-and-span.

Japanese

Over the past few years in Singapore, there has been a sudden interest in all things Japanese, no doubt partly because of the influx of Japanese tourists, but also because of the very large Japanese community here. Japanese restaurants (and supermarkets stocking imported Japanese produce) are all over the island, and Singapore can now offer Japanese cuisine equal to the best served in Japan.

The Japanese eat with studied grace. Dishes look like still-life paintings; flavors and textures both stimulate and soothe. Waitresses quietly appear and then vanish; the cooks welcome you and chat with you.

In Singapore you can savor a modified form of the high art of *kaiseki* (the formal Japanese banquet) in popular family restaurants. It was developed by the samurai class for tea ceremonies and is influenced by Zen philosophy. The food is served on a multitude of tiny dishes and offered to guests as light refreshments. Regulations govern the types of foods that can be served: the seasoning is light, the color schemes must be harmonious, and the foods, whenever possible, must be in their natural shapes. Everything presented is intended for conscious admiration. This stylistic approach is the perfect way to mark a special occasion.

More fun for some are the forms of Japanese dining in which guests can watch the chef exercise his skills right at the table. At a sushi bar, for example, the setting and the performance of the chef as he skillfully wields the knife to create the elegant, colorful pieces of sushi (vinegared rice tinged with wasabi, or green horseradish, and topped with a slice of raw fish) make the meal special. Savor the incredibly fresh flavor and you will be hooked forever. Also watch the chef perform stylistic movements, including knife twirling, at places serving *teppanyaki:* on a large griddle around which diners are seated, fish, meat, vegetables, and rice are lightly seared, and flavored with butter and sake. Sukiyaki, too, is grilled at the table, but the meat is strictly beef and the soup is sweeter; noodles and bean curd are served at the end of the meal as fillers.

Yakitori, a Japanese *satay,* is meat and vegetables grilled to perfection and glazed with a sweet sauce. *Yakiniku* is a grill-it-yourself meal of thin slices of beef, chicken, or Japanese fish. *Shabu-shabu* is a kind of fondue: seafoods and meats are lightly swished in boiling stock, then dipped in a variety of sauces. Tempura is a sort of fritter of remarkable lightness and delicacy; the most popular kinds are made of prawns and vegetables. The dipping sauce is a mix of soy sauce and *mirin* (sweet rice wine), flavored with grated giant white radish and ginger.

Malay and Indonesian

Malay cuisine is often hot and rich. Turmeric root, lemongrass, coriander, *blacan* (prawn paste), chilies, and shallots are combined with coconut milk to create fragrant, spicy gravies. A basic method of cooking is to gently fry the *rempah* (spices, herbs, roots, chilies, and shallots ground to a paste) in oil and when the mixture is fragrant, add meat and either a tamarind liquid, to make a tart spicy-hot sauce, or coconut milk, to make a rich spicy-hot curry sauce. Dishes to look for are *gulai ikan* (a smooth, sweetish fish curry), *sambal telor* (eggs in hot sauce), *empalan* (beef boiled in coconut milk, then deep-fried), *tauhu goreng* (fried bean curd in peanut sauce), and *ikan bilis* (crispy fried anchovies).

Perhaps the best-known Malay dish is *satay*—slivers of marinated beef, chicken, or mutton threaded onto thin coconut sticks, barbecued, and served with a spicy peanut sauce. At most hawker centers, you will find at least one satay seller sitting over his charcoal fire and fanning the embers to grill sticks of satay. Tell the waiter how many of each type of meat you want, and he'll bring the still-smoking satay to your table.

Unlike the Chinese, who have a great tradition of eating out and a few classical schools of restaurant cooking, most Malay families continue to entertain at home, even when celebrating special events, such as marriages. As a consequence, there are very few stylish Malay restaurants.

Indonesian food is very close to Malay; both are based on rice and cooked with a wide variety of spices, and both are Muslim and thus do not use pork. A meal called *nasi padang*—consisting of a number of mostly hot dishes, such as curried meat and vegetables with rice, that offer a range of tastes from sweet to salty to sour to spicy—originally comes from Padang in the Indonesian province of West Sumatra. Ready-cooked dishes are usually displayed in glass cases from which customers make their selections.

Nonya

The first Chinese immigrants to this part of the world were the Hokkien. When they settled on the Malay Peninsula, they acquired the taste for Malay spices and soon adapted Malay foods to their cuisine. Nonya food is one manifestation of the marriage of the two cultures, which is also seen in language, music, literature, and clothing. This blended Peranakan culture was called *baba,* as were the men; the women were called *nonya,* and so was the cuisine, because cooking was considered a feminine art.

Nonya cooking combines the finesse and subtlety of Chinese cuisine with the spiciness of Malay cooking. Many Chinese ingredients are used—especially dried foods like Chinese mushrooms, fungus, anchovies, lily flowers, soybean sticks, and salted fish—along with the spices and aromatics used in Malay cooking. A favorite Chinese ingredient is pork, and pork satay is made for the Peranakan home (you won't come across Malay pork satay, since Muslims do not eat pork).

The ingenious Nonya cook uses *taucheo* (preserved soybeans), garlic, and shallots to form the rempah needed to make *chap chye* (a mixed-vegetable stew with soy sauce). Other typical dishes are *husit goreng* (an omelet fried with shark's fin and crabmeat) and *otak otak* (a sort of fish quenelle with fried spices and coconut milk). Nonya cooking also features sourish-hot dishes like *garam assam,* which is a fish or prawn broth made with pounded turmeric, shallots, *galangal* (a type of ginger), lemongrass, and shrimp paste. The water for the broth is mixed with preserved tamarind, a sour fruit that adds a delicious tartness.

A few years ago, Nonya cuisine appeared to be dying, like Peranakan culture itself, but since the publication of many Nonya cookbooks, there has been a resurgence of interest.

Thai

Thai cuisine, while linked with Chinese and Malay, is distinctly different in taste. Most Thai dishes are hot and filled with exciting spices and fish aromatics. On first tasting a dish, you may find it stingingly hot (tiny chilies make the cuisine so fiery), but the taste of the fresh herbs will soon surface. Thai food's characteristic flavor comes from fresh mint, basil, coriander, and citrus leaves; extensive use of lemongrass, lime, vinegar, and tamarind keeps the sour-hot taste prevalent.

Thai curries—such as chicken curry with cashews, salted egg, and mango—use coconut milk and are often served with dozens of garnishes and side dishes. Various sauces are used for dipping; *nam pla,* one favorite, is a salty, fragrant amber liquid made from salted and fermented shrimp.

A popular Thai dish is *mee krob,* crispy fried noodles with shrimp. Other outstanding Thai dishes: *tom yam kung;* hot and spicy shrimp soup (few meals start without it); *gai hor bai toey,* fried chicken wrapped in pandanus leaves; *pu cha,* steamed crab with fresh coriander root and a little coconut milk; and *khao suey,* steamed white rice, which you'll need to soothe any fires that may develop in your mouth.

The larger Thai restaurants are actually seafood markets where you can pick your own swimming creature and tell the waitress how you want it cooked. For drinks, try Singha beer, brewed in Thailand, or *o-liang,* the national drink—very strong black iced coffee sweetened with palm-sugar syrup.

INDEX

✕ = *restaurant,* 🏨 = *hotel*

WHEREVER YOU TRAVEL, *H*ELP IS NEVER FAR AWAY.

From planning your trip to providing travel assistance along the way, American Express® Travel Service Offices are always there to help you do more.

> ### *Singapore*

American Express International, Inc.
300 Beach Rd.
The Concourse, 18F
(65) 2998133

Chan Premier Travel (R)
150 South Bridge Rd.
05/02 Fook Hai Bldg.
(65) 7334471

Travel Bug Holidays (R)
75 Amoy St.
(65) 2224101

do more **AMERICAN EXPRESS**

Travel

www.americanexpress.com/travel

And just in case.

We're here with American Express® Travelers Cheques and Cheques *for Two*.® They're the safest way to carry money on your vacation and the surest way to get a refund, practically anywhere, anytime.
Another way we help you...

do more ®

Travelers Cheques

In case you're running low.

We're here to help with more than 118,000 Express Cash locations around the world. In order to enroll, just call American Express before you start your vacation.

do more

In case you want to be welcomed there.

We're here to see that you're always welcomed at establishments everywhere. That's why millions of people carry the American Express® Card – for peace of mind, confidence, and security, around the world or just around the corner.

do more®

Cards